Exploring the Metaverse

Redefining reality in the digital age

Kuldeep Singh

www.bpbonline.com

First Edition 2024

ISBN: 978-93-55519-306

LIMITS OF LIABILITY AND DISCLAIMER OF WARRANTY

Distributors:

BPB PUBLICATIONS
20, Ansari Road, Darya Ganj
New Delhi-110002
Ph: 23254990/23254991

DECCAN AGENCIES
4-3-329, Bank Street,
Hyderabad-500195
Ph: 24756967/24756400

MICRO MEDIA
Shop No. 5, Mahendra Chambers,
150 DN Rd. Next to Capital Cinema,
V.T. (C.S.T.) Station, MUMBAI-400 001
Ph: 22078296/22078297

Published by Manish Jain for BPB Publications, 20 Ansari Road, Darya Ganj, New Delhi-110002 and Printed by him at Manipal Technologies, Manipal

www.bpbonline.com

Dedicated to

*My grandfather, **Shri Bhagirath Verma**, my source of inspiration and guide. My heartfelt dedication also extends to my parents, my beloved wife **Ritu**, and my sons **Lakshya** and **Lovyansh***

Forewords

The concept of the metaverse has been around us for decades, an enduring quest to seamlessly integrate artificial reality into our physical existence. Our entire journey of digital transformation and modernization revolves around embracing an alternative reality through trusting digital images and videos, forging our social lives in the realm of digital media. As we navigate the diverse landscapes of enterprise and consumer metaverse use cases, each with its unique concerns, it's evident that this phenomenon is still evolving, awaiting a comprehensive definition, and striving to reach the stature of the next internet. The critical question is, how are we adapting to this imminent reality, and are we actively contributing to its evolution?

I commend Kuldeep for dedicating his efforts to craft the book *Exploring the Metaverse.* It's truly inspiring to see Kuldeep openly dissect the loosely defined definitions, building blocks, characteristics, and the metaverse's journey towards becoming the next internet. He delves into our own evolutionary trajectory, examining how we've welcomed technology into our lives. By analyzing the current state of technology and identifying the driving forces behind the metaverse, he paints a vivid picture of our proximity to the next stage of the internet.

This book brilliantly explores a number of use cases where the metaverse will revolutionize not only entertainment and gaming but also our approach to health and fitness, interpersonal connections, livelihoods, lifestyle, and education. Kuldeep fearlessly addresses the challenges associated with metaverse adoption, highlighting concerns about identity preservation, privacy protection, sustainability, and ethical considerations. He places a strong emphasis on the development of metaverse standards and practices, advocating for shared and open development—a sentiment closely aligned with Lenovo's commitment to shaping an Open Ecosystem in the ThinkReality XR product lines and the OpenXR ecosystem.

Kuldeep calls for collective metaverse development, urging enterprises, educational institutions, governing bodies, and individuals to come together and collaboratively build the future. In this call to action, he emphasizes the crucial role each entity plays in this collective effort, encouraging safe, ethical, and responsible technology adaptation.

I extend my congratulations to Kuldeep for producing this exceptional work, and I wish him the best of luck in the future. This book is poised to serve as an indispensable guide to the metaverse.

—Vishal Shah

General Manager of XR(ARVR) and Metaverse, Lenovo

Our industry is ripe with hype and promises for the next new thing that will solve all our problems, make everything easier, engage our customers better, and much more. However, these promises do not often result in the large-scale transformation of how we deliver value to our customers. It is often overlooked that many foundational technologies do end up resulting in important changes to how we deliver systems. We continue to see advances in the underlying technologies for the metaverse, with the most prominent being virtual reality and their virtual worlds. This book serves as a guidepost to some of those technologies and their applications within our systems.

Kuldeep's approach to this topic is wide ranging, where he begins with an analysis of the technology revolutions that have come before metaverse, beginning with the first industrial revolution. He tackles the complex issue of what exactly is the metaverse, or more precisely to me, a metaverse. The lack of an agreed definition plagues discussions of the metaverse, and Kuldeep tackles this by stating his own and justifying it. The exploration of the supporting technologies, such as AI and VR hardware, grounds the subsequent sections where he explores a variety of applications of the technology to both, more and less obvious scenarios.

In the later sections, he addresses the concerns with utilizing features of metaverse, including privacy, safety, security, and sustainability. All technologies come with a cost and our job as responsible technologists is to evaluate them, and do what we can to mitigate anticipated costs. We should also work to expand our horizons and uncover costs and risks that aren't immediately obvious. These technologies will become common as we understand more about deriving value from them, through the use cases explored in the earlier sections of this book. We can be responsible technologists and still experiment with deriving value from these technologies. Such experimentation is essential to advance our capabilities in the underlying metaverse technologies.

Kuldeep's experience of working with these technologies' grounds the section on the practicalities. He appropriately highlights the critical role standards should play in allowing interoperability. He understands and communicates to the reader what it takes to make these technologies deliver value.

While the science fiction version of the metaverse may not come to pass anytime soon, technology will continue changing how we approach designing systems to deliver value to our customers. Kuldeep's book provides a broad roadmap to not only the technologies and their uses, but also the practical issues that to be addressed. This roadmap guides us to our own roadmaps for experimentation in understanding how metaverse technologies will impact our organizations today and in the future.

– Dr. Rebecca J Parsons

Chief Technology Officer Emerita, Thoughtworks

It gives me immense pleasure to learn that Mr. Kuldeep Singh is bringing out a book titled *Exploring the Metaverse* embarking the ongoing technological advancements and unleashing the transformative potential for the impetus to solve the global challenges.

Bharat has taken a leap forward in the technology-dominated era. The New Age Governance requires technology-based solutions for amicable redressal of local as well as global concerns. The Digital India program aims to transform the nation into a knowledge-based economy and a digitally empowered society by ensuring digital services, digital access, digital inclusion, digital empowerment and bridging the digital divide. Society and Science always co-evolves, and tech-based tools always become an important bridge in this process. The changing paradigm of the digital age has made an imperative to redefine the realities of the digital age for betterment of the humanity. The success of the digital public platforms like Aadhaar, UPI, Digilocker, UMANG, Cowin, AarogyaSetu, GeM, UMANG, Diksha, E-Sanjeevani, E-Hospital, E-Office, Tele-Law, Tele-medicine, and AI-assisted tools like Bhashini, OpenNyAI have been phenomenal. These platforms not only facilitated "Ease of Living" but also empowered the lives of common citizens.

As the Nation is now poised to internationalize India's most significant contribution to the Digital world in this Techade, this book is a commendable effort towards showcasing technological acumen for the reference of the tech fraternity. Considering the challenges of the digital world, the emphasis of the book to build upon responsible tech is an appreciable intervention. This skillfully and lucidly written book emerges as an essential addition to the library of any reader interested in the innovations and reflections of technology as well as its multidimensional application for the global good. I convey my best wishes for the successful publication of the book and the author's future endeavors.

– Arjun Ram Meghwal

Minister of State (I/C) for Law and Justice and
Minister of State for Parliamentary Affairs and Culture
Government of India

Testimonials

It is with great pride that I introduce Kuldeep Singh's upcoming book, *Exploring the Metaverse: Redefining reality in the digital age.* Having collaborated with Kuldeep on technological innovation, especially in Extended Reality, I have witnessed his profound insights and futuristic perspective. This book serves as a timely compass in our rapidly evolving digital landscape, expertly navigating the intricate layers of the metaverse.

Kuldeep seamlessly combines technological expertise with a storyteller's finesse, offering a comprehensive narrative and real-world use cases. The book is an invitation to a transformative journey, catering to both seasoned technology professionals and newcomers. Beyond speculation, it provides practical insights into the metaverse's impact on industries, societies, and individuals.

As we witness the digital revolution, Kuldeep's guide explores augmented and virtual realities, blockchain, and artificial intelligence, unraveling the metaverse's building blocks. This work is a testament to Kuldeep's passion for innovation, demystifying complex technology topics and issuing a call to action to rethink our digital reality. I am confident that readers will find inspiration and enlightenment within these pages, echoing the privilege I've had collaborating with Kuldeep.

– Kanchan Ray
Chief Technology Officer, Nagarro

There are many misconceptions and myths associated with the word "Metaverse". Touted as the window to the dystopian world, this is one concept that remains largely misunderstood. This book in my mind addresses this challenge. It takes a logical view on technological advancements and how the human relationship with it has evolved over time.

It provides a comprehensive understanding of Metaverse as a holistic concept, its association with various technologies and most importantly the business case for why it makes sense.

– Vanya Seth
Head of Technology, Thoughtworks India and Middle East

Kuldeep's book navigates the complex landscape of recent technological advancements, from the convergence of our physical and digital worlds to the rise of the Metaverse and the accessibility of emerging technologies. In a clear and accessible manner, he demystifies these concepts and provides valuable insights for both technologists and businesses. By incorporating practical software engineering concepts and standards, especially in the context of XR, Kuldeep ensures a practical and adaptable dimension. Drawing from his extensive experience with global enterprises, the book offers a well-rounded perspective on how emerging technologies can benefit various industries. With a thoughtful exploration of topics like privacy and sustainability, this book is a valuable read for both tech enthusiasts eager to learn and businesses contemplating the adoption of emerging technologies.

– Venkatesh Ponniah

Global Head of Emerging Tech, Thoughtworks

Future of Metaverse in India presents a captivating parallel to the concept of Maya, a concept that has existed for centuries in the country. Kuldeep offers insights, analyses, and visions that collectively contribute to a deeper understanding of the Metaverse and its transformative potential. In this remarkable journey through the pages of this book, the readers are invited to explore the impacts and the challenges of this uncharted territory of a digital universe that has the potential to transcend the confines of screens and pixels to become an integral part of our everyday existence soon. This book has highlighted the need for a collective effort from industry, government, academia, and people to make this Metaverse come true. The role of academia in the Metaverse is multifaceted and dynamic. As the Metaverse continues to evolve, academia stands as a guiding force, illuminating the path toward a more interconnected and knowledge-rich digital reality. I hope the readers would embark with an open mind and an adventurous spirit, for the Metaverse awaits.

– Prof. M Manivannan,

Head of Experiential Technologies Innovation Center (XTIC),

IIT Madras

The Metaverse stands as one of the most recent advancements in a series of technologies with the potential to profoundly shape humanity's future. It holds the promise of transforming the ways we work, connect, and communicate. Acting as a bridge between the real and virtual worlds, the Metaverse allows individuals to metamorphose into new 'amphibians' capable of seamlessly navigating between these realms. This book is a valuable resource for anyone embarking on the exploration of this transformative technology. By demystifying technical jargon and presenting content in a learner-friendly structure, this book provides a comprehensive overview of the Metaverse domain. Additionally, it stands out as a suitable textbook for introductory courses catering to students, employees, and professionals, including executive education programs.

– Ravindra Dastikop

Assistant Professor, Co-founder Pixuate

Author Metaverse Glossary: Your Gateway to the Future

In the heart of India, Kuldeep Singh stands out as a visionary, guiding us through the uncharted territories of the Metaverse in his groundbreaking work, "Exploring the Metaverse: Redefining Reality in the Digital Age". As the founder of Imaginate XR, that mirrors the innovation pulsating from this vibrant nation, I find parallel inspiration in both Kuldeep's journey and our collective mission.

Kuldeep's exploration transcends geographical boundaries, skillfully weaving together a narrative that resonates with anyone seeking a deeper understanding of our digital future. From unraveling the origins of the Metaverse to dissecting its various forms, he paints a vivid picture of this evolving landscape.

In the spirit of Trishanku Swarg । त्रिशंकु स्वर्ग, symbolizing a celestial realm between heaven and earth, Kuldeep's work becomes a guiding light—a delicate balance between the known and the unknown.

As we read the chapters spanning XR, AI, IoT, and Blockchain, it becomes evident that Kuldeep's vision transcends the local and resonates globally. *Exploring the Metaverse* is not just a book, it's an invitation to join a collective exploration where ideas born in India shape the broader narrative of the digital age.

Congratulations, Kuldeep, on this remarkable endeavor! Wishing him the very best as his work contributes to the global conversation on the future of the Metaverse.

– Hemanth Kumar Satyanarayana

Founder Imaginate XR, MIT-TR35 Young Innovator, TEDx Speaker

I am thrilled with the publication of this comprehensive and insightful book on the Metaverse. It's more than just a guide; it's an insightful exploration of the Metaverse, a concept often mistaken for an overnight success but is a product of persistent research and learning from setbacks. This book explores the Metaverse's complex layers, offering a thorough examination of its development and presenting a perspective beyond superficial understandings. The author skillfully demystifies technical jargon, making complex concepts accessible to not just experts, but to all readers. It serves as an empowering tool for creative minds, entrepreneurs, students, and professionals, providing deep insights into the Metaverse and encouraging exploration and contribution to this dynamic field. Whether you're a seasoned professional or a curious novice, this book is your gateway to the immense possibilities that await in the world of the Metaverse.

– Dinker Charak

Principal Product Manager, Thoughtworks,

Author #ProMA, Product Management Untangled and more

We are standing at the cusp of a revolutionary era where the digital and physical will be intertwined and interchangeable. For decades, we've been making strides, unlocking different use cases with immersive experiences. For example, we help customers be more productive in enterprise, shop with confidence in retail, and have a more enjoyable gaming experience through overlaying the digital layer over the physical. Through his book, "Exploring the Metaverse", Kuldeep brilliantly lays out all the milestones that had led us to this point in time, where all the dots are connecting to a multifaceted and multi-layered phygital (physical and digital) world. He walks the readers through a thorough breakdown of the different use cases and gives actionable advice to those interested in actively participating in this field. This comprehensive guide is a must read for anyone interested in diving deep into the virtual vast ocean that is the Metaverse.

– Mayan Shay May Raz,

AR Lead at Amazon

For executives and technologists, the metaverse is intriguing and confusing in equal measure. That is what makes me glad to see a book that unlocks the secrets of this technological frontier. Kuldeep's book, Exploring the Metaverse, is your guide for understanding the metaverse, beyond all the hype. You will learn not just about how we got here, but also about the potential the metaverse holds for businesses and society. This book does not shy away from its challenges either. It gives you a realistic view of the pitfalls and how to navigate them. What sets this book apart is its emphasis on not just understanding but also embracing the metaverse, urging us to see it as an opportunity rather than a threat. Forget the jargon; this book speaks your language, making the complex simple and paving the way for you to navigate this digital landscape responsibly. It is not just an academic read; it is your companion in this journey to discover the next evolution of computing and tech-led experiences.

The question for you is - are you ready to redefine reality?

– Sumeet Gayathri Moghe
Product Manager, Thoughtworks
Author of The Async-First Playbook

A comprehensive book covering a range of metaverse related topics including: Metaverse related emerging technologies, Business and Technology perspectives, Opportunities and Challenges. Knowing Kuldeep and the great work he has been/is doing for quite a few years, I would expect nothing less from him. Wishing him all the best for this book.

– Pradeep Khanna
Executive Director VRAR Association
CEO Global Mindset, Co-Founder INSquare, Adjunct Professor

About the Author

Kuldeep Singh is a seasoned technology professional with a rich background spanning nearly two decades, where he has consistently demonstrated expertise in various roles. His journey has encompassed diverse positions, from a software developer and enterprise architect to an engineering director, practice head, and technical product manager. Currently associated with Thoughtworks Technologies (India) Pvt Ltd., he has also significantly contributed to Nagarro Software (India) Pvt Ltd and Quark Media House during his illustrious career.

In the tech industry, Kuldeep stands out as a trailblazer, playing a pivotal role in pioneering Centers of Excellence for emerging technologies like IoT, AR/VR, and Web3. His leadership extends to overseeing complex data projects in estimations, forecasting, and optimization, designing highly scalable, cloud-native, and microservices-based architectures. He emphasizes bringing technology to the core of the business and advocates for development practices such as CI/CD, Test-Driven Development (TDD), and eXtreme Programming (XP). His extensive experience spans diverse domains, including manufacturing, aviation, education, retail, telecom, healthcare, commodity trading, and more.

Beyond his technical roles, Kuldeep is a prolific writer and speaker, actively sharing insights on technology, leadership, and motivation. His extensive portfolio includes over 100 articles, some of which have gained recognition in esteemed publications such as Economics Times, Tech.de, industry4o.com, Thoughtworks Insights, and Analytics India magazine.

Academically, Kuldeep holds a B. Tech. in Computer Engineering from NIT, Kurukshetra. His commitment to knowledge includes active involvement in events, mentoring and judging initiatives, and volunteering for ideations, hackathons, and nonprofit causes, collaborating with organizations like NASSCOM, Meta, Ministry of Electronics and Information Technology (MeitY) - Government of India, Smart India Hackathon, Digital India, Federation of Indian Chambers of Commerce & Industry (FICCI), AICTE, IEEE, The VRARA, Metaverse India Policy and Standards (MIPS), and academic institutions like IIT, NITs, and other universities across India. He is also engaged with World Metaverse Council, Responsible Metaverse Alliance, and others to collectively build and share the community by open source.

With a passion for empowering others and a steadfast commitment to innovation, Kuldeep stands as a thought leader in the ever-evolving landscape of technology.

About the Reviewer

Raju Kandaswamy is a strategic and innovative principal consultant renowned for his passion for driving technological innovation and product excellence. With a specialization in Generative AI applications and Extended Reality (XR) technologies, he holds a master's degree in Software Systems from BITS Pilani. He has contributed to a leading XR platform, co-inventing six software patents. His commitment to technological advancement and community development is further evidenced by his invitation to speak at KaniTamil-2024 by the TN state government and his active role in leading an AI/ML community.

He co-founded a startup that develops industrial robots showcasing his entrepreneurial spirit and innovation. With 23 years of diverse experience, he is a frequent speaker, sharing his deep knowledge in XR and AI at esteemed conferences and community events. As a mentor and contributor to educational standards, he has played a pivotal role in aligning curricula with industry demands and fostering a culture of learning and innovation.

Acknowledgement

I want to express my deepest gratitude to my friends and family for their unwavering support and motivation throughout my life and during the journey of this book.

I am grateful to Raju Kandaswamy, a distinguished expert in XR, Robotics, and AI and a valued Thoughtworks colleague. Raju has been a great collaborator, offering technical insights, reviewing the manuscript, and providing invaluable suggestions for the content. My appreciation extends to my co-workers Neelarghya, Vaibhav, Nāg, Razin Memon, Arijit, Hari, Deepak, and many more, who supported me in brainstorming and creative ideation and showed a willingness to challenge traditions shaping the XR practices.

I also want to express my gratitude to Thoughtworks, its leadership, and various communities for fostering an environment that encourages the pursuit of passion. Special appreciation goes to Santosh Mahale, Prasanth Soman and Mushtaq Ahmed for guidance in shaping my goals and expectations at Thoughtworks. Authors such as Neal Ford, Martin Fowler, Vinod, Mangalam, Sumeet, and Dinker from Thoughtworks have been instrumental in shaping the author within me, providing valuable mentorship and guidance in professional writing.

I began my journey of writing and sharing insights during my tenure at Nagarro, mostly for internal audiences, but it provided me with a robust foundation. Later, Thoughtworks' content team played a key role in enhancing my storytelling and editing skills. Their support has allowed my articles to find a home in Thoughtworks Insights and other avenues. It gave me the confidence to set up a personal blog site, thinkuldeep.com, and all these efforts became the energy for this book.

Special thanks to the diverse set of leaders from industry, academia, government, and startups who reviewed the book, wrote forewords, and provided testimonials. Engaging with them on various social platforms and discussing ideas with friends at VRARA and Lenovo significantly shaped various narratives in this book. Conversations with Chuck Thota, Feroz Mohummed, Vikram Sharma, Hassan Mahini, and Mayan Shay at various forums were invaluable.

A special acknowledgment to BPB Publications and their exceptional team of content reviewers, editors, and technical reviewers. Thanks for providing me with the opportunity to embark on and drive this enlightening journey.

Lastly, I want to acknowledge that this book encapsulates not just my experiences but those of many directly or indirectly in the metaverse or XR domain, influencing today's and tomorrow's internet. With deep appreciation and a sense of anticipation, let the journey into the metaverse commence!

Preface

The metaverse, a loosely defined term, has gone from a virtual game world to the next internet and sparks conversations on technology's potential. Despite eye-rolling at terms like metaverse and eXtended Reality (XR), immersive technologies are silently becoming part of our daily life through social media, virtual collaboration, and digitized experiences. We seamlessly embrace digital tools, scanning codes, engaging in virtual trials, and altering reality through digital filters. In this evolving landscape, computer vision and AI consistently redefine our perception of reality.

Strategic investments are crucial for technological evolution, but a delicate balance is needed. Even though businesses hesitate to invest without a clear outcome, an initial investment is required to ascertain them. Technology adoption, following the Diffusion of Innovations theory, varies—some invest early, others wait. Hype can drive uninformed investments, emphasizing the need to separate the hype and reality. Identifying promising opportunities in the metaverse is vital, demanding careful consideration and awareness of potential pitfalls.

Understanding our responsibility to adapt to new technologies is crucial in a dynamic era of ever-evolving technology and human interactions. With this recognition and a sense of responsibility, I embark on the journey of writing this book. My goal is to provide insights that distinguish between exaggerated expectations and genuine opportunities of the metaverse, and guiding readers to have a balanced and informed perspective on its promises and challenges. This book moves across **16 chapters**, neatly organized into five parts.

Chapter 1: Exploring the Metaverse Origin - explores the evolution of technology and human interactions, from industrial revolutions to the digital web, and traces the origin of the metaverse.

Chapter 2: Metaverse : Various Forms and Interpretations - examines the expert perspectives and the loosely defined nature of the metaverse and tries to define it with its characteristics. The chapter also addresses myths and reality of the evolving metaverse landscape.

Chapter 3: Understanding XR: Metaverse Foundation - explores the crucial role of XR technologies in enabling the metaverse. It introduces different forms extending the realities (AR, VR, MR, and more) and its immersive capabilities.

Chapter 4: AI Empowering the Metaverse - explores the crucial role of Artificial Intelligence (AI) in enabling intelligent and seamless interactions within the metaverse.

Chapter 5: IoT, Cloud, and Next-gen Networks – covers technological advancements in the Internet of Things (IoT), cloud-based solutions, and next-generation networks, which are instrumental to realizing the full potential of the metaverse.

Chapter 6: Decentralization and the Role of Blockchain – discusses the need for decentralized architectures to make the metaverse open, interoperable, and accessible. It covers the evolution of Blockchain and its role in shaping the metaverse economy.

Chapter 7: Gaming Redefined: The Metaverse Revolution – discusses how the metaverse would redefine the gaming and entertainment industry. It covers immersive experiences in confined spaces like museums, gaming studios, amusement parks, and location independent collaborative internet. Also covers the filmmaking and visualizations in the metaverse.

Chapter 8: Connecting and Engaging in the Metaverse – covers the transformative use cases of the metaverse in connecting people and engaging the world, from easing the communications barriers to redefining physical and virtual travels and tourism.

Chapter 9: Revolutionizing Fitness and Healthcare – covers the metaverse experiences for fitness and sports and how it would revolutionize healthcare by seeing inside more deeply and naturally.

Chapter 10: Exploring the Metaverse Economy – uncovers the metaverse potential of redefining traditional notions of commerce, property, and value. It reimagines digital commerce, digital property, and real states, and is backed by associated digital value in the metaverse economy.

Chapter 11: Skilling and Reskilling in the Enterprise Metaverse – discusses the metaverse's potential to revolutionize the education industry, enterprise training, onboarding, and shaping up the enterprise metaverse.

Chapter 12: Identity Preservation and Privacy Protection – discusses safeguarding the metaverse identity and protecting privacy in the metaverse. It addresses the need to mitigate these risks and ensure trust in metaverse environments.

Chapter 13: Metaverse and Sustainability – presents an understanding of sustainability, the challenges introduced by the metaverse, and the sustainability considerations for shaping up the metaverse.

Chapter 14: Getting Started with Metaverse Development – lays the foundation for metaverse development by exploring the metaverse solutions ecosystem, essential development tools, techniques, and infrastructure.

Chapter 15: Metaverse Practices, Standards, and Initiatives – explores the essential practices for creating engaging metaverse experiences. It also sheds light on the emerging standards and collective initiatives shaping the metaverse landscape.

Chapter 16: Metaverse: A Way Forward - wraps up the book by giving us all a plan on how to use and build the metaverse responsibly. It tells us that we can't avoid the natural evolution and changes happening, so it's better to get ready and adapt to them.

Coloured Images

Please follow the link to download the
Coloured Images of the book:

https://rebrand.ly/kywf4jd

We have code bundles from our rich catalogue of books and videos available at **https://github.com/bpbpublications**. Check them out!

Errata

We take immense pride in our work at BPB Publications and follow best practices to ensure the accuracy of our content to provide with an indulging reading experience to our subscribers. Our readers are our mirrors, and we use their inputs to reflect and improve upon human errors, if any, that may have occurred during the publishing processes involved. To let us maintain the quality and help us reach out to any readers who might be having difficulties due to any unforeseen errors, please write to us at :

errata@bpbonline.com

Your support, suggestions and feedbacks are highly appreciated by the BPB Publications' Family.

Piracy

If you come across any illegal copies of our works in any form on the internet, we would be grateful if you would provide us with the location address or website name. Please contact us at **business@bpbonline.com** with a link to the material.

If you are interested in becoming an author

If there is a topic that you have expertise in, and you are interested in either writing or contributing to a book, please visit **www.bpbonline.com**. We have worked with thousands of developers and tech professionals, just like you, to help them share their insights with the global tech community. You can make a general application, apply for a specific hot topic that we are recruiting an author for, or submit your own idea.

Reviews

Please leave a review. Once you have read and used this book, why not leave a review on the site that you purchased it from? Potential readers can then see and use your unbiased opinion to make purchase decisions. We at BPB can understand what you think about our products, and our authors can see your feedback on their book. Thank you!

For more information about BPB, please visit **www.bpbonline.com**.

Join our book's Discord space

Join the book's Discord Workspace for Latest updates, Offers, Tech happenings around the world, New Release and Sessions with the Authors:

https://discord.bpbonline.com

Table of Contents

Part - 1
Introduction: Unveiling the Metaverse

The introduction sets the stage by offering a concise overview of the metaverse and providing a glimpse into the key insights discussed in the chapters of Part 1. We will start the book with *Chapter 1, Exploring the Metaverse Origin*, delving into the historical context, tracing the metaverse's roots from the evolution of the digital web. This exploration offers valuable insights into how the concept has evolved over time and sets the foundation for understanding its significance.

In *Chapter 2, Metaverse various Forms and Interpretations*, we expand on the diverse interpretations and forms that the metaverse can take. It showcases the breadth of experiences within the metaverse, demonstrating that it is not limited to a singular definition or confined to specific technologies. Part 1 of the book illuminates the extensive possibilities and highlights the dynamic nature of the metaverse.

Collectively, these chapters provide readers with a comprehensive introduction to the metaverse, its origins, and its various forms. By setting the stage and piquing curiosity, readers are primed for the immersive exploration of the metaverse that lies ahead in the subsequent parts of the book.

CHAPTER 1
Exploring the Metaverse Origin

Introduction

This chapter explores the evolution of technology and human interactions, from industrial revolutions to the digital web, and origin of the metaverse. The digital web has transformed how we access and interact with information. Web 1.0 enabled reading static content, Web 2.0 introduced user-generated content and social interactions, and Web 3.0 focuses on personalized immersive experiences with technologies like blockchain, **Internet of Things** (**IoT**), **Artificial Intelligence** (**AI**), and AR/VR.

The chapter also examines visionary ideas from science fiction, the impact of online gaming and virtual worlds, technological advancements in internet technologies, and the concept of the metaverse. By tracing the metaverse's inter-connected realms back to the digital web, readers gain insight into its origins and its transformative potential for human interaction and digital experiences.

Structure

In this chapter, we will discuss the following topics:

- Industrial revolutions and the origin of digital web
- The digital web and human interactions
- Metaverse: The origin

Objectives

The objective of this chapter is to provide readers with an understanding of the evolution of technology and human interactions over time. By exploring the influence of the industrial revolution and the digital web on society, readers will gain insights into how these advancements have shaped human imagination and the possibilities for the future. Additionally, the chapter aims to shed light on how this collective imagination has led to the origin of the metaverse, a concept that embodies interconnected virtual worlds and immersive experiences. Through this exploration, readers will gain a deeper appreciation for the interplay between technology, society, and human imagination in shaping the metaverse.

Industrial revolutions and the origin of digital web

Evolution is an inherent part of human existence, constantly driving us forward through periods of innovation and transformative change. Throughout history, we have witnessed remarkable shifts in technology that have revolutionized the way we live. While the forms and sizes of these technological advancements may vary across different eras, they have always held a profound impact on society. In the present age, the pace of technological evolution is accelerating, propelling us into the future at an unprecedented rate.

In the upcoming sections, we will delve into the intricate relationship between humans and technology across various industrial revolutions. These revolutions mark significant milestones in our collective journey, shaping the course of human progress. *Figure 1.1* serves as a visual representation of this remarkable journey, highlighting the transformative path we have traversed.

Through an exploration of the past, we will gain a deeper understanding of how technological advancements have propelled us forward, unlocking new possibilities and reshaping our world. Each industrial revolution has left an indelible mark on human history, and by examining their significance, we can better appreciate the profound impact technology has had on our lives.

Pre-industrial era

The pre-industrial revolution period in human history is characterized by the transition from stone to bronze and iron materials. During this era, human focus and ingenuity were directed towards discovering and utilizing different materials to improve their homes, tools, and utensils. The primary concern was to adapt to and thrive in their immediate environments.

"Necessity is the mother of all inventions."

Human interactions during this time revolved mainly around needs in the physical world and the manipulation of materials. As societies evolved, people began to expand their horizons, seeking connections and interactions beyond their immediate surroundings. This drive to explore and socialize with others led to the development of new tools and techniques that would ultimately pave the way for the first industrial revolution.

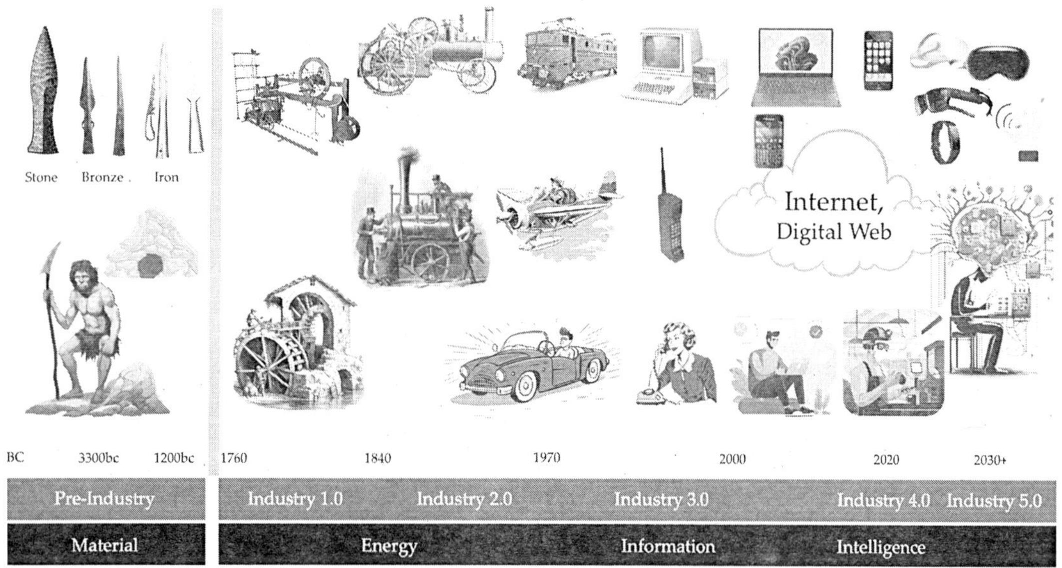

Figure 1.1: *Human history and industrial revolutions*

First industrial revolution

The first industrial revolution or *Industry 1.0* occurred from the late 18th century to the early 19th century, marking a significant shift in human history and the economy. During this period, mechanization and the use of new energy sources revolutionized industries, replacing agriculture as the dominant economic sector.

One of the key developments in this era was the emergence of machines. With the extraction of coal and the invention of the steam engine, a new and powerful source of energy became available. This led to the rapid expansion of manufacturing, particularly in the production of textiles, consumer goods, and transportation through the construction of railroads. The focus of this revolution was on harnessing and utilizing energy from natural resources, such as coal and steam, to drive machinery and accelerate economic growth.

Industry 1.0 also brought significant changes in societal structures and modes of production. Factory systems emerged, leading to urbanization as people moved to work in these factories. New forms of employment, trade, and economic systems developed, transforming the way people worked and earned a living. The interaction between humans and machines became increasingly intertwined, with humans becoming dependent on machines for productivity and efficiency. This dependence on machines and the ongoing evolution in machinery set the stage for subsequent industrial revolutions.

The second industrial revolution

The second industrial revolution, also known as Industry 2.0, emerged in the late 19th century, and brought about significant technological advancements that transformed industries and society. One of the key developments during this period was the introduction of new sources of energy, namely electricity, gas, and oil. These energy sources replaced earlier forms of power, such as steam engines, and enabled more efficient and widespread industrialization.

Industry 2.0 also witnessed the rapid growth of the internal combustion engine, which revolutionized transportation and led to the invention of automobiles and airplanes. These innovations drastically reduced the limitations of physical distance, enabling faster travel and the ability to connect with people and places previously inaccessible. Additionally, the development of steel production techniques and chemical synthesis further fueled industrial growth during this time. Another pivotal aspect of the second industrial revolution was the advancement of communication technologies. The telegraph, telephone, and television became integral tools for transmitting information over long distances, facilitating faster and more efficient communication between individuals and businesses.

The combined effects of these advancements in energy, transportation, materials, and communication paved the way for unprecedented industrial growth and laid the foundation. In fact, Industry 2.0 is often regarded as one of the most important periods in history, as it propelled humanity into a new era of technological progress and set the stage for further transformative developments in Industry 3.0 and beyond.

The third industrial revolution

The third industrial revolution, Industry 3.0, emerged in the second half of the 20th century, marking significant advancements in technology and energy sources. During this revolution, nuclear energy became a prominent source of untapped power, however, this era is primarily known for the rise of electronics, telecommunications, and computers. These technological breakthroughs played a crucial role in transforming communication, making distance more relevant, and opening doors to space expeditions, research, and biotechnology. The invention of **Programmable Logic Controllers** (**PLCs**) and robots introduced the concept of machines performing tasks on behalf of humans, leading to advanced industrial automation.

This era also witnessed the increasing importance of information and its role in connecting and separating the world. The transition from analog to digital became normalized, with computing devices such as portable mobile phones laying the foundation for the devices we rely on today. A significant development during this period was the establishment of the **Internet**, which enabled the transfer of digital information among various computers. The introduction of the **Transfer Control Protocol / Internetwork Protocol (TCP/IP)** as a communications protocol paved the way for the **digital web** and the belief in digital content as a tangible reality.

The fourth industrial revolution and the future

The fourth industrial revolution, Industry 4.0, represents the era we are in. While previous industrial revolutions took decades or even centuries to unfold, Industry 4.0 is characterized by rapid advancements and paradigm shifts happening within a short span of time. In today's digital age, breakthroughs are occurring at an astonishing rate, and the pace of change is expected to accelerate even further in the future.

In Industry 4.0, the focus remains on information, as seen in the previous revolution, but with a shift towards harnessing intelligence from that information. The IoT plays a significant role in this revolution, with an increasingly connected world and an abundance of data. Machines are now capable of collecting information, making sense of it, and generating knowledge. This enables them to provide actionable insights for both humans and machines, leading to better and faster decision-making.

The advent of generative AI is opening new possibilities in Industry 4.0 and beyond. Machines can generate intelligence, revolutionizing various aspects of our lives. This ongoing technological evolution is transforming the world into a new digital realm, a virtual world that was once only imaginable. It allows us to transcend the limitations of physical reality and explore new frontiers.

Human interactions with machines are also evolving in this era. Traditional methods of input, such as physical keyboards, are no longer the limit. We are entering a phase where interaction with the virtual world goes beyond 2D screens, providing immersive and intuitive experiences.

In the upcoming section, we will explore how human interactions have evolved alongside the development of the digital web, leading us to a new era of spatial computing and the potential realization of the metaverse.

The digital web and human interactions

The industrial revolutions played a crucial role in the development of computing machines capable of processing digital information. These machines have evolved over time, transitioning from room-sized devices to more compact and portable forms, such as laptops and mobile phones. Additionally, wearable devices like smart glasses and smartwatches have further contributed to the digitization of our world.

With constant internet connectivity, these computing devices have given rise to the digital web. The digital web is a vast network that facilitates the storage, retrieval, and sharing of digital information. It has brought about a revolution in the way we access and interact with data, making it easily accessible through the web. This transformation has had a profound impact on various aspects of human interactions, ranging from communication and information retrieval to entertainment and commerce.

In the subsequent sections, we will explore the evolution of the digital web over time and delve into how humans interact with this digital landscape. We will also discuss the exciting possibilities and advancements that lie ahead as we continue to navigate the ever-evolving digital realm.

Pre web era

During the pre-web era, which began during *Industry 2.0*, the journey towards digitization commenced. This era was characterized by advancements in mechanics and energy sources, which eventually led to the invention of computing machines capable of processing information in digital formats. However, these early computing machines were large and slow, with limited interactivity.

In the early stages of digitization, users had to feed punched cards into the computer to input data and receive output in physical forms. This era, referred to as the **Batch age** in *Figure 1.2*, lacked real-time interaction with the computing machines. Results were obtained after hours or even days of processing. As technology progressed, improvements were made to provide a better user experience. Display screens and keyboards were introduced, marking the **Command Line Interface (CLI)** age. Users could now receive alerts and display information on the screen, as well as input commands for further processing. Companies like Apple and Xerox made significant investments during this period, although many of their products were not commercially successful. Nonetheless, their contributions paved the way for future technological advancements. Microsoft's DOS and Unix/Linux shell gained prominence during the CLI Age. The internet was invented during this time, and network protocols allowed access and sharing over CLI.

Overall, the pre-web era witnessed the initial steps towards digitization, with computing machines gradually becoming more interactive and user-friendly. These advancements set the stage for the rapid development and transformation of technology that would follow in the coming decades and become the foundation for *Industry 4.0* described earlier. The following figure illustrates the evolution of human integrations in the digital web:

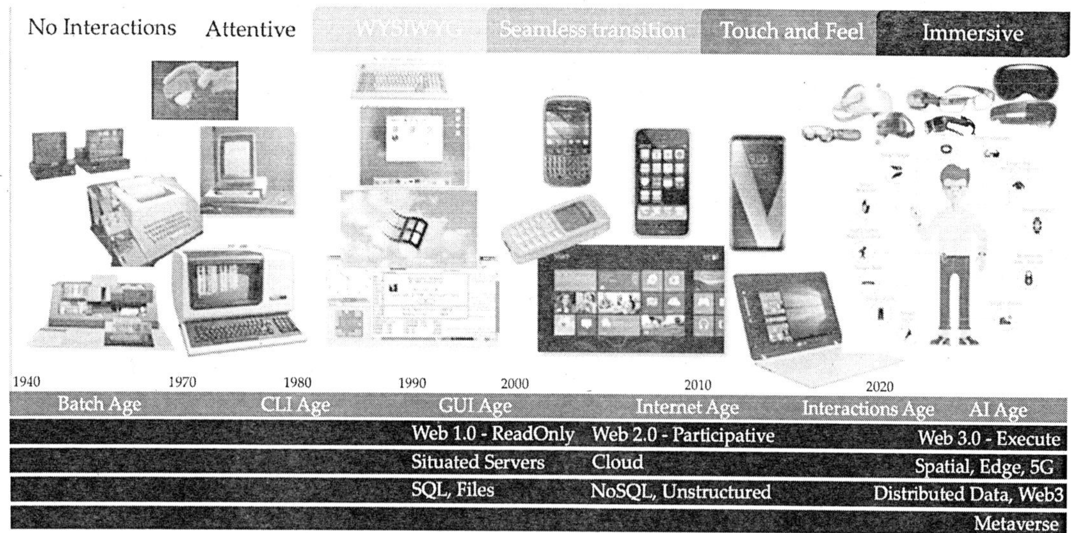

Figure 1.2: Evolution of human integrations in the digital web

Web 1.0

Web 1.0, also known as the Read-only web, marked a significant milestone in the evolution of the web. During this era, which emerged in the late 1980s, the focus was on the development of **Graphical User Interfaces (GUI)** and user-friendly interactions.

The **GUI age** began in the early 1980s, with advancements in technology leading to the introduction of window-based interfaces and **What You See Is What You Get (WYSIWYG)** interactions. Companies like Xerox and Apple made costly attempts to popularize GUI through products like Xerox Star and Apple Lisa. However, it was Microsoft and Apple's efforts with Windows 1.0 and Macintosh in the mid-1980s that gained significant traction. GUI interfaces became widely adopted, and the GUI age continued to evolve with improvements in software and hardware technologies to accommodate various screen sizes.

In the late 1980s, the concept of the **World Wide Web** (**WWW**), or the web was introduced as a global information medium. Users could access the Web through computers connected to the Internet using protocols like **HyperText Transfer Protocol** (**HTTP**). The first web browser and WYSIWYG HTML editor, called WorldWideWeb[1], was developed. Subsequently, several web browsers were introduced to display static web content created using HTML. This marked the establishment of Web 1.0 as a platform where users could read, and access static content hosted on web servers.

During the Web 1.0 era, **Structured Query Language** (**SQL**) and **Database Management Systems** (**DBMS**) also got its shape and became a crucial technology for server-side data storage, enabling efficient data querying and retrieval. The focus was on providing users with the information they were seeking, making SQL an essential tool for serving static content on the web. This period saw the rise of web pages, home pages, file/web servers, search engines, email services, peer-to-peer file sharing, content portals, and enterprise portals.

Web 1.0 laid the foundation for the modern web, establishing the concept of a global information network accessible through computers. However, during this phase, the web was primarily a one-way communication channel, with limited interactivity and user-generated content.

Web 2.0

Web 2.0 represented a significant shift in the evolution of the web, transitioning from a read-only platform to a more participatory and interactive experience. After approximately 15 years of advancements in the GUI age, the web began to take shape as a platform that allowed users to actively contribute and share content. The focus shifted towards shared web resources and the emergence of various interactive features. People started tagging individuals, creating web profiles, forming web communities, and engaging in activities such as blogging and contributing to wikis. This period also saw the rise of information portals that encouraged user-generated content and collaboration. It can be seen as an era of shaping and molding the web to fit the needs and interests of its users, and believing in the virtual identities of social media, thousands of virtual connections.

This phase is often referred as the *Internet age* (*Figure 1.2*), as mobile phones became ubiquitous, and user interactions started transitioning from desktop-based GUIs to web or mobile app-based GUIs. The web became more programmable, with technologies like JavaScript that enabled dynamic and editable web experiences, and AJAX allowed for desktop-like partial GUI rendering on web pages, enhancing the interactivity and responsiveness of the user interface.

During this period, there was an increasing emphasis on seamless GUI transitions across devices. Mobile devices were becoming more powerful and prevalent, leading to a growing demand for mobile-first GUI designs. Keypads and display screens were the primary input and output interfaces for most devices. Companies like Nokia, Motorola, and Blackberry played significant roles in the cell phone market, with QWERTY keypads becoming popular. Laptops and tablets with external keyboards largely replaced traditional desktop PCs.

A significant change in human interactions came with the popularization of touch screen interfaces, spearheaded by the release of the Apple iPhone in 2007. The touch and feel experience gained momentum, with various manufacturers, including Samsung, contributing to the mass adoption of touch-based interactions. Touch screen interfaces surpassed physical keypads, while Nokia and Blackberry still relied on the haptic feedback provided by physical buttons, but people accepted touch-based interaction as the new normal. *Figure 1.3* shows mobile phones with variety of physical keypads and without keypads:

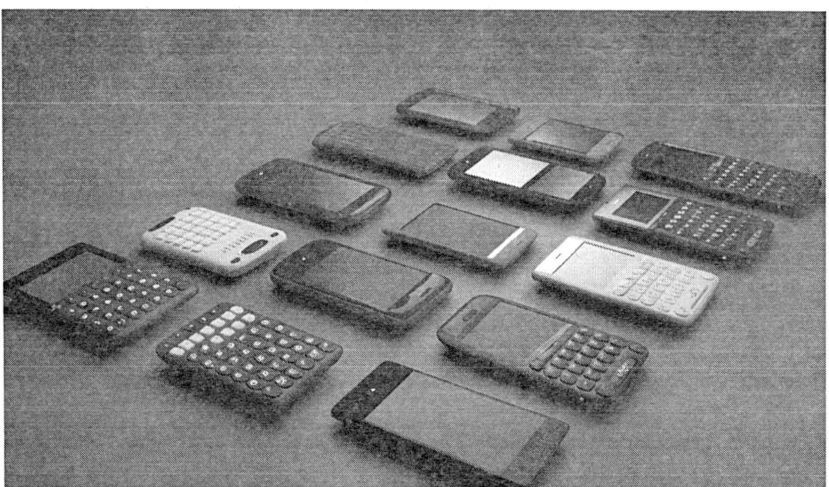

***Figure 1.3**: Various mobile devices with and without physical keypad*

Throughout the Internet age, advancements in technology, such as IoT and cloud-based infrastructure for web servers, further enhanced internet connectivity and interactions. The phone transformed into a smartphone, bringing devices closer to humans to the point where they could be worn and interacted with physically. The Internet age gradually transitioned into the Interactions age, with the Digital web paving the way for the future development of Web 3.0.

Web 3.0 and later

Web 3.0, building upon the foundations laid by Web 2.0, represents the era of the **Interaction age** that emerged around 2010 and continues to evolve, refer *Figure 1.2*. In this period, our reliance on technology has grown significantly, leading to an abundance of recorded interactions and a massive increase in data. Data has become a powerful asset, driving the development of Web 3.0.

Web 3.0 is often referred to as the executable web, also referred as semantic web, characterized by distributed and decentralized architectures, including technologies like blockchain. These architectures aim to address the need for personalization and localized trust-ability. Trust in technology has grown to the extent that traveling with strangers is no longer a concern. For example, transportation services like Uber, Ola, have gained our trust, transforming the way we interact with transportation services. Text-based interactions have gained prominence over phone calls, and social media has become a powerful platform due to these changes.

In the Web 3.0 era, we are increasingly treating digital content as real. Conversational user interfaces powered by generative AI have become prevalent, mimicking human-like responses. Instead of navigating through websites or bulky portals, we can simply send a text or voice message to a bot, and it will provide us with the desired result. Voice interfaces, exemplified by devices like Google Home and Amazon Echo, are gaining popularity. IoT empowers voice based conversational interfaces, enabling numerous enterprise use cases. Devices have become increasingly integrated into our lives, to the point where we can wear them and experience their functionalities firsthand. The smartphone serves as the central processing unit, controller, and internet gateway for wearable and sensing devices. Lightweight communication protocols such as MQTT and BLE have been developed to facilitate communication with IoT and wearable devices.

Figure 1.4: *Immersive interactions in Web 3.0 era*

Smart glasses and smartwatches are examples of products that provide more immersive interactions, blurring the lines between the physical and virtual worlds. The next level of immersive interactions comes from technologies like **Augmented Reality (AR)** and **Virtual Reality (VR)**. These interactions occur within computer-generated environments that are mapped onto real-looking environments. AR and VR technologies are also being integrated into future mobile applications. *Figure 1.4* depicts the immersive experience, and we will cover these advancements in depth in *Part 2* of this book:

Moreover, the development of **Brain-Computer Interfaces (BCI)** is shaping the web. Ongoing research in this field aims to establish direct communication between computers and the brain. BCI has the potential to enable individuals with visual disabilities to see through camera streams directly in their brain or assist those with mobility challenges by enabling movement through brain-implanted chips. The convergence of AR, VR, and AI will play a significant role in shaping these immersive interactions.

AI is instrumental in making these interactions look and feel more realistic. Hardware is becoming more flexible, regeneratable (3D printable), and wearable. Devices are shrinking in size to the point where they can be taken as a pill[2] and controlled externally. Technology is increasingly aligning with its context and application. Examples include:

- BLE-enabled contact lenses for eyes,
- Printed stickers for monitoring vital signs like blood pressure and heart rate,
- Smart shoes to guide foot movement,
- Smart glasses to record visual experiences,
- Smart gloves to assist with work tasks, and
- Smart shirts to ensure comfort and regulate body temperature,
- Smart edible pills to help diagnose internals disorders

The possibilities are vast and ever-expanding.

In summary, Web 3.0 and the onward journey represents the era of immersive interactions, where technology integrates seamlessly into our lives. It encompasses advancements in AI, wearable devices, AR/VR, and the exploration of BCI. The web is evolving to become more context-aware and tailored to individual needs. It is an exciting age of innovation and limitless possibilities.

Metaverse: the origin

While exploring industrial revolutions and the digital web, we explored how technology evolution has shaped human interactions and the significance of technology in our lives. People readily adopt technology that not only eases their work but also provides a sense of enjoyment. Various forms of media, such as movies, games, and books, have sparked imagination and allowed people to view the world differently.

The term "Metaverse" originated in 1992 from a science fiction novel *Snow Crash by Neal Stephenson*. It describes a persistent, immersive, shared virtual world where individuals interact. Similar concepts have been revisited in sci-fi works like Ernest Cline's Ready Player One, which portrays the **Ontologically Anthropocentric Sensory Immersive**

Simulation (OASIS) as a massively multiplayer online simulation accessible through haptic devices.

Figure 1.5: The metaverse - an imagination becoming a reality

> **"People come to Oasis for all the things they can do, because of all the things they can be."**
>
> -- *a dialogue from Real Player One*[3]

The dictionary meaning of the word *Meta* means *beyond*, suggesting that the Metaverse represents a universe beyond real life. In *Neal Stephenson's Snow Crash*, the Metaverse is controlled by the fictional Global Multimedia Protocol Group, while in Ready Player One, it is owned by Innovative Online Industries. While social networks follow winner-take-all economics, virtual spaces offer diverse experiences and defy the same path.

> **"If you are traveling beyond this life, where the weight of tradition cannot follow..."**
>
> -- *a dialogue from Second Life commercials*[4]

Human interactions and the digital web have evolved to closely resemble the concepts depicted in science fiction. People can participate in these virtual spaces through digital representations of themselves, known as avatars or skins, taking on any desired form. Restrictions may arise from terms of service, community standards, intellectual property, or licensing requirements. Currently, the Metaverse is viewed as a collective set of online, connected experiences, where the "player" (human) is connected to an online framework that enables live content changes, social connections, and monetization. The Metaverse is a living multiverse of interconnected worlds.

While there are multiple definitions and interpretations of the Metaverse, enterprises define it based on their business narrative. Some may use alternative terms like cyberspace, spatial environment, spatial computing, semantic web, spatial web, extended world, or extended reality. The key aspect of the Metaverse being discussed today is the technological advancements that have made imagination a possibility. Whether called the Metaverse or given a new name, we are progressively approaching a connected and immersive world.

Conclusion

In this chapter, we have explored the evolution of technology throughout different industrial revolutions and its profound impact on society. We have witnessed how human interactions with machines have evolved, and the digital web has rapidly advanced alongside technology. As technology has progressed, so has our imagination for what the future holds. Art and culture have also evolved in tandem with technological advancements, shaping new forms of expression and experiences.

One fascinating concept that was once considered purely science-fiction is now becoming a reality: the Metaverse. With the advancements in technology, the Metaverse is emerging as a convergence of virtual reality, augmented reality, and immersive technologies. It holds the potential to revolutionize how we interact with digital worlds, bridging the gap between the physical and virtual realms.

In the next chapter, we will delve deeper into the Metaverse by exploring its various definitions and interpretations.

Points to remember

Here are some points to remember from this chapter:

- Technology is evolving at an unprecedented rate, with industrial revolutions now occurring in shorter time frames compared to the past.
- Human interactions and imagination have evolved alongside technology, envisioning possibilities for the future.
- The term "metaverse" originated in science fiction and is now becoming a reality with advancements in technology and digital web.
- The metaverse encompasses multiple interpretations and definitions, representing a convergence of virtual reality, augmented reality, and immersive technologies.

References

1. World Wide Web - **https://www.pewresearch.org/internet/2014/03/11/world-wide-web-timeline/**

2. **https://new.nsf.gov/news/smart-pills-help-diagnose-gut-disorders**
3. READY PLAYER ONE - Official Trailer 1 - **https://youtu.be/cSp1dM2Vj48**
4. Second Life Commercial - **https://youtu.be/BqeyN77nLyQ**

CHAPTER 2
Metaverse: Various Forms and Interpretations

Introduction

The chapter covers the diverse manifestations and interpretations of the metaverse. From its portrayal as a game, virtual world, and **eXtended Real (XR)** world to its role as a new social media platform and collaboration hub, the chapter delves into the different facets of the metaverse. It examines expert perspectives and the loosely defined nature of the concept, while also discussing the metaverse's potential as the next evolution of the internet. The chapter explores metadata and people networks, characteristics of the metaverse, immersive experiences, and their impact across various sectors. It also addresses misconceptions and trends, guiding navigating the evolving metaverse landscape.

Structure

In this chapter, we will discuss the following topics:

- Metaverse: a game
- Metaverse: a virtual world
- Metaverse: an extended real world
- Metaverse: a social collaboration platform
- Metaverse: as defined by the experts

- Defining the metaverse
- Metaverse: the next internet
- Metaverse: myths vs reality
- Navigating the evolving metaverse landscape

Objectives

The objective of the chapter is to provide readers with a comprehensive understanding of the diverse interpretations of the metaverse concept and the reasons behind its loose definition. By exploring different perspectives and examining myths and realities surrounding the metaverse, readers will gain insights into the evolving nature of this concept. Additionally, this chapter aims to establish a common definition and outline the key characteristics associated with the metaverse. Upon completing this chapter, readers will have a solid foundation for comprehending the metaverse and its implications in future discussions.

Metaverse: a game

Digital gaming has played a significant role in driving the adoption of technology. From preloaded card games to iconic titles like Super Mario on personal computers and the Snake game on Nokia mobile phones, gaming has been instrumental in shaping entertainment and technology adoption. The influence of gaming on technological advancements can be traced back to science fiction games and entertainment, making it natural to view the metaverse as a game, while the term itself originated from a science-fiction novel.

Here is a dialogue from the science-fiction movie *Free Guy*, where an ordinary guy gets into the game, accidentally and sees the world from the eyes of a player. A game character explains to him about the world by saying:

"Guy, this world, it's a video game, and it's full of bad guys, we need you to be the good guy...[1] "

Multiplayer online games have flourished with the advent of the digital web. Games like *World of Warcraft*[2], *Star Wars Galaxies*[3], and *MxO*[4] have brought together millions of players, requiring substantial technological infrastructure to support shared world sessions and collaborative tasks. Inventions like *Xbox*[5], *PlayStation*[6] also took gaming to the next level. These games simulate various activities such as sports, racing, combat, music concerts, and social interactions. Additionally, players can earn and trade within these digital games.

Platforms like *Linden Lab's Second Life*[7] go beyond being just a game by introducing their currency and providing open access to users through digital avatars. These online games aim to replicate and reimagine the real world in the virtual game, offering players limitless possibilities and imaginative experiences. *Figure 2.1* below depicts a player playing a multiplayer online game on a laptop.

***Figure 2.1**: Multiplayer online game*

The list of such games is endless, with titles like *Fortnite*[8], *Decentraland*[9], *Sandbox*[10], and more emerging as community-based co-creation and play-to-earn platforms. Some people refer to these games as metaverses, connecting people and enabling them to transcend physical boundaries, allowing them to be and do whatever they desire within the virtual realm. However, the metaverse cannot just be what we see while playing a game, it has potential beyond the game screen. Let us see more interpretations.

Metaverse: a virtual world

Facebook's dominant position in the realm of social media and its significant investments in virtual world devices and applications has solidified its presence as a key player in the metaverse landscape. Through their rebranding as *Meta*, they have embarked on a mission to establish the metaverse as a virtual world that faithfully replicates the real world. In this envisioned metaverse, individuals would be able to assume virtual identities known as avatars and seamlessly connect to this virtual world in a manner like how they connect to the internet. It is essential, however, to recognize that *Meta's* endeavors should not be equated with the entirety of the metaverse concept. While their efforts are noteworthy and influential, the metaverse encompasses a broader scope beyond *Meta's* specific initiatives. *Figure 2.2* below depicts a virtual world imagination.

***Figure 2.2:** The virtual world*

Numerous other companies, including *Samsung, HTC, Sony, Lenovo,* and many more, have also ventured into the development of virtual worlds by creating devices and enabling the creation of applications for immersive 3D environments. This expansion has not only revolutionized the gaming and entertainment industry but has also unlocked new possibilities for realistic simulations, such as providing virtual tour experiences or facilitating immersive medical procedures. Industries are actively exploring the potential of virtual world simulations in various fields, including painless surgeries, psychological therapy, immersive training, onboarding, and education.

It is worth noting that while the replication of the real world and the immersive experiences offered by virtual worlds are often referred to as aspects of the metaverse, the metaverse encompasses a broader range of interpretations and applications. The subsequent sections will delve into more alternative understandings.

Metaverse: an extended real world

Niantic Labs[11], renowned for popularizing **Augmented Reality (AR)** through games like *Pokémon Go,* defines the metaverse as an enhanced version of the existing universe, referring to it as the *real world metaverse. Niantic's* objective is to build 3D maps and augment the entire world using its *Lightship platform*[12], which is accessible to developers and creators. *Google CEO Sundar Pichai*[13] views the metaverse as immersive computing in the realm of AR. Even *Apple's VisionPro*[14] touted as a spatial computer, affirms the idea that the evolution of the metaverse extends beyond purely virtual worlds, emphasizing the seamless integration of digital elements into the physical world. *Figure 2.3* below depicts an eXtended world seen using smart glasses:

Figure 2.3: The extended real world

Perceiving the world through a different lens leads us into a realm that transcends physical reality, qualifying it as a metaverse. This presents an opportunity to not only connect with people but also connect with everything in the world, as every object in the physical realm can have an associated digital context that can be shared among individuals. The impact of technologies like *Google Maps* on travel and logistics demonstrates how we rely on technology to navigate and access contextual information. With features such as real-time traffic updates, automatic rerouting, and the integration of nearby restaurants, accidents, congestion, and toll information, *Google Maps* extends the real-world experience. When such information is linked to devices like heads-up displays in cars, helmets, or smart glasses, it evokes a sense of living in a science fiction movie. Imagine billboards transforming into augmented assistants, and a hyper-personalized world where every individual encounter personalized advertisement within the same physical space. This vision of the metaverse, where individuals have the power to redefine the world according to their preferences, is widely accepted and embraced. Physical locations would become hubs for communication and become more important when people see social context mapped / tagged to these locations.

In essence, the metaverse as an extended real-world encompasses the integration of digital and physical elements, providing a rich and personalized experience that goes beyond traditional boundaries.

Metaverse: a social collaboration platform

Facebook, now known as *Meta*, has emerged as a company that has revolutionized social collaboration. Through strategic investments and acquisitions of platforms like *Instagram* and *WhatsApp*, *Meta* has established itself as a leader in this domain. These social platforms have transformed communication, eliminating the need for traditional telephone calls, much like how telephones replaced the need for physical meetings in many contexts. The introduction of video conferencing / calling features on these social collaboration platforms, as well as tools like *Zoom* and *Microsoft Teams*, has further enhanced alliance by allowing participants to see each other and express themselves in real-time. *Figure 2.4* below depicts a social collaboration using smart glasses or with advanced display:

Figure 2.4: *Social collaboration platform*

Given their expertise in social collaboration, it is natural for companies like *Meta* (formerly *Facebook*) and *Microsoft* to extend this concept into the realm of virtual worlds. In these virtual spaces, individuals can collaborate with personalized and imaginary identities, creating and defining virtual environments where they can invite others to join them. *Meta* has launched *Horizon World*[15], while *Microsoft* has introduced an immersive version of *Microsoft Teams* called *Mesh*[16]. These advancements have revolutionized video calls, with features such as filters that enable users to change their surroundings, backgrounds, and even real-time facial expressions and gestures, which can be shared with collaborators. These filters allow people to work remotely and present themselves in different ways, altering their appearance, attire, and even the environment in which they are seen. These dynamic collaboration environments can be seen as a form of metaverse, and when integrated with advanced AR and **Virtual Reality (VR)** devices, they provide a seamless transition for users into an all-new world, called the metaverse.

While *Facebook's* social platforms have redefined human connection, this type of metaverse introduces the concept of multiple identities that can be entirely distinct from one's physical self. It opens new possibilities for social interaction and collaboration, where individuals can assume different roles and personas within virtual spaces.

Metaverse: as defined by the experts

We find several definitions of the metaverse, based on different understandings and interests, and the intentions of people and industry. *Cathy Hackl* tried to collect inputs from industry experts and published a report in *Forbes*[17], that the metaverse is defined differently and even named it differently. Some call it metaverse, while others call it *a collective virtual shared space, Mirrorworld, Omniverse, the Nth Floor, AR Cloud, Spatial Internet, 3D Internet*, or *Spatial Web*. While defining the term is not easy, one thing is probably true. The term will not be defined by one single person or company, it will be defined by many, and it will evolve. The language we use to describe the future today is ever-changing. The report covers definitions and perspectives on the metaverse shared by 20 professionals. The definitions are primarily in the following categories:

The virtual universe and open digital space

Most of the experts defined the metaverse as a virtual universe or open digital space where all digital experiences exist for all. It encompasses the idea of a vast, observable digital universe comprising countless digital galaxies. These definitions highlight the potential for individuals to engage in new and immersive ways, creating their worlds and connecting with others in a digitally constructed environment. They envision the metaverse as a connective tissue between humanity, allowing for full interactive reality and the integration of virtual experiences into various aspects of our lives.

Seamless integration of physical and digital realities

A couple of experts defined the metaverse as a concept that blurs the boundary between physical and digital realities. They highlight the metaverse as a bridge between actual and virtual realms, where individuals can navigate and interact with both worlds simultaneously. These definitions emphasize the convergence of the digital and physical realms, often envisioning the use of advanced technologies like AR and VR to create a seamless and immersive experience that extends beyond the limitations of physical space.

Immersive and interactive experience

The experts from the user experience designing side have emphasized the metaverse as an immersive and interactive experience. They describe the metaverse as a space where individuals can create memories and engage in activities that rival physical experiences in scope, meaning, and value. These definitions emphasize the importance of social connection and authentic interactions within the metaverse, enabling hyper-social co-experiences and deep connections with others. They often highlight the potential for shared spatial awareness, agency, and participation in a virtual economy within the metaverse, with significant societal impact.

In summary, we can say that the definitions provided by professionals across various industries offer unique perspectives on the metaverse, reflecting its potential as a virtual universe, a bridge between physical and digital realities, and an immersive and interactive experience. These definitions serve as starting points for understanding and exploring the concept, providing insights into the diverse range of ideas and visions surrounding the metaverse.

In the coming decade, as technology progresses, the metaverse will likely undergo further development and transformation. It will require ongoing exploration, innovation, and collaboration across disciplines to fully comprehend and shape its potential. As brands, companies, and individuals seek to embrace the metaverse, it becomes increasingly important to reflect on its meaning and consider how it can be leveraged to create meaningful and inclusive experiences for all.

Defining the metaverse

Defining the metaverse is a multifaceted and ever-evolving undertaking. As technology rapidly progresses and our digital environment expands, the lines between our physical and digital lives become progressively more indistinct. The metaverse envisions a future where these realms harmoniously merge, creating a virtual universe that presents limitless opportunities. In this context, we embark on a quest to comprehend and propose an additional definition for the metaverse, considering its dynamic nature and the myriad interpretations surrounding it.

Metadata and people network

The concept of the metaverse encompasses various elements that emerge from a careful examination of definitions provided by enterprises and experts. These include co-creation, openness, currency, self-sustainability, communities, sharing, collaboration, and networks. To better grasp the metaverse, it is essential to first comprehend two fundamental terms: **metadata** and **Internet**. *Figure 2.5* below depicts the metadata and their network:

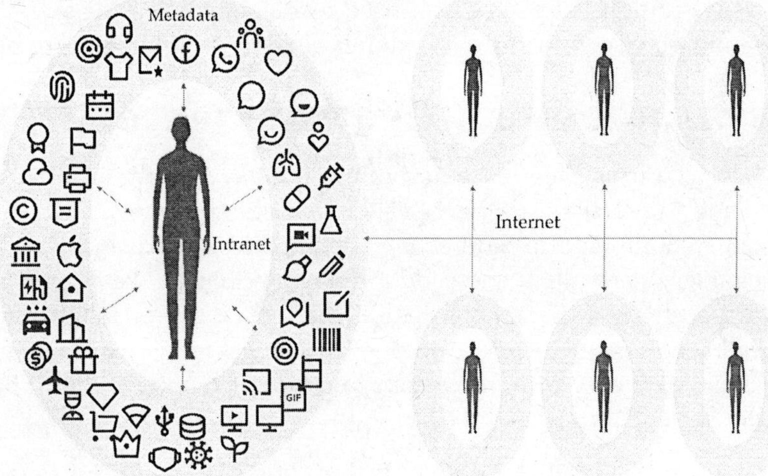

Figure 2.5: *Metadata and Internet*

Metadata refers to additional or supplementary data that characterize various aspects of an individual, such as their email address, phone number, address, interests, preferences, possessions, and places they frequently visited, and more. This metadata can be seen as forming an **Intranet of Metadata** when connected to an individual. Similarly, when all individuals' metadata connections are considered collectively, it can be referred to as the **Internet of Metadata**. Understanding these concepts lays the foundation for a more comprehensive definition of the metaverse.

Metaverse and its characteristics

Having established the relationship between metadata, its internet, and the metaverse, we can now refine our definition of the metaverse.

"The metaverse is a vast digital universe that is constructed upon the network of metadata connected to and about individuals. In this universe, the boundaries between the real and the virtual blur, and avatars serve as representations of individuals, interacting with virtual identities, intellectual properties, assets, societies, and currencies unique to this digital realm. It is a space where the physical and digital intertwine, enabling immersive experiences and a new dimension of social interaction and economic opportunities."

To further enhance our understanding of the metaverse, it is crucial to consider its defining characteristics as listed below:

- **Open and independent:** The metaverse should be open for use and development, allowing individuals to freely access and contribute to its ecosystem. It should not be controlled by any single entity or organization.
- **One and interoperable:** The metaverse should be a unified entity, providing a seamless and integrated experience across different software and hardware platforms. It should enable interoperability, allowing various systems and technologies to work together within the metaverse.
- **For everyone and self-sustainable:** The metaverse should be accessible to all individuals, regardless of their background or resources. It should offer opportunities for people to earn, buy, and sell within its virtual environment, creating a self-sustaining economy.

These characteristics emphasize the importance of inclusivity, openness, and sustainability in shaping the metaverse, ensuring that it remains a collaborative and thriving digital space for all participants.

Metaverse: the next internet

When we delve into the definition and characteristics of the metaverse, we begin to see a striking resemblance to the current state of the internet. The metaverse, like the internet, is envisioned as an open and inclusive space, welcoming individuals from all walks of life. It is a realm where people can connect, collaborate, and interact with each other, transcending physical boundaries. Just as the internet revolutionized the way we access information and communicate, the metaverse represents the next natural step in this evolution - **The Next Internet**.

The metaverse holds immense potential for a plethora of applications and experiences. It encompasses virtual identities, photo-realistic avatars, and virtual intellectual properties/assets, enabling individuals to navigate a universe where the lines between the real and the virtual blur. Within the metaverse, communities, and societies can form, fostered by shared interests, interactions, and virtual currencies that facilitate transactions and economic activity. It becomes a self-sustaining ecosystem where individuals can not only exist but also thrive.

As we move forward, the notion of connecting to the internet and opening a specific web page published over the internet will transform into joining the metaverse and entering into a specific space published in the metaverse or browsing the metaverse applications. The metaverse will become an integral part of our digital lives, seamlessly integrated with our daily experiences. This evolution is not a matter of personal choice or preference, but an organic process driven by advancements in technology and the ever-expanding digital landscape. Just as the internet transformed the world, the metaverse holds the potential to reshape how we interact, create, and explore in the digital realm. So, in simple terms, the metaverse is a stage internet, and what we are seeing is just some metaverse applications and technological advancements that take would us to that stage, though the current stage is far from the true metaverse.

While opinions and sentiments may vary regarding the metaverse, its emergence is an inevitable outcome of our collective technological progress. It is a testament to our innate curiosity and desire to push the boundaries of what is possible. As we embark on this journey towards a more interconnected and immersive digital future, the metaverse stands as a testament to the ever-evolving nature of technology and its transformative impact on society.

Metaverse: myths vs reality

In this section, we delve into the prevalent myths and misconceptions surrounding the metaverse and contrast them with the reality of this emerging digital phenomenon. The metaverse has captured the imagination of many, but it is essential to separate fact from fiction to gain a clearer understanding of its true nature and potential. *Table 2.1* covers myths or misconception and the reality of the metaverse:

Myth / Misconception	In reality
Meta is metaverse, Metaverse means Facebook/Meta.	*Meta* is the name of a technology company that was formerly known as *Facebook*. The metaverse is a broader concept and stage of the internet that refers to a virtual digital universe where people can interact with each other and digital environments in real time. While *Meta* (formerly *Facebook*) has expressed its interest in developing metaverse-related technologies, the metaverse encompasses a much larger ecosystem beyond any single company.
Metaverse is simply a gaming gimmick or limited to the gaming industry.	The metaverse goes beyond gaming and has implications in various sectors and aspects of life. While gaming is an important component of the metaverse, it is not the sole purpose or definition of this concept.
Metaverse means virtual space, Metaverse means virtual reality. Metaverse means virtual, We can only visit the metaverse through augmented reality or virtual reality.	The metaverse encompasses a broader concept that includes both virtual and physical realities, and it is not solely reliant on VR/AR technology. It is a stage of internet evolution where metaverse applications would be interoperable and accessible across hardware, software, technology, and tools.

Myth / Misconception	In reality
The metaverse will be a single, centralized space owned by some company. The metaverse will be a monopoly.	The true vision of the metaverse is a decentralized and open digital universe that transcends any individual entity's control. It would be just like the Internet, it is not owned by anyone, and what people own is web resources like IP, domains, websites, and more, similarly the metaverse would be open but people will own their resources in it. However, we are yet to reach that stage, initially, companies may build their own metaverse implementation called metaverse applications and as we grow common standards and practices would evolve to make their applications interoperable.
There will not be a single metaverse; there will always be multiple applications like Omniverse, Metaversity, SecondLife Viewer, Ready Player One, Roblox, and more.	The metaverse is comparable to the internet. Internet today, where there are numerous applications and websites, but we do not refer to these individual entities as **the Internet**. Similarly, there will be multiple metaverse applications to cater to different industries and use cases. However, these individual applications are not the metaverse itself; rather, the metaverse represents a broader concept.
Metaverse is NFT, Metaverse must use blockchain Metaverse must use a cryptocurrency	The metaverse is not limited to NFTs or Blockchains. While they have gained popularity and are just one aspect of the metaverse. The metaverse encompasses a broader concept of a virtual universe where people interact and engage with immersive experiences. It includes technologies like VR, AR, AI, and virtual economies, offering diverse opportunities beyond NFTs or cryptocurrency. While blockchain technology can play a role in the metaverse, it is not a requirement. *Chapter 6, Decentralization and the Role of Blockchain* would cover it in detail.
Metaverse is only for GenZ, Alpha	No metaverse is not targeted to a particular generation, it has wide use cases across the verticals and age, race, location, etc.
There is no **ROI (Return on Investment)** in the metaverse	There is ROI potential in the metaverse applications. Businesses and individuals can generate value through immersive advertising, virtual commerce, digital asset trading, and more. Strategic investments in the metaverse can lead to brand recognition, customer engagement, revenue generation, and other benefits.

Myth / Misconception	In reality
The metaverse will replace the real world.	The metaverse is not intended to replace the real world but rather complement it. It will offer an additional layer of virtual experiences and opportunities while still acknowledging the importance of the physical world. People will have the choice to engage with the metaverse for various activities like work, socializing, entertainment, and creativity, but the real world will continue to exist and play a significant role in our lives. The metaverse is about enhancing and augmenting our reality, not replacing it. Like the internet today, it has not replaced basic human aspects however physical things like paper-based storage got replaced by their digital versions, and this type of evolution would continue, few things we rely on today will go and be replaced by some new things.
The metaverse will be a utopia.	No, it will not, as it is evolved there will be rules and regulations for the metaverse too. It will be shaped by the interactions and contributions of its users. Just as the internet today has both positive and negative aspects, the metaverse will have its own set of advantages and challenges. The metaverse's potential for positive impact depends on responsible development, inclusive design, and ethical considerations. It is essential to approach the metaverse with a realistic understanding of its potential benefits and the need for careful navigation and management of its complexities.
The metaverse is a fad. The metaverse is dead	The metaverse is not just a passing trend or a short-lived fad, or dead. It represents a significant shift in how we interact with digital spaces (Internet) and opens new possibilities for communication, collaboration, and entertainment. While the concept of the metaverse is still in its early stages of development, it has gained substantial attention and investment from major technology companies and industry leaders. The metaverse has the potential to transform various aspects of our lives, including work, education, socializing, and more. As technology continues to advance and evolve, the metaverse will likely become an integral part of our digital future, rather than a mere fad. Refer to Part 2.
The metaverse is already here	While various VR, AR, and online platforms offer immersive and interactive experiences, it is incorrect to claim that the metaverse is already fully realized. The concept of the metaverse entails a fully interconnected and shared virtual universe that integrates seamlessly with the physical world. The current state of technology and platforms falls short of achieving this vision. While we may see glimpses and early manifestations of the metaverse, it is still in its early stages and has a long way to go before becoming a comprehensive and fully functional digital realm.

Myth / Misconception	In reality
The generative AI wave has moved the industry focus away from the metaverse	While generative AI has garnered significant attention and advancements in recent years, it does not imply that the industry focus has shifted away from the metaverse permanently. The metaverse concept encompasses a broad range of technologies, including AI. These technologies are all interconnected and play crucial roles in the development of metaverse applications. Generative AI can be a valuable tool within the metaverse, enabling the creation of immersive experiences, realistic avatars, and dynamic environments. The metaverse remains a prominent area of interest and investment, with various companies and industries actively exploring its potential applications. The advancement of generative AI complements and enhances the development of the metaverse, rather than diverting attention from it.
The metaverse is a mind-changing technology that would cause a lot of mental issues.	While the metaverse has the potential to transform how we interact with digital environments, it is not inherently a technology that would cause mental issues. Like any technology, the impact on mental health depends on how it is used and the individual's relationship with it. The metaverse can offer immersive and interactive experiences, but it is up to users to maintain a healthy balance and set boundaries for their engagement. Responsible design and user education can mitigate potential negative effects and promote well-being within the metaverse. Additionally, mental health concerns associated with technology are not unique to the metaverse and can apply to various digital platforms and devices. It is important to approach the metaverse with mindfulness, emphasizing user agency, well-being, and ethical considerations to ensure a positive and inclusive experience for all users.
No rules and regulations are being built for the metaverse.	The development of the metaverse is accompanied by ongoing discussions and efforts to establish rules and regulations. As the metaverse expands and becomes more integrated into our lives, it raises various legal, ethical, and societal considerations. Governments, policymakers, industry organizations, and experts are actively exploring the potential implications and working towards creating a regulatory framework for the metaverse. These discussions cover areas such as privacy, data protection, intellectual property rights, virtual currencies, virtual asset ownership, content moderation, and user safety. To recognize the need for responsible governance, there are initiatives underway to address these issues and ensure that the metaverse operates within legal and ethical boundaries, fostering trust and safeguarding user rights and interests.

Myth / Misconception	In reality
The metaverse is not inclusive, and it will leave society inaccessible or cause people to live in isolation.	The metaverse aims to be an inclusive and connected digital space, fostering community, and overcoming isolation. Efforts are underway to address accessibility challenges and ensure equal participation. While there may be risks and challenges, ongoing discussions and initiatives prioritize inclusivity, bridging the digital divide and promoting connectivity for all. Making technology inclusive takes time, but with a focus on accessibility, the metaverse can create a sense of community and enhance connectivity in the digital realm.
The metaverse requires excessive resources and is not environmentally sustainable	While the metaverse will undoubtedly require resources, there is a growing emphasis on addressing environmental sustainability concerns. Efforts are being made to optimize energy usage, explore renewable energy sources, and implement eco-friendly practices in the development and operation of metaverse platforms. Furthermore, advancements in technology and infrastructure can lead to more energy-efficient systems. The goal is to ensure that the metaverse evolves in a way that minimizes its environmental impact and promotes sustainability.
Spatial computing is the way to go, while the metaverse is an outdated term	Apple has popularized spatial computing terms with their new XR device launch and called it a spatial computer. Spatial computing and the metaverse are not mutually exclusive terms or concepts. Spatial computing technologies are a crucial component of the metaverse, providing the means to deliver immersive experiences within virtual environments. The metaverse encompasses a broader vision of a fully immersive and interconnected world that transcends the limitations of individual spatial computing technologies. Both spatial computing and the metaverse have transformative potential in various industries, including gaming, entertainment, education, and more. It is important to recognize that spatial computing is a part of the larger concept of the metaverse and that both contribute to the evolution of immersive experiences.

Table 2.1: Metaverse myth vs reality

Navigating the evolving metaverse landscape

Navigating the evolving metaverse landscape requires an understanding of its potential value and the challenges that lie ahead. As a new computing platform and content medium, the metaverse is expected to generate trillions of dollars in value. In its full vision, it becomes the gateway to digital experiences and a fundamental component of physical ones, transforming labor platforms and offering diverse opportunities. Companies that become key participants in the metaverse stand to gain significant economic upside, much like the leading Internet companies today. However, this shift will also lead to the emergence of new players and the decline of present-day incumbents.

Beyond economic implications, the metaverse has the power to redefine resource allocation and monetization. Virtual labor will enable individuals to participate in the high-value economy regardless of their physical location. As consumer spending increasingly moves toward virtual goods and services, it will impact where we live, the infrastructure we build, and the nature of different tasks. The value of virtual work, such as in-game trade economies, will expand as the metaverse grows.

Matthew Ball, a renowned metaverse expert, emphasizes the need for patience, collaboration, and adaptation in realizing the metaverse's potential, as the realization of the metaverse's full vision is still decades away, it requires significant technological advancements, regulatory considerations, and behavioral shifts. Overcoming technical challenges in achieving real-time synchronization for millions of users is a priority, as is addressing legal and ethical aspects through appropriate regulation. Businesses and individuals must adapt their strategies and behaviors to effectively participate in this digital realm.

Conclusion

In conclusion, this chapter delved into the various forms and interpretations of the metaverse concept, aiming to establish a common definition. It became evident that the metaverse is an evolving landscape with no fixed boundaries, representing the future state of the internet. While many applications and solutions may be labeled as metaverse applications, it is important to recognize that they are not the metaverse itself. Throughout the chapter, we debunked myths surrounding the metaverse and provided a clear understanding of its realities. As the metaverse continues to develop, it is crucial to stay aware of its implications and the direction in which it is heading. By doing so, we can navigate this evolving digital realm and harness its potential for the future.

Points to remember

Here are the key points to remember from this chapter:

- The definition of the metaverse varies among different entities and individuals based on their specific use cases and interests.
- The metaverse is not limited to being just a game or a virtual world; it encompasses a broader concept.
- The metaverse should not be confused with the company *Meta* (formerly known as *Facebook*).
- The metaverse is not necessarily tied to blockchain technology or non-fungible tokens (NFTs).

- The metaverse represents a stage of the internet where people can have immersive experiences.
- While we are already witnessing some metaverse applications, it is important to note that these applications are not the metaverse itself.
- The metaverse is not a utopia or a replacement for the real world; rather, it is intended to enhance the world we live in.

In this part of the book, we have uncovered the concept of the metaverse, tracing its origins and exploring different interpretations. Although challenges and prerequisites lie ahead, the advancements in technology discussed in *Part 2* of this book, coupled with societal changes, bring us ever closer to the eventual realization of the metaverse. By navigating these challenges and seizing the opportunities presented by the metaverse, we have the power to shape its future and unlock its immense potential.

References

1. Free Guy | Official Trailer | 20th Century Studios - **https://youtu.be/X2m-08cOAbc**
2. Game: World of Warcraft - **https://worldofwarcraft.blizzard.com/en-us/**
3. Game: StartWars Galaxies - **https://swglegends.com/**
4. Game: The Matrix Online - **https://matrix.fandom.com/wiki/The_Matrix_Online**
5. Xbox - **https://www.xbox.com/en-IN/**
6. Sony Playstation - **https://www.playstation.com/en-in/**
7. Second Life from Linden Labs - **https://en.wikipedia.org/wiki/Second_Life**
8. Fortnite Game - **https://www.fortnite.com/**
9. Decentraland - **https://decentraland.org/**
10. Sandbox Game - **https://www.sandbox.game/en/**
11. Niantic Labs - **https://nianticlabs.com/products# pokemongo**
12. Lightship platform – building real-world metaverse **https://lightship.dev/**
13. **https://9to5google.com/2021/11/17/sundar-pichai-google-metaverse/**
14. **https://www.apple.com/apple-vision-pro/**
15. **https://www.meta.com/horizon-worlds/**
16. **https://www.microsoft.com/en-us/mesh**
17. **https://www.forbes.com/sites/cathyhackl/2021/05/02/defining-the-metaverse-today/?sh=633409606448**

Part - 2
Metaverse: A Result of Technological Evolutions

In *Part 1,* we extensively explored the diverse interpretations and definitions of the metaverse. As technology and businesses continue to advance, the metaverse is on the brink of gaining wider acceptance and a more precise definition. Although we have yet to unlock its immense potential fully, the current buzz surrounding the metaverse reflects the constant evolution of technology and the convergence of various elements. The key question remains whether the metaverse will retain its loose definition or witness the emergence of a more concrete definition. Nonetheless, adopting the metaverse will be driven by significant progress in the foundational building blocks and technologies underpinning its existence.

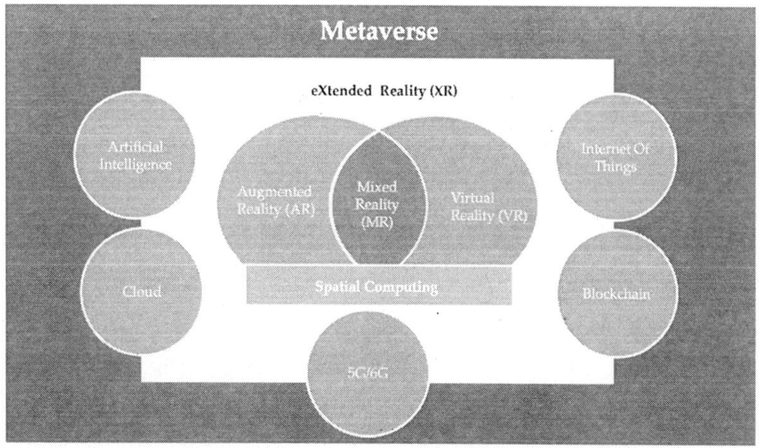

Figure Part 2: Metaverse building blocks

The preceding figure depicts the crucial elements shaping the metaverse's current stage. In the upcoming chapters, we will embark on a detailed exploration of these foundational building blocks. We will closely examine the evolutionary advancements within each domain, highlighting the notable enhancements that shape the trajectory of the metaverse and its transformative potential. Through this comprehensive understanding, we will gain insights into how these advancements enable metaverse applications and propel us closer to the next stage of the internet.

In *Chapter 3, Understanding XR: Metaverse foundation,* we will explore **Extended Reality (XR)** as the foundation of the metaverse. XR combines **Augmented Reality (AR)** and **Virtual Reality (VR)** to push the boundaries of the physical world by integrating digitally generated content. This chapter will delve into the immersive experiences offered by XR and its role in shaping the metaverse.

Moving on to *Chapter 4, AI empowering the metaverse,* we will delve into pivotal technologies such as **Artificial Intelligence (AI)** and spatial computing that bolster the capabilities of XR and contribute to the evolution of the metaverse. These technologies enable intelligent interactions, adaptive content creation, and seamless integration of virtual and physical worlds.

Chapter 5, IoT, cloud, and next-gen networks, will focus on the role of **Internet of Things (IoT)**, cloud/edge computing, and high-speed networks (5G/6G) in providing dynamic and distributed computing power and scalability to metaverse applications. We will explore how these technologies enable real-time data processing, seamless connectivity, and the ability to handle massive scale of data generated in the metaverse.

Additionally, *Chapter 6, Decentralization and the role of blockchain,* will discuss the rise of decentralized architectures and their impact on growth of the metaverse. We will delve into blockchain technology, decentralized storage, and peer-to-peer networks that empower users and communities, fostering a more open and participatory metaverse.

Read on as we dive into these exciting chapters, uncovering the technologies and innovations that shape the metaverse and lay the groundwork for its future possibilities.

CHAPTER 3
Understanding XR: Metaverse Foundation

Introduction

This chapter explores the crucial role of XR technologies in enabling the metaverse. It introduces different forms extending the realities (AR, VR, MR and more) and its immersive capabilities. It covers advancements in AR, integration into the metaverse, and versatile applications. It also examines the impact of VR and the role of virtual environments. The chapter addresses advancements in XR devices, infrastructure, and the importance of robust XR infrastructure for the metaverse's success. This chapter provides a comprehensive understanding of XR's transformative potential and its role in shaping the future of digital interactions.

Structure

In this chapter, we will discuss the following topics:

- The reality
- Augmenting the reality
- Virtual Reality
- eXtended Reality
- Evolution in XR technologies and tools
- XR enabling the metaverse

Objectives

The objective of this chapter is to provide readers with a comprehensive understanding of **Extended Reality (XR)** as a fundamental building block of the metaverse. XR encompasses technologies such as **Augmented Reality** (**AR**) and **Virtual Reality** (**VR**) that redefine reality and create immersive experiences.

Readers will gain insights into the different types of reality technologies, their evolution, and their significance in enabling metaverse applications. By understanding XR, readers will have a clear understanding of how it is taking us closer to the next phase of the internet - the metaverse.

The reality

Understanding reality is fundamental before delving into the concept of the XR and metaverse. Reality encompasses our visual perceptions, auditory experiences, and sensory interactions with the world around us. It is the environment and objects that surround us, shaping our understanding of the physical world. Throughout our lives, we learn to navigate and engage with our surroundings effortlessly, developing a deep sense of familiarity and trust in the predictability of our reality. This innate belief in the reliability of our environment allows us to interact with it seamlessly, in a way reality is just a belief and illusion.

Reality is merely an illusion, albeit a very persistent one - *Albert Einstein*

A visual representation provided below in *Figure 3.1* is of a specific reality of the world as observed by an observer at a given location. Embracing the power of transformative technologies allows us to reshape our perception of reality, giving rise to a new realm of possibilities.

***Figure 3.1**: The reality - the real world – a white, brown cow near mountains* [1]

In the upcoming sections, we will explore various manifestations of this new reality, each offering a distinct form and experience. From augmented reality to virtual reality, mixed reality, and beyond, these immersive technologies unlock the potential for unprecedented encounters with the digital world. Prepare yourself to embark on a journey where boundaries are blurred, and the fabric of reality is woven with innovation and imagination.

Augmenting the reality

Augmenting reality is akin to decorating the world with digitally generated content, transforming the way we perceive and interact with our surroundings. Overlaying virtual elements onto the physical environment is called Augmented Reality, and it creates a unique blend of the real and digital realms. *Figure 3.2* illustrates a captivating example of how the real world is augmented by the artificial donkeys standing near a real white, brown cow:

***Figure 3.2:** Augmented Reality*[2]

The virtual elements (digital content) in AR can take various forms, including textual information, videos, audio, and 3D content, all of which serve to enhance reality and assist users in their interactions. When AR is specifically used to provide helpful information and guidance, it is often referred to as **Assisted Reality**. In this mode, users can invoke content augmentation on-demand, accessing relevant information when they need it. Alternatively, in most advanced AR use cases can intelligently detect the environment and dynamically present context-aware AR experiences, seamlessly integrating digital content with the user's surroundings. This flexibility in content delivery and interaction is a key characteristic of AR, enabling users to engage with digital information in a manner that suits their specific needs and preferences.

Another fascinating aspect of reimagining reality is the ability to merge the real world with a digitally generated environment. As depicted in *Figure 3.3*, we can witness the same cow from the real world seamlessly integrated into entirely new and interactive virtual surroundings. This captivating phenomenon represents a form of Augmented Reality known as **Augmented Virtuality,** where the real-world objects are augmented in a virtual environment. This innovative blend of the real and virtual realms opens exciting possibilities for immersive experiences and interactive storytelling.

Figure 3.3: *Augmented Virtuality* [3]

Virtual Reality

Virtual Reality (VR) takes the concept of reality to a whole new level by taking users into a fully artificial and digitally generated environment, and users are completely immersed in a virtual world, and do not see the real world around them. *Figure 3.4* exemplifies this by showcasing a computer-generated environment where every element, including digital twins of real-world objects, is meticulously replicated:

Figure 3.4: *Virtual Reality* [4]

VR not only provides a visually captivating experience but also replicates real-world interactions, enabling users to engage with and manipulate objects within the virtual realm. It offers a profound sense of presence and allows individuals to explore and interact with a seemingly boundless virtual world.

eXtended Reality

Today, advancements in technology have brought about a new level of immersion and interaction, surpassing the capabilities of traditional AR and VR experiences. This progress has given rise to the term **Mixed Reality (MR)**, which refers to the merging of the real and virtual worlds to create a cohesive reality where physical and digital elements coexist and interact seamlessly in real time. In MR experiences, users can perceive and engage with virtual objects that are integrated into their actual environment, enhancing their perception of reality.

Within the broader landscape of immersive technologies, we find XR, an umbrella term that encompasses AR, VR, and MR. XR represents a holistic concept aimed at extending human perception and interaction beyond the constraints of the physical world. It enables the fusion of real and virtual elements, allowing users to immerse themselves in rich and interactive experiences that blur the boundaries between the physical and digital realms.

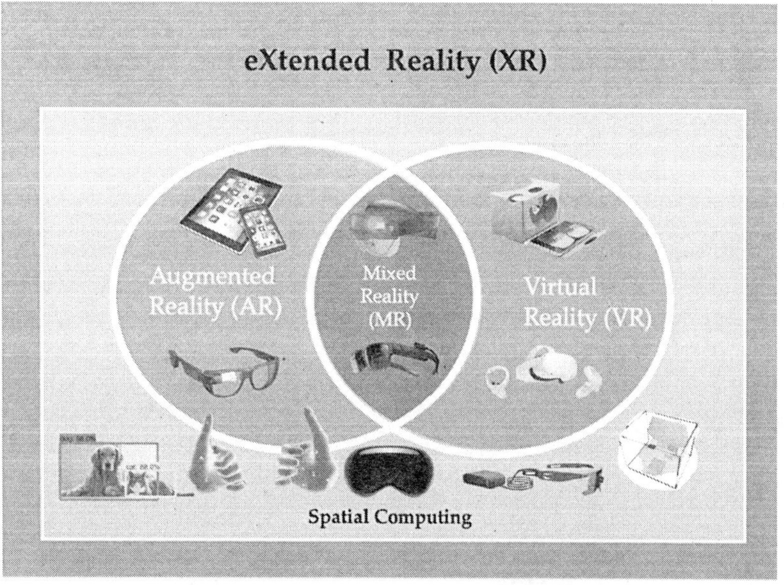

Figure 3.5: *Extended Reality*

XR serves as a comprehensive framework that encompasses a range of technologies and approaches, providing a versatile platform for innovation and exploration in the realm of extended reality. Ultimately, XR is about extending our beliefs, fulfilling our imagination, and bringing us closer to a reality that transcends our traditional boundaries.

Evolution in XR technologies and tools

The realm of XR is made accessible through a diverse array of tools and technologies designed to alter our perception of the world. Whether it is through specialized glasses, cameras, or mirrors, these devices act as gateways to a new reality. Additionally, advancements in display technologies have allowed us to seamlessly blend virtual worlds with our physical environment, creating immersive experiences even visible to the naked eye without wearing special eye gear. In this section, we will delve into the fascinating world of XR tools and technologies, exploring their evolution and the remarkable possibilities they bring forth.

Head Mounted Display

Head Mounted Displays (HMDs) play a crucial role in delivering immersive experiences in XR, particularly in the realm of VR. These devices are worn on the head, covering the eyes and sometimes the ears, to create a visual and auditory environment that transports the user to a virtual world.

In VR, HMDs serve as the primary interface between the user and the virtual environment. They typically consist of high-resolution displays, lenses, and motion sensors. By wearing an HMD, users can view and explore virtual landscapes, interact with virtual objects, and engage in various experiences that go beyond the confines of the physical world.

Many VR HMDs are tethered to a PC, meaning they rely on a wired connection to a powerful computer for processing and rendering the virtual content. This configuration allows for more sophisticated and visually stunning experiences, as the computational load can be offloaded to the PC. Tethered HMDs provide high-fidelity visuals, precise tracking, and the ability to run graphically intensive applications, making them popular among gamers, professionals, and enthusiasts seeking immersive VR experiences. By leveraging the power of a PC, tethered HMDs can deliver realistic graphics, smooth performance, and intricate interactions within the virtual environment. However, the tethered nature of these devices restricts mobility, as users are physically connected to the PC.

Figure 3.6: Virtual reality with head mounted display device

Popular HMD devices on the market include Oculus Quest (rebranded as Meta Quest)[5], Oculus Go, HTC Vive[6], Sony Playstation VR[7], Samsung GearVR[8], and many more. Over time, VR headsets have undergone significant advancements and standalone VR devices are reducing the reliance on PC tethering, allowing for greater freedom of movement and untethered VR experience. These standalone devices initially offered **three degrees of freedom (3DOF)**, allowing users to track head movements and experience rotational motion by tilting or moving their heads up, down, left, or right. However, the latest VR devices now support **six degrees of freedom (6DOF)**, introducing translational movements that track users' physical movements in a 3D space. This enhanced freedom enables users to move within the virtual environment, going beyond static positions. 6DOF has become the industry standard for creating immersive VR experiences, and we can expect further advancements in the future.

***Figure 3.7**: AR headset with mixed reality - Microsoft HoloLens 1*[9]

The advancements made by *Microsoft*[10] and *Magic Leap*[11] have played a significant role in popularizing AR headsets with MR capabilities. These AR headsets bring immersive virtual reality experiences into the real world. Several similar devices available in the market now offer advanced tracking features. These devices can not only track head and body movements but also detect gestures, poses from hands and fingers, and even sense eyeball and iris movement. The line between AR and VR is becoming increasingly blurred with the introduction of MR devices like *Meta Quest 2*[12], *Pico 4*[13], *Lenovo ThinkReality VRX*[14] and *Apple VisionPro*. These devices incorporate a pass-through mode that allows users to view the real world while still being in a virtual reality environment. This integration of real-world elements within a virtual reality setting creates a seamless and immersive experience.

The human eye has a **field of view (FOV)**[15] of over 200°, which provides us with a wide and comprehensive view of our surroundings. In comparison, current XR devices have a limited field of view, that affect the peripheral vision and gives a confined window effect, that impacts the level of immersion and realism experienced in XR. However, the newer devices are being developed with larger FOV and better display resolution, and frame rates to match the capabilities of the human eye. Meta's recent revelation of a retinal-resolution varifocal display device signifies a significant stride towards achieving a more natural and realistic virtual reality experience[16].

XR devices are continually evolving to cater to the diverse needs of both general consumers and specialized enterprise applications. A wide range of XR devices is available in the market, offering unique features and capabilities. To get an overview of the progress in XR, you can refer to a consolidated list of 200+ XR devices as shown in *Figure 3.8*. These devices showcase the evolutions and innovations in XR technology.

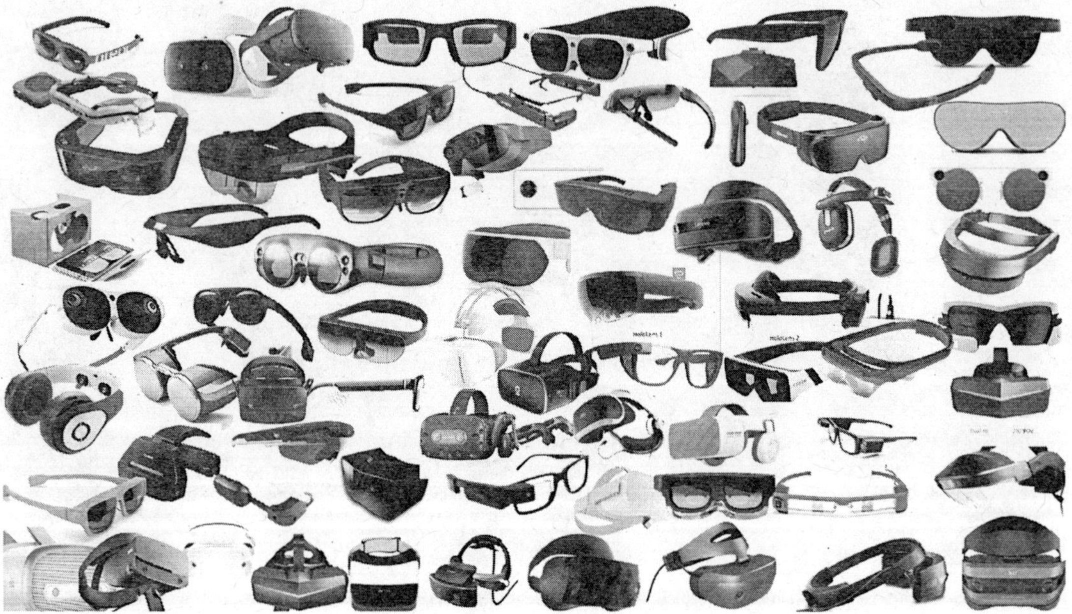

***Figure 3.8:** Growing list of XR devices*[17]

XR technology is rapidly maturing, and the industry is eagerly awaiting a groundbreaking moment like the iPhone/Apple moment in smartphones; it has already started with VisionPro announcement. As HMD devices become more refined and capable, they enable increasingly immersive and comfortable experiences. Physical controllers are being replaced by natural input modalities like gestures, gaze, eye, voice commands, and even direct brain control, enhancing immersion and interactivity. As it continues to advance, we can expect even more groundbreaking applications and experiences in XR, pushing the boundaries of what is possible. The future holds promise of increasingly immersive, realistic, and transformative XR experiences that have the potential to reshape industries and redefine our interaction with virtual environments.

Smart glasses

The concept of smart glasses has emerged as a natural progression in the era of smart devices. Just like smartphones, watches, and TVs have become smart, it was inevitable for glasses to follow suit. *Google Glass*[18], introduced in the past, played a significant role in paving the way for a new generation of smart glasses. These devices feature compact designs and utilize projection technology to overlay digital information onto the user's field of view. Companies like *Epson*[19], *Vuzix*[20], and *Realwear* (shown in *Figure 3.9*) have also entered the market with their own versions of smart glasses, incorporating small LED screens that display digital content directly in the user's field of view. It has gone as small as a contact lens[21]. These advancements in XR technology have pushed the boundaries of what is possible with smart glasses, offering new possibilities for immersive experiences and practical applications.

Figure 3.9: *Realwear smart glasses for industrial use cases* [22]

Smart glasses excel in Assisted Reality use cases, where they provide users with digital content such as text, audio, video, or step-by-step instructions to assist them in their tasks. They are particularly useful in scenarios where users may not require full immersion but still need lightweight access to relevant information. Over time, smart glasses have become more accessible and versatile, finding applications in various industries, including sports, healthcare, and industrial settings. We are witnessing the adaptation of this technology on the consumer side. Smart eyewear for sports has become more accessible, allowing users to receive vital information while engaging in activities like racing, cycling, or workouts. Users can interact with their smart glasses, access navigation features, and even enjoy music playback, showcasing the adaptability and functionality of these devices.

One of the key advantages of smart glasses is their lightweight design, making them comfortable to wear for extended periods. These glasses are equipped with features like hot-swappable batteries and voice command interactions, offering a new range of eyewear devices that combine full AR capabilities with MR functionality. Currently, devices like the

ThinkReality A3[23] (shown in *Figure 3.10*), and *Nreal* (now *XReal*)[24] are the popular ones, resembling normal glasses while still providing MR capabilities. These glasses offload computing tasks to connected smartphones or small compute units, and are powered by the Qualcomm Snapdragon XR[25] chipsets and supported by the OpenXR[26] ecosystem.

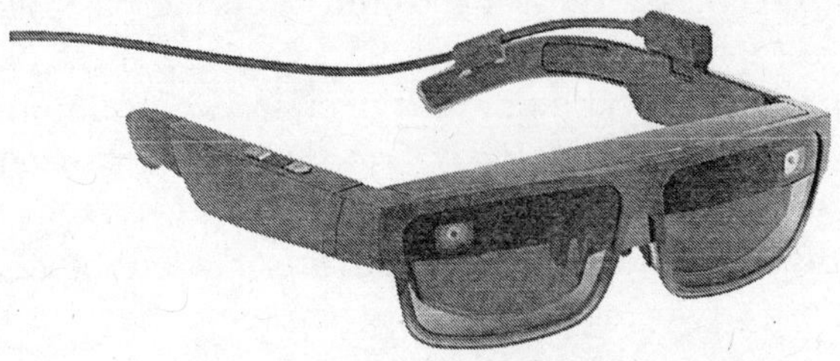

Figure 3.10: *Lenovo ThinkReality A3 MR smart glass*

An exciting trend in the evolution of smart glasses is the transition from bulky head-mounted displays to lightweight, normal-looking glasses. Future iterations may even eliminate the need for wires, becoming wireless or remotely tethered. These devices are also being utilized as private widescreens for laptops[27], hinting at a potential future where laptops may go screenless, as demonstrated by innovations like *Spacetop*[28]. These advancements in smart glasses are not only enhancing individual experiences but also contributing to the development of a real-world metaverse, as highlighted by *Niantic*[29].

Mobile XR

Mobile phones have become an integral part of our reality, with over 15 billion devices worldwide[30]. They offer much more than just telephony or internet browsing, as we now spend a significant amount of time on them. As we discussed tethered HMDs and smart glasses earlier, it is important to note that XR experiences are not limited to these devices alone. In fact, smartphones and tablets have the capability to provide XR experiences through their cameras. For example, *Pokemon Go*[31] (*Figure 3.11*) an AR Game by *Niantic labs*.

ARCore[32] by Google and ARKit[33] by Apple power the XR experiences on mobile devices. Smartphones are continuously evolving to include advanced capabilities such as depth sensing and semantic scene understanding right out of the box, for example, RoomPlan by Apple[34]. These advancements enable the creation of immersive experiences that integrate seamlessly with the real world. For instance, Google Maps can overlay arrows, directions, and distance markers onto your surroundings, making navigation easier and more intuitive. Niantic has even set out to map the entire world, further pushing the boundaries of mobile AR experiences.

Figure 3.11: *A still from mobile AR Game - Pokemon Go*

Mobile devices can also be used for playing VR applications and 360-degree videos. It just needs Google Cardboard[35] based devices like Virtual Box starting from $5. Place your phone inside these devices and the phone becomes an HMD. In VR mode, the phone screen splits in two parts, one for each eye for stereo rendering, 3D perception. These devices also come with adjustable distance between lenses to adjust to the user's IPD as shown in *Figure 3.12*:

Figure 3.12: *Mobile VR*

Powerful tools like the Unity 3D Engine[36], and Unity AR Foundation, along with other 3D engines like Unreal[37], Vuforia[38] , have significantly contributed to scaling XR experiences to the next level. These engines provide developers with the necessary tools and frameworks to create immersive and interactive XR content for mobile devices. Mobile XR acts as a catalyst for the metaverse, offering convenience, accessibility, and immersive capabilities. It allows users to connect, interact, and experience the metaverse on the go, fostering a new era of digital engagement and transforming the way we perceive and engage with our surroundings.

WebXR

WebXR represents a significant advancement in the accessibility and adoption of XR experiences. As the internet remains the most widely accessible medium, web-based applications and websites provide an open and seamless entry point into the XR world without the need for special downloads or dedicated XR devices.

Companies like Google[39] have embraced WebXR, revolutionizing the browsing experience by enabling 3D browsing directly from web browsers. For example, Google Search offers immersive search results with View in 3D capability, allowing users to interact with 3D models and objects right from their browser. This capability extends to any webpage, empowering developers to create XR-enabled experiences that can be accessed by users directly through their web browser as depicted in *Figure 3.13:*

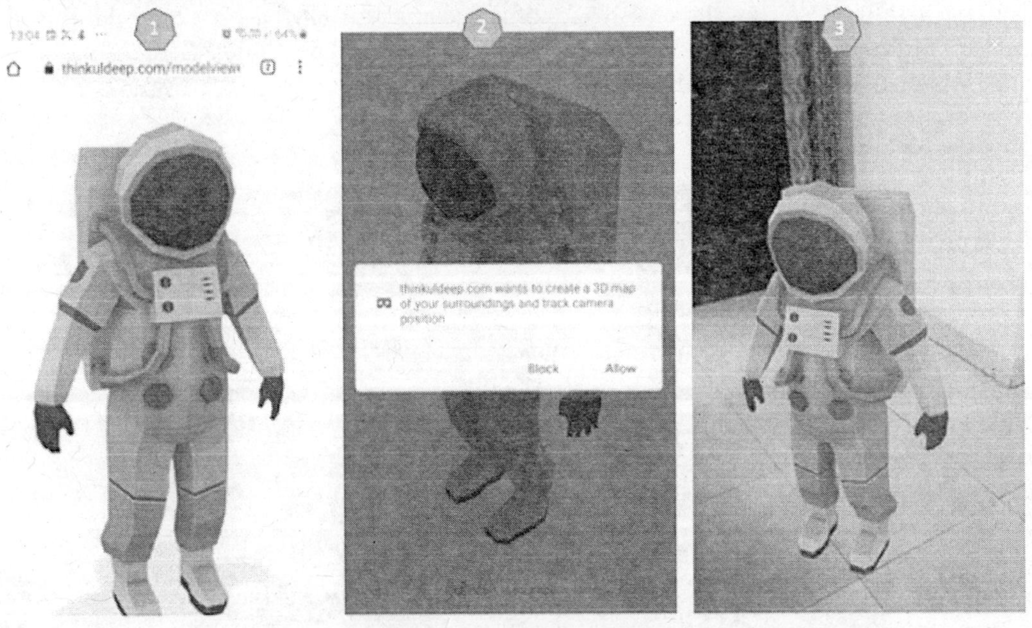

Figure 3.13: *WebXR from Google*[40]

Various technologies and libraries, such as traditional WebGL or JavaScript libraries like ThreeJS[41], BabylonJS[42] or likes of 8th Wall[43], enable the development of XR experiences on the web. These tools provide the necessary frameworks for creating interactive and immersive XR content that can be accessed by a broad audience. Web-based XR also fosters collaboration and social interaction. Platforms like Spatial.io[44] (*Figure 3.14*) enable multiple users to collaborate and interact within a shared XR environment, accessible through web browsers. This collaborative aspect paves the way for immersive experiences in the metaverse, where users can connect and engage with others seamlessly.

Figure 3.14: *A virtual space created in WebXR platform - Spatial.io*

When accessing XR-enabled websites through XR-capable smartphones or tablets, users can leverage the full capabilities of their devices, including more degrees of freedom and XR features. This integration enhances the immersive experience and expands the possibilities of web based XR applications. In essence, web based XR serves as a crucial entry point for the adoption and integration of XR in the metaverse. Its accessibility, openness, and compatibility with various devices make it a powerful tool for democratizing XR experiences and paving the way for a more interconnected digital realm.

3D displays

3D displays play a crucial role in fueling the advancements of XR and the metaverse. These displays are capable of conveying depth to viewers, and technologies such as stereoscopic displays in HMDs and smart glasses provide a stereoscopic effect by presenting offset images to each eye. This simulates the way human eyes perceive depth and enables immersive 3D experiences. From 3D cinemas to 3D goggles and TVs, we have witnessed the evolution of stereoscopic displays bringing 3D content in our homes.

In recent years, we have seen further developments in 3D display technologies that go beyond stereoscopy[45]. Light-field display, also known as holographic display, has emerged as a transformative concept. Projects like *Google Startline*[46], explore innovative approaches to enhance realistic collaboration by harnessing light-field technology, which enables individual pixels to emit light at varying intensities, resulting in a display that exhibits distinct appearances from different visual angles. Other technologies such as **Micro Mirror Array Plate (MMAP)**[47] and **Aerial Imaging by Retro-Reflection** (AIRR)[48] are getting implemented for 3D signage and more. These approaches enable realistic 3D perception without the need for specialized glasses.

Figure 3.15: *Volumetric display*[49]

Moreover, advancements in 3D displays extend to volumetric displays (*Figure 3.15*), which operate on the concept of voxels rather than pixels. Volumetric displays create true representations of 3D models by emitting, scattering, or relaying illumination in 3D space. This technology allows viewers to observe objects from any direction, providing a realistic sense of depth, perspective, and scale. By mimicking the characteristics of actual material objects, volumetric displays enhance the immersive nature of XR experiences, enabling users to interact with virtual objects in a more natural and intuitive manner.

As 3D display technologies undergo continuous evolution, they offer users increasingly captivating and lifelike visual experiences. This enables individuals to delve into virtual landscapes with an enhanced sense of presence and immersion.

See-through glass and mirrors

The evolution of see-through glass and mirrors has played a significant role in fueling the development of XR. Various everyday objects such as car windshields, bike helmet glass, and window glasses in our homes can serve as platforms for XR experiences. These transparent surfaces provide opportunities for overlaying digital information onto our field of view, creating augmented reality experiences.

Heads-Up Displays (HUDs) have already revolutionized flight vision[50] and have made their way into cars, helmets, and other applications. By projecting important information directly into the line of sight, HUDs enhance decision-making and improve situational awareness. This technology allows crucial data to be displayed without requiring users to divert attention from their surroundings.

Moreover, advancements in smart window glasses have opened up new possibilities. These glasses can automatically adjust darkness to maintain optimal temperature, providing a natural and energy-efficient solution. Additionally, smart window shades eliminate the need for manual adjustments, bringing convenience and comfort to our living spaces. By integrating XR capabilities into these glass surfaces, digital content and information can also be seamlessly integrated into our everyday environment.

Similarly, mirrors have also undergone customization to augment the reality they reflect. This customization allows for virtual trial experiences, like the effects achieved with selfie cameras. Users can see themselves in different ways, enhancing their self-perception and exploring new virtual identities.

Overall, the advancements in see-through glass and mirrors have expanded the reach of XR into our surroundings. By leveraging these everyday objects, we can bring digital possibilities to every corner of the world, enhancing our perception, interactions, and overall experiences in the XR realm.

Peripherals

XR development is not limited to visual experiences alone; it encompasses a broader range of sensory immersion. Peripheral devices play a crucial role in enabling these immersive experiences by extending beyond visual perception. For example, VR Treadmill[51] is bringing the immersive gaming and fitness together.

Haptic gloves [52] have emerged as a significant development, allowing users to physically touch and feel virtual objects. These gloves provide feedback through vibrations or pressure sensors, enhancing the sense of presence and interaction with the virtual environment. Users can now shake hands with virtual avatars, manipulate objects, and feel the textures and shapes within the XR space. In addition to haptic gloves, other wearable devices, such as wristbands[53] and smart rings[54] and bodysuits[55] (*Figure 3.16*) will track hand movements and body posture with precision, enabling accurate and natural interactions within the XR environment.

Figure 3.16: TeslaSuit full body tracking

Users can use gestures, hand poses, and body motions to navigate and interact with virtual objects, further enhancing the immersive experience. By incorporating these peripheral devices into XR setups, the realm of possibility expands beyond visual and graphical enhancements. Users can engage multiple senses, including touch and motion, enabling a more comprehensive and realistic XR experience.

XR enabling the metaverse

One key aspect of XR that is driving the metaverse forward is the advancement of immersive devices. From HMDs to smart glasses and even mobile devices, XR hardware is becoming more refined, lightweight, and capable. These devices provide users with the ability to seamlessly enter and interact with virtual environments, bridging the gap between the physical and digital worlds. Whether it is through fully immersive VR experiences or overlaying digital information onto the real world with AR, XR devices are instrumental in shaping the metaverse.

Furthermore, XR is not limited to specialized hardware. Web-based XR applications are emerging as a highly accessible medium for experiencing the metaverse. With technologies like WebXR, users can access XR content directly through web browsers, eliminating the need for additional downloads or installations. This allows a broader range of audience to engage with XR experiences, expanding the reach of the metaverse and democratizing access to immersive content.

Another significant driver of the metaverse enabled by XR is the evolution of 3D display technologies and peripheral devices. From stereoscopic displays to light-field displays and volumetric displays, advancements in visual rendering bring virtual worlds to life with greater realism, depth, and interactivity. Wearables with advanced sensing capability create a sense of presence and immersion, enhancing the overall metaverse experience and enabling users to interact with virtual objects and environments in a natural and intuitive manner.

Everything we call real is made of things that cannot be regarded as real

-- Niels Bohr

Conclusion

This chapter has provided a comprehensive understanding of XR as the foundation for the metaverse. XR encompasses technologies such as VR, AR, and MR, which are evolving and converging to create immersive and interconnected virtual experiences. We discussed advancements in XR tools and technologies, which play a crucial role in enabling the metaverse by offering immersive devices, web-based experiences, advanced 3D displays, and social interaction capabilities. As XR continues to evolve, it will contribute to the development of a connected virtual world where people can explore, create, and interact in new and exciting ways. The future of the metaverse relies heavily on the continued evolution and integration of XR technologies.

In the next chapter, we will delve into the profound role of artificial intelligence as the catalyst for enabling the metaverse.

Points to remember

Here are the key points to remember from this chapter:

- XR forms the foundation of immersive metaverse applications.
- Advancements in XR technology are propelling us closer to the metaverse.
- The combination of AI and XR technology has the potential to accelerate this progress even further.
- The lines between AR and VR are becoming increasingly blurred, with devices supporting both.
- The metaverse encompasses both AR and VR to enable a wide range of virtual and real-world use cases.
- It is not necessary to have Head Mounted Devices or Smart glasses to experience XR; it can also be enjoyed using mobile phones or other display technologies.

References

1. Picture credit: **https://www.pexels.com/photo/white-and-brown-cow-nearby-mountains-1390200/**
2. 3D model credits: **https://pngimg.com/image/25046**
3. Background artwork derived from: **https://www.artstation.com/artwork/oO6zNk**
4. 3D model credits: **https://www.cgtrader.com/free-3d-models/animals/mammal/comic-toy-golden-bull**
5. Meta Quest - **https://www.meta.com/quest/**
6. HTC Vive - **https://www.vive.com/eu/**
7. Sony Playstation VR - **https://www.playstation.com/en-in/ps-vr/**
8. Samsung GearVR - **https://www.samsung.com/us/business/support/owners/product/gear-vr-with-controller-sm-r325/**
9. Picture credit - **https://www.thoughtworks.com/insights/blog/extending-reality-ar-and-vr-part-i**
10. **https://learn.microsoft.com/en-us/hololens/hololens1-hardware**
11. **https://www.magicleap.com/ml1-devices**
12. Passthrough feature Quest - **https://developer.oculus.com/blog/mixed-reality-with-passthrough/**
13. Passthrough feature Pico - **https://www.youtube.com/watch?v=vtz5MlvRHj4**
14. Lenovo ThinkReality VRX – passthrough - **https://www.lenovo.com/in/en/thinkrealityvrx**
15. Field of View (FOV) - **https://www.interaction-design.org/literature/topics/field-of-view-fov-in-extended-reality**
16. **https://mixed-news.com/en/meta-vr-headset-retinal-resolution-varifocal-display-siggraph-2023/**
17. **https://medium.com/xrpractices/the-growing-list-of-xr-devices-f102262e4a58**
18. Google Glass - **https://blog.google/products/devices-services/glass-enterprise-edition-2/**
19. **https://www.epson.co.in/moverio-augmented-reality**
20. **https://www.vuzix.com/**
21. **https://www.extremetech.com/extreme/337691-mojo-vision-details-its-first-smart-contact-lens**
22. **https://realwear.at/en/**

23. https://www.lenovo.com/us/en/thinkrealitya3/
24. https://xreal.com/
25. https://www.qualcomm.com/products/mobile/snapdragon/xr-vr-ar/xr-vr-ar-device-finder
26. https://www.khronos.org/openxr/
27. https://www.tcl.com/global/en/glasses/tcl-nxtwear-g
28. https://www.sightful.com/
29. https://nianticlabs.com/news/building-the-real-world-metaverse?hl=en
30. https://www.statista.com/statistics/245501/multiple-mobile-device-ownership-worldwide/
31. https://pokemongolive.com/?hl=en
32. https://developers.google.com/ar
33. https://developer.apple.com/augmented-reality/arkit/
34. https://developer.apple.com/augmented-reality/roomplan/
35. https://en.wikipedia.org/wiki/Google_Cardboard
36. https://unity.com/
37. https://www.unrealengine.com/en-US
38. https://developer.vuforia.com/
39. https://arvr.google.com/
40. https://thinkuldeep.com/modelviewer/
41. https://threejs.org/
42. https://www.babylonjs.com/
43. https://www.8thwall.com/
44. https://www.spatial.io/s/Understanding-XR-647174d2ac5745d9ae8fa081?share=8228641953723972584
45. https://www.nttdata.com/global/en/about-us/focus/floating-3d-display-next-generation-technology-for-xr
46. https://blog.google/technology/research/project-starline/
47. https://ieeexplore.ieee.org/document/9090633
48. https://ieeexplore.ieee.org/document/9347425
49. Picture Credit: https://en.wikipedia.org/wiki/File:VX1_DICOM.jpg

50. **https://www.federalregister.gov/documents/2001/06/18/01-15333/special-conditions-enhanced-vision-system-evs-for-gulfstream-model-g-v-airplanes**
51. **https://www.kat-vr.com/**
52. **https://haptx.com/**
53. **https://dl.acm.org/doi/10.1145/3126594.3126604**
54. **https://wearable-technologies.com/news/apples-patent-suggests-smart-ring-that-could-let-you-control-other-devices**
55. **https://teslasuit.io/products/teslasuit-4/**

Chapter 4
AI Empowering the Metaverse

Introduction

This chapter explores the crucial role of **Artificial Intelligence (AI)** in the metaverse, enabling intelligent and seamless interactions within virtual environments. It covers how AI capabilities contribute to immersive and interactive experiences in the metaverse, encompassing user identification, natural language interactions, visual perception, physical interactions, spatial awareness, audio experiences, and advanced data processing. It also touches up on the research that connects the brain to computers and manipulates dreams and thoughts to bring magic of technology.

> **Any sufficiently advanced technology is indistinguishable from magic**
>
> -- *Arthur C. Clarke*

Structure

In this chapter, we will discuss the following topics:

- Artificial Intelligence
- Importance of AI
- Evolution in AI
- AI enabling metaverse

Objectives

The objective of this chapter is to provide readers with a comprehensive understanding of AI and its significance in the digital era. After reading this chapter, the readers will have understood the evolution of AI and its role in shaping the future of the internet, specifically in relation to the emerging concept of the metaverse. Readers will gain insights into the advancements in AI that are propelling us closer to the next internet age and the potential implications of AI in realizing the metaverse.

Let us start with understanding AI.

Artificial Intelligence

AI is a field of computer science that involves the development and management of technology capable of learning, making decisions, and performing tasks. It is also referred to as machine intelligence. AI encompasses various technologies and is a broad term that includes components such as machine learning, computer vision, natural language understanding, and **Natural Language Processing** (**NLP**). Rather than being defined by a specific structure or function, AI is more focused on the process and ability to quickly analyze data and make informed decisions.

AI systems typically operate by collecting large amounts of labeled training data, analyzing it to identify correlations and patterns, and utilizing these patterns to predict future outcomes. Learning, reasoning, and correction are key cognitive skills of AI. Learning components of AI programs involve collecting data and establishing rules to transform it into valuable knowledge. AI algorithms are sets of rules that provide step-by-step instructions for carrying out tasks on computer systems. Selecting the most optimal algorithm to achieve a desired outcome is a fundamental aspect of AI programming logic. Correction processes are implemented to fine-tune algorithms regularly, ensuring that they produce the most accurate and reliable results possible.

In brief, AI is a part of computer science that deals with making technology learn, make decisions, and perform tasks. It includes different technologies and involves analyzing data, finding patterns, and using them to make predictions. AI algorithms guide computer systems, and we make ongoing improvements to make them work better.

Importance of AI

The importance of AI stems from its ability to provide businesses with previously inaccessible insights and its potential to outperform humans in certain tasks. AI systems can perform operations quickly with minimal errors, making them valuable for repetitive and detail-oriented activities. Here are some key benefits of AI:

- **Execution of risky tasks:** AI robots can be deployed in situations where human interaction is risky, such as space exploration, bomb defusing, or deep-sea exploration. By using AI robots, we can bypass many hazardous constraints faced by humans.

- **Faster task completion:** By combining AI with other technologies, computers can make decisions and carry out tests more quickly than humans. While humans evaluate various factors emotionally and practically before deciding, AI-driven machines focus on the task at hand and generate results swiftly.
- **Reduced need for human intervention:** Digital assistants and chatbots has reduced the need for human personnel in customer interactions. Chatbots have advanced to the point where it becomes difficult to distinguish between conversing with a person or a machine, leading to significant reductions in human resources.
- **Management of repetitive tasks:** AI algorithms excel at handling repetitive tasks that do not require complex thinking. Machines can think much faster than humans and multitask, leading to greater productivity and outcomes.
- **AI does not need breaks:** This characteristic makes AI particularly valuable in applications where continuous operation is required. Unlike humans, machines running AI algorithms do not experience fatigue or become distracted, allowing them to work tirelessly for extended periods.

In summary, AI enables businesses to gain insights, execute risky tasks, complete tasks faster, reduce human intervention, and handle repetitive tasks efficiently. Its capabilities contribute to improved productivity, enhanced decision-making, and expanded possibilities across various industries.

Evolution in AI

Evolution is a natural process, and AI evolutions are going little beyond nature, and extending nature. Here are some evolutions that are shaping the metaverse application, that aim to bring us into another universe.

Identity definition and recognition

Identity is now being defined in more comprehensive and sophisticated ways with the integration of AI. While traditional identification relied on personal information, modern identity detection methods focus on capturing unique physical or behavioral traits through biometrics. Biometrics provide a more reliable and secure means of identification since they are based on individual-specific characteristics that are difficult to forge or replicate.

AI has played a pivotal role in defining identity by enabling the analysis and recognition of various biometric attributes. For example, facial recognition algorithms can analyze facial features, including the structure, contours, and unique patterns, to create a digital representation of an individual's face. This representation is then used for identity verification and recognition. Additionally, AI has facilitated the development of advanced algorithms for voice recognition, iris recognition, fingerprint scanning, and DNA profiling. These methods offer distinct advantages in accurately identifying individuals based on their physiological or behavioral characteristics.

The use of AI and machine learning algorithms has allowed identity detection systems to continuously learn and improve their accuracy over time. These systems can analyze large datasets and identify patterns and correlations that may not be apparent to human observers. As a result, the process of defining identity has become more precise and efficient. Furthermore, AI has enabled the integration of multiple biometric factors in identity detection systems, creating multimodal approaches. By combining different biometric modalities, such as facial recognition and voice/speech recognition, these systems enhance the accuracy and robustness of identity verification.

***Figure 4.1:** Evolution of AI in face identification*

AI is not only boosting physical identity verifications but also evolving in the context of defining new virtual identities as Avatars (also called meta-human) and **Non-Player Characters (NPCs)**. Avatars are 3D representations of individuals in virtual environments, allowing users to create characters that resemble their identified characteristics or define new characteristics altogether. Avatars serve as a means for users to interact with other users or computer agents in the metaverse. They can take various forms, including human-like characters, animals, or imaginary creatures, and can be created in applications or games. To create more realistic virtual environments, a wide variety of avatar representations is required. *Figure 4.2* depicts an avatar of a person:

Figure 4.2: Avatar the new identity

Furthermore, avatars can also be utilized as NPCs. NPCs are characters within the metaverse that are not controlled by players and do not represent real individuals. With the increasing realism in the gaming sector, NPCs have evolved to enhance the metaverse experience. AI plays a crucial role in NPC development by mimicking intelligent behaviors that provide high-quality entertainment and meet players' expectations. This includes control strategies, realistic graphics, voice capabilities, and lifelike character animations. AI allows these NPCs to behave like humans, interact, and communicate, whether connected to real humans or not. Lip sync solutions like iClone[1] make it more real.

"They can be in the metaverse, what they can't be in the real world"

In summary, by utilizing biometrics and advanced algorithms for reliable identification, AI has revolutionized the way identity is defined. This has paved the way for creation of advanced avatars and NPCs in the metaverse, enhancing the immersive experience. As AI continues to advance, identities will become more comprehensive and realistic, both in the metaverse and the real world.

Environment definition and recognition - the spatial computing

In the context of AI evolutions powering the metaverse, the environment plays a crucial role in creating a realistic and immersive experience. The environment encompasses various elements such as objects, lighting, sound, and temperature, which have a significant impact on our interactions within it. Recognizing and understanding the environment is essential for seamless navigation and interaction. *Figure 4.3* depicts scanning and mapping the environment in real time.

***Figure 4.3:** Environment scanning and mapping*

AI technology has enabled spatial computing, and it is integrated into devices to scan and sense the environment continuously. This process, known as **Simultaneous Localization and Mapping (SLAM)**, enables the generation of a virtual representation of the environment and its ongoing tracking. By detecting objects, images, and plane surfaces, AI facilitates the development of solutions tailored to the recognized environment. Augmenting virtual objects in the real environment, considering occlusion, collision, and gravity, relies on the capabilities of AI and physics engines.

Digitization of the environment takes different forms.

- **Digital model**: Digital replica of physical entity refers to digital model. There is no interaction between the metaverse and the physical world.
- **Digital shadow**: In digital shadow, you can see the digital representation of a physical entity. If the physical entity changes, the digital shadow also changes.
- **Digital twin**: This type of digitization revolves around the interconnectedness of the physical and virtual worlds, where changes in one realm have a direct impact on the other.

Tools like *RoomPlan*[2], *RealityScan*[3], and *Matterport*[4] enable the scanning and creation of digital models of the environment, which can be further enhanced and integrated with environment sensors to form digital twins. AI aids in fast-tracking scanning processes and object detection under various conditions. Semantically understanding the scanned scene is vital for sharing the environment in the metaverse or creating its digital twin. Devices and **Software Development Kits** (**SDKs**) come with built-in image and object recognition, as well as plane detection capabilities. Tracking detected objects accurately, even when occluded by real or virtual objects, is a critical aspect of this process.

Moreover, advancements such as live video processing, deep learning, and environmental sensing contribute to the development of useful technologies for the metaverse. Innovations like *NVIDIA Instant NeRF*[5], and similar Google Research[6] can convert simple images into 3D environments, expanding the possibilities of environment creation and recognition.

In summary, AI plays a crucial role in defining and recognizing the environment in the metaverse. Through techniques like SLAM and object detection, AI enables the creation of realistic virtual environments and facilitates interactions with virtual objects. The digitization of the environment includes digital models, shadows, and twins, with tools and technologies aiding in efficient scanning and understanding. Advancements in live video processing and deep learning contribute to the conversion of images into immersive 3D environments.

Human machine interactions

Machines have undergone significant advancements, and along with them, human-machine interactions have also evolved. The digital revolution began with computer screens, keyboards, and mouse as the primary means of interacting with the digital world. With the advent of mobile devices, virtual keypads on touch screens replaced physical keyboards, and AI played a crucial role in enabling precise typing on these virtual interfaces.

Now, we are moving beyond the limitations of the 2D world and keyboard, entering the era of 3D interactions. The future where we are heading to with the rise in Ubiquitous Computing (Pervasive Computing), Artificial Intelligence, Ambient Intelligence, and IoT devices are blurring the lines between humans and technology. To interact with these machines to its full potential, the interaction needs to be implicit and as natural as possible, which requires enhancing or augmenting our senses. The hardware needs to fade into the background and become a part of the environment, leaving only the software for users to interact with, so we interact with these machines as naturally as possible.

Spatial Computing helps us to partner with these machines, in which the device retains and manipulates real objects and spaces around us as a medium to interact with technology. Using the 3D space which we humans are familiar with helps us to utilize the underused capabilities of our senses in understanding the complex information in the world. Interactions in the 3D space aim to be as seamless as our interactions in the real world, considering the third dimension: depth. In the **Extended Reality** (**XR**) world, the cursor is known as the **Gaze pointer**, while the equivalent of a laser beam is called a **raycast**. *Figure 4.4* depicts interactions in space with gaze, hand, and head movements:

Figure 4.4: Interactions in space

These techniques, enabled by AI, allow for interactions with virtual content in XR environments. The Gaze pointer is typically controlled by head movements, hand tracking or additional controllers. Once the Gaze pointer focuses on interactive elements, actions can be triggered through physical buttons on smart glasses, controllers, trackpad touch, or by maintaining gaze on the interactable for a specific duration. Some devices even incorporate eye tracking, where blinking can trigger interactions. All these interactions are made possible by AI.

However, gaze and hand-based interactions alone may have limitations. Continuous gazing can be tiring, and some users may have difficulty focusing their head for gaze interactions. Therefore, alternative methods are required. Advanced AI techniques now enable devices to track finger movements and hand-gestures, facilitating real-life interactions such as pinch-zoom, scale, rotate, and object manipulation. Even body pose detection is possible, although prolonged use of these interactions can cause fatigue. Another natural interaction modality is **voice-based** interactions, leveraging natural language processing. This allows users to communicate with devices and the virtual world using their voice, emulating real-world conversations. Wearing the devices like *AI Pin*[7] would change the way we have been interacting with machines. However, this form of interaction may disturb people in the surrounding environment. The next stage of evolution involves interactions through thoughts that we will discuss in the *Chapter 5, IoT, Cloud, and Next-gen Networks*.

In summary, the evolution of human-machine interactions has transitioned from traditional input devices to touch screens and now to 3D interactions. AI has been instrumental in driving these advancements and is responsible for enabling interactions through hand gestures, voice commands, and brain-computer interfaces. These developments indicate a shift towards a more connected, user-friendly, and digitally immersive world, which aligns with the concept of the metaverse.

Generative AI

Over the years, Google search has become synonymous with the internet itself. It has been the go-to tool for people to check their internet connection and find answers to almost anything. However, the rise of AI-based technologies has disrupted these established norms. *OpenAI's ChatGPT*[8], for instance, has emerged as the de facto standard in the textual content revolution, challenging the supremacy of traditional search engines. Google, recognizing the potential, has even launched its own AI-powered model called *Bard*[9].

This evolution in AI is recognized as generative AI, a remarkable subset of artificial intelligence techniques and models designed to generate new content or data. Unlike conventional AI models that rely on existing data to recognize patterns or make predictions, generative AI models possess the incredible ability to create original content. They can produce images, music, text, and even entire virtual environments by learning from vast amounts of training data and leveraging that knowledge to generate outputs with similar characteristics or patterns.

***Figure 4.5:** Generative AI for 3D content generation*

In the context of the metaverse or XR, where the belief in another universe built over content is paramount, generative AI plays a crucial role. Creating dynamic and scalable 3D content for XR poses challenges due to various content generation siloes. This is where AI comes to the rescue. While conversations surrounding generative AI often focus on **Large Language Models (LLMs)** that revolutionize text-based communication, recent advancements in the text-to-image domain have opened exciting possibilities. **Latent Diffusion Models (LDMs)** such as OpenAI's DALL-E[10] and Stability's Stable Diffusion[11] have empowered generative AI to convert natural language inputs into photorealistic images or ultra-realistic art. These LDMs learn from training data and use it to generate visually stunning imagery. The building blocks of an LDM are training and inference, allowing them to bridge the gap between textual prompts and visual representations. *Figure 4.5* shows an example of 3D content created using generative AI.

The journey of using generative AI for 3D content generation in the metaverse involves several steps:

1. **Text to photography**: Generative AI starts from a textual description, called a prompt. Many of the images generated for this book uses MidJourney that generates images based on text description. *Adobe FireFly*[12] and Generative Fill feature of photoshop that transform creativity at new heights with simple text prompts.
2. **Photo to 3D point cloud**: In this step, AI brings volume into the scene from sparse sets of photographs. NVIDIA Instant NeRF can convert simple images into 3D environments, similarly *Google's Dream Fusion*[13] can take a **Neural Radiance Fields (NeRF)** model and use a mathematical process called probability density distillation and gradient descent to perfect the 3D model created from a single image. It generates a point cloud, the 3D representation in points. Few other ways are also evolving to sense depth from monocular photos.
3. **3D point cloud to 3D mesh**: 3D point cloud is not directly consumed in business applications, these point clouds are further processed into 3D meshes using techniques like Marching Cubes[14] or Poisson Mesh, accompanied by textures derived from RGB color values.

Generative AI and LDMs[15] not only impact XR applications but also find utility in various other fields such as media/entertainment, building simulation environments for autonomous vehicles, and more. From generating music and videos to creating PowerPoint slides or assisting in software development (for example, GitHub Copilot)[16], the possibilities are vast. These advancements in generative AI bring us closer to the scalability and immersive potential of the metaverse, where content creation plays a pivotal role.

AI beyond reality

AI is pushing the boundaries of reality even further, with researchers exploring the possibility of programming dreams. Ongoing studies are investigating the nature of dreams and methods to manipulate them[17]. In the future, it may be conceivable to sleep with a problem, contemplate it during sleep, and awaken with a solution at hand.

Figure 4.6: Control brain to change the reality

As mentioned previously, the integration of chips into the brain has the potential to alter physical reality. Remarkable advancements have been made, such as a paralyzed individual regaining the ability to walk using AI tools[18]. *Figure 4.6* depicts AI interacting with brain.

By simply thinking or intending to walk, these individuals can be assisted by implanted brain chips. **Deep Brain Stimulation (DBS)** techniques[19], like pacemakers, use electrical pulses to potentially reduce the need for medications and enhance overall quality of life.

AI also has the capacity to break language barriers, facilitating communication between individuals of different origins through translation. Additionally, it enables communication with individuals who have hearing or speech disabilities by detecting and converting sign language. Avatars, our digital representations in the metaverse, have the potential to surpass our physical selves in power and capability, akin to the actor's portrayal in the movie *Avatar*.

AI enabling metaverse

In conclusion, AI is playing a pivotal role in enabling the metaverse, a digital realm where individuals can immerse themselves in virtual experiences. Through its various applications and advancements, AI is transforming the way we interact with and create content for the metaverse.

One of the key contributions of AI to the metaverse is in the field of generative AI. This subset of artificial intelligence focuses on generating new content or data, such as images, music, and text. Generative AI models can create original and diverse outputs, learning from vast amounts of training data and exhibiting similar characteristics or patterns. This opens possibilities for creating dynamic and immersive virtual environments within the metaverse. AI also contributes to the content creation process for the metaverse. Text-to-image models can convert textual descriptions into photorealistic images, while AI algorithms can generate 3D models and meshes from photographs, adding depth and volume to virtual scenes. These capabilities facilitate the creation of 3D objects and environments, essential for building immersive metaverse experiences.

Furthermore, AI enables spatial computing, which further enables natural and intuitive interactions within the metaverse. Hand gestures, voice commands, and even brain-computer interfaces allow users to engage with virtual content in a seamless and realistic manner. AI techniques track hand movements, finger gestures, and even interpret spoken language to perform actions like pinch-zoom, scale, rotate, and move objects. These interactions bring us closer to replicating real-life experiences within the metaverse. Moreover, AI aids in overcoming language barriers and enhancing communication within the metaverse. Translation tools powered by AI enable real-time language translation, enabling individuals from different linguistic backgrounds to interact and collaborate. AI can also detect and convert sign language, making communication accessible to people with hearing or speech disabilities.

Conclusion

In conclusion, AI's contributions to the metaverse are multidimensional. From generative AI to intuitive interactions, content creation, and communication enhancements, AI is propelling the development and realization of the metaverse. As AI continues to advance, it holds the potential to create even more captivating, user-friendly, and immersive virtual worlds, further blurring the line between the physical and digital realms.

In the next chapter, we will delve into the exciting progress in IoT, cloud technology, and the next generation of networks that are driving the evolution of the metaverse.

Points to remember

Here are the key points to remember from this chapter:

- The adoption of digital identity is becoming increasingly common, with AI-powered systems playing a crucial role in identity detection.
- Avatars, our digital representations, will serve as our identities in the metaverse, offering the potential for both realistic and imaginative identities.
- The field of spatial computing is experiencing rapid growth due to advancements in AI, enabling natural interactions between humans and machines.
- Generative AI will play a vital role in fuelling the content needs of metaverse applications.
- We are approaching a future where brain-controlled interfaces and seamless collaboration between humans and machines are becoming more feasible.

References

1. https://www.reallusion.com/iclone/lipsync-animation.html
2. https://developer.apple.com/augmented-reality/roomplan/
3. https://www.unrealengine.com/en-US/realityscan
4. https://matterport.com/
5. https://developer.nvidia.com/blog/getting-started-with-nvidia-instant-nerfs/
6. https://ai.googleblog.com/2023/06/reconstructing-indoor-spaces-with-nerf.html
7. https://hu.ma.ne/aipin
8. https://openai.com/chatgpt
9. https://bard.google.com/
10. https://openai.com/dall-e-2
11. https://stablediffusionweb.com/
12. https://www.adobe.com/sensei/generative-ai/firefly.html
13. https://dreamfusion3d.github.io/
14. https://graphics.stanford.edu/~mdfisher/MarchingCubes.html
15. https://thinkuldeep.com/post/generative-ai-for-3d-content-in-xr-and-beyond/
16. https://github.com/features/copilot
17. https://www.scientificamerican.com/article/how-to-control-dreams/
18. https://opendatascience.com/paralyzed-man-walks-again-thanks-to-ai-powered-tool/
19. https://mayfieldclinic.com/pe-dbs.htm

CHAPTER 5
IoT, Cloud, and Next-gen Networks

Introduction

This chapter will explore the crucial role of the **Internet of Things (IoT)**, cloud-based solutions, and next-generation networks in enabling the metaverse. These technological advancements are instrumental in creating the infrastructure and capabilities necessary to realize the full potential of the metaverse.

We begin by examining the evolution of IoT and its significance in bridging the gap between the physical and virtual worlds. IoT devices act as connectors, collecting and transmitting data from the physical environment to the digital cloud realm over the next-gen networks super-fast network. This seamless integration allows for the creation of immersive and interactive experiences within the metaverse.

Structure

In this chapter, we will discuss the following topics:

- Internet of Things
- Scaling the metaverse with cloud-based solutions
- Accelerating the metaverse with next-generation networks

Objectives

This chapter aims to provide readers with a comprehensive understanding of the evolution of IoT, cloud computing, and next-generation networks. These advancements are crucial in fueling the development of metaverse applications and transitioning us toward the next stage of the internet, known as the metaverse. By exploring the capabilities and implications of IoT, cloud computing, and next-generation networks, readers will gain insights into how these technologies shape the future of immersive and interconnected virtual experiences.

Internet of Things

The **Internet of Things (IoT)** is revolutionizing the physical world by connecting everyday objects to the internet, making them smarter and more interconnected. It goes beyond simple connectivity and encompasses a wide range of services. IoT involves not only connecting things but also analyzing the data generated by these interconnected devices. Through data analysis, IoT enables the discovery of new insights, pattern recognition, prediction of situations, solution recommendations, and the ability to instruct ordinary objects to make decisions and optimize their operations.

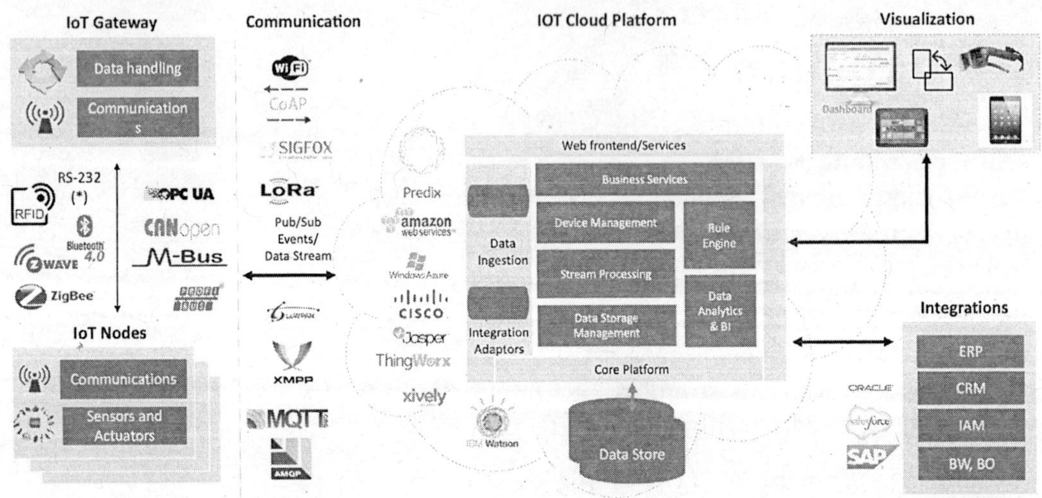

Figure 5.1: A typical IoT ecosystem

A comprehensive IoT ecosystem comprises various essential components, as illustrated in *Figure 5.1*. At the core of this ecosystem are IoT devices, which can be embedded with internet capabilities or connected through gateway devices. These devices are equipped with sensors to perceive the environment and can respond to commands received via connected networks.

IoT devices are connected to cloud platforms, which serve as the central hub for managing and processing the data generated by these devices. The cloud platforms collect, process, and store the data, extracting meaningful insights and enabling businesses to derive value from it. Actionable data is then sent back to the IoT devices, empowering them to take appropriate actions based on the insights received. The IoT cloud platform provides extended computing capabilities to the IoT devices, augmenting their processing power and enabling sophisticated analysis. Communication protocols play a vital role in ensuring seamless connectivity and interoperability between IoT devices. These protocols have evolved over time to facilitate efficient data exchange and enable effective collaboration among devices within the IoT landscape.

Furthermore, the IoT ecosystem leverages edge computing, which involves performing data processing and analysis near the IoT devices or gateways. This approach reduces latency, optimizes network bandwidth, and enables real-time decision-making. Edge computing enhances the responsiveness and efficiency of IoT devices, enabling them to process and act on data quickly.

By embracing IoT, businesses and industries can unlock new possibilities and harness the power of connected devices to enhance efficiency, improve decision-making, and create innovative solutions.

The integration of IoT and XR: A closer human-machine relationship

Combining IoT and **Extended Reality** (**XR**) enables a closer relationship between humans and machines, fostering an immersive and interactive experience. XR devices, which encompass technologies like **Virtual Reality** (**VR**), **Augmented Reality** (**AR**), and **Mixed Reality** (**MR**), are not only capable and connected but can also function as IoT gateways within the IoT ecosystem. In fact, XR devices can be considered as evolved IoT devices, as they possess both communication and computing capabilities to process data and act upon instructions from connected systems. Additionally, XR devices can connect to other IoT devices using various IoT protocols, enhancing their understanding of the environment.

Figure 5.2: *XR devices are the evolved IoT*

In industrial settings, the integration of XR and IoT creates a more productive ecosystem. For instance, when a user is in proximity to a machine, the connected ecosystem can provide contextual information about that machine. By merging multiple identification methods like image/object recognition and IR/proximity data, the machine can be accurately identified, and relevant information can be presented to the user.

Moreover, XR devices can establish a seamless connection with the IoT ecosystem, allowing for data exchange and interaction. XR devices can serve as the eyes and ears for traditional IoT devices, bridging the gap between humans and machines. This convergence is a key aspect of the enterprise metaverse, where humans and machines collaborate closely to achieve common goals.

Digital twins and simulations

Digital twins are virtual representations of physical IoT devices in the digital world, replicating their behavior by synchronizing data collected from IoT sensors. These virtual copies serve as powerful tools for simulating workflows and industrial processes, allowing us to visualize and analyze the outcomes before implementing them in the real world. For instance, simulations can be used to test scenarios like fire environments, car safety features such as airbags, and more.

Simulations can also extend to the training of autonomous vehicles using XR technology. Self-driving cars exemplify the capabilities of artificial intelligence today, built upon extensively trained machine learning algorithms. These algorithms require vast amounts of data to effectively model all the possible scenarios.

Figure 5.3: Autonomous vehicle training in XR

Digital twins provide a valuable resource for data scientists, enabling them to generate the necessary data to train complex **Artificial Intelligence (AI)** models in a cost-effective manner. Digital twins are particularly useful in training self-driving cars, where a digital model of the car acts as an agent and is immersed within a simulated city environment. By incorporating rigid-body physics elements to simulate mass and gravity, the agent can learn through reinforcement, determining the right and wrong moves in different hypothetical situations. This is called reward modelling, a part of reinforcement learning where we guide the AI to find an optimal solution by giving rewards for success and penalty for failures. This iterative learning process allows for the efficient development of AI for autonomous vehicles during the prototyping stage. Similar approaches can be applied in the realm of industrial robotics, aiding in the training of path-planning and optimization for moving robots.

In summary, XR simulations utilizing digital twins to train machine learning models offer a rapid prototyping solution for industrial AI applications. By leveraging the power of virtual simulations, data scientists can expedite the development and testing of AI algorithms, specifically in areas such as autonomous vehicles and industrial robotics. This methodology enables faster innovation, optimization, and deployment of AI systems, ultimately enhancing efficiency and safety in various industrial domains.

Drone swarming and 3D displays

Drone swarming is a fascinating development that combines the capabilities of drones with 3D displays, enabling immersive visual experiences both indoors and outdoors. In the realm of IoT, drones serve as mobile sensors, collecting valuable data and transmitting it to cloud applications or analytics services. They can also be utilized as remote inspection devices, assisting in maintaining and monitoring IoT endpoints and other components.

Drones, often referred to as Flying IoT[1], have undergone significant advancements in size and functionality. They have become as small as bees, and the ability to control them programmatically has made swarming a natural phenomenon. By incorporating LED lights, drones transform into a powerful 3D visualization system. These visually captivating displays can be enjoyed with the naked eye, making them suitable for outdoor and indoor settings. The integration of drone swarming and 3D displays holds tremendous potential for future metaverse experiences. This technology enables the visualization of vast cityscapes, creating immersive environments on a city scale. Additionally, it opens possibilities for enhancing stadium experiences, delivering captivating visual displays that engage and delight audiences.

Figure 5.4: 3D drone show

Drone swarming and 3D displays represent a remarkable fusion of technology, allowing us to explore new frontiers in visual storytelling and entertainment. With their ability to merge physical and digital worlds seamlessly, these advancements hold promise for the future of immersive experiences in the metaverse.

Cybernetics: Enhancing the user experience in the metaverse

The section describing IoT advancements at the next level, known as cybernetics, explores the integration of electronic and biological systems to create a seamless interaction between humans and machines. Through technologies like **Brain-Computer Interfaces (BCIs)** and haptic feedback systems, cybernetics aims to enhance the user experience in the metaverse.

Brain-computer interfaces enable direct communication between the human brain and digital systems, opening new possibilities for interaction in the metaverse. By wearing a BCI headset, users can control virtual objects and navigate virtual environments using their thoughts, providing a more natural and intuitive interface.

This technology relies on tracking brain patterns through **electroencephalogram (EEG)** and converting them into commands, allowing individuals with limited physical abilities to interact with devices without relying on gestures or physical movements. Brain implants will be common in the coming years; *Neuralink*[2] , *Blackrock NeuroTech*[3] and *Apple's new AirPod*[4] are heading towards that.

Figure 5.5: *Interactions just by thinking*

Haptic feedback systems are another key area of focus in advanced IoT. These systems provide tactile sensations to users, allowing them to feel and touch virtual objects within the metaverse. By using haptic gloves or suits, users can experience the texture, weight, and even the temperature of virtual objects, blurring the boundaries between the physical and virtual worlds. In addition to haptic feedback, audio technologies play a crucial role in creating immersive experiences. Spatial audio can recreate realistic soundscapes, providing users with directional and distance-based sound cues, further enhancing immersion in the metaverse.

The implications of cybernetics extend beyond entertainment and gaming. In the field of medicine and rehabilitation, cybernetic technologies can significantly impact the life of individuals. Prosthetic limbs integrated with sensory feedback systems enable amputees to have more natural and intuitive control over their artificial limbs, improving their quality of life. The advancement in cybernetic technologies has the potential to revolutionize not only entertainment but also healthcare, communication, and various other industries.

IoT and metaverse: Bridging the physical and virtual worlds

In conclusion, the integration of IoT and the metaverse holds great potential for transforming our digital experiences and bridging the gap between the physical and virtual worlds. IoT technology, which connects physical objects to the internet and enables data analysis and automation, plays a crucial role in building a comprehensive ecosystem for the metaverse.

We can gather data from the physical world through IoT devices, analyze it, and derive valuable insights. This data-driven approach enhances our understanding of the environment and enables us to make informed decisions. Moreover, IoT devices can act as connectors between the physical and virtual worlds. Metaverse benefits from the advancements in IoT by leveraging scalable infrastructure; this enables IoT devices to act as the eyes and ears of the metaverse, bringing humans and machines closer together in a collaborative environment.

XR devices, such as virtual reality headsets and augmented reality glasses, can serve as IoT gateways, connecting to other IoT devices and providing a deeper understanding of the environment. This integration allows users to interact with virtual objects and environments using their thoughts, thanks to cybernetics, which integrate electronic and biological systems. It further enhances the user experience by creating a seamless interaction between humans and machine BCIs and experience realistic tactile sensations through haptic feedback systems.

As IoT continues to evolve and connect more devices, and as the metaverse becomes increasingly immersive and interconnected, the possibilities for innovation and transformation are endless. The integration of IoT and metaverse represents a significant step forward in creating a digital realm that seamlessly blends with our physical reality, opening new opportunities for communication, collaboration, entertainment, and beyond.

Scaling the metaverse with cloud-based solutions

Cloud-based solutions are pivotal in scaling the metaverse and addressing the limitations of XR devices. As XR devices become more powerful and capable, they face challenges such as reduced battery life, larger form factors, overheating, and increased complexity. These limitations hinder the extended and continuous usage of XR devices.

Cloud-based XR solutions provide a scalable alternative by harnessing the capabilities of cloud infrastructure, relieving battery and resource constraints on XR devices, thereby extending their operational duration. Within the realm of cloud technology, the competition among private, public, and hybrid clouds has fostered the development of robust practices, enabling organizations to tailor their cloud usage according to their specific requirements for security, control, and scalability. Furthermore, these solutions streamline infrastructure management and maintenance, offering a more efficient approach. This evolution will be explained across different categories in the subsequent sections.

Live streaming

The rise of live streaming has brought about a shift in the way we perceive being online. It is no longer just about being connected to the internet; it now encompasses being available on live streaming applications. Live streaming creates a virtual face-to-face experience, allowing multiple individuals to come on camera simultaneously and communicate as if they were in each other's presence. However, this experience is currently limited to a 2D screen, with interactions confined within that boundary.

However, with the integration of XR and the metaverse, 3D live streaming is now possible, along with the sharing of spatial environments. This means that people can not only see each other face to face but also interact, touch, and feel within the virtual space.

To facilitate this, cloud solutions play a crucial role. Common sessions hosted over cloud infrastructure, with popular technologies like WebRTC and WebSocket-based communication for real-time bi-directional interaction, enable seamless live streaming experiences. Various protocols, such as **HTTP Live Streaming (HLS)**[5], **Real-Time Messaging Protocol** (**RTMP**), and MPEG-DASH, have emerged to cater to different streaming needs. Nowadays, most cloud infrastructure providers offer comprehensive services tailored for live streaming.

In XR streaming, the experience is akin to streaming content frame by frame, like a video stream. The advancements in cloud-based live streaming technologies have made certain use cases possible in XR, where immersive and interactive experiences can be delivered seamlessly.

Cloud rendering

Cloud rendering is becoming crucial in addressing the limitations of XR content on devices. Generating XR content can impose a heavy load on XR devices, making it challenging to develop all types of XR content seamlessly. Efforts are being made to optimize XR content for different devices, but there are still restrictions when it comes to using photorealistic content. The need to balance battery life, weight, resource consumption, and overheating issues often results in sub-optimal experiences, compromising the believability of virtual content.

To overcome these challenges, the concept of cloud rendering has emerged. Cloud rendering offloads the computational burden from XR devices to powerful cloud infrastructure, allowing for more complex and realistic XR experiences. By leveraging cloud resources, XR content can be rendered remotely and streamed to the XR device in real time. This enables the delivery of high-quality, immersive content that would be otherwise difficult to achieve on the device.

To support cloud rendering, developers have created **Software Development Kits** (**SDKs**) for devices that facilitate automatic switching between local rendering and the closest cloud rendering options. It makes the intelligent decision based on the computational requirements of the rendering process and passes on the rendered to the CloudXR client, which is connected to the corresponding CloudXR server, as described in *Figure 5.6*. Examples of cloud rendering solutions include Azure Remote Rendering[6] and NVIDIA

CloudXR, which provide the infrastructure and tools to support cloud rendering for XR applications.

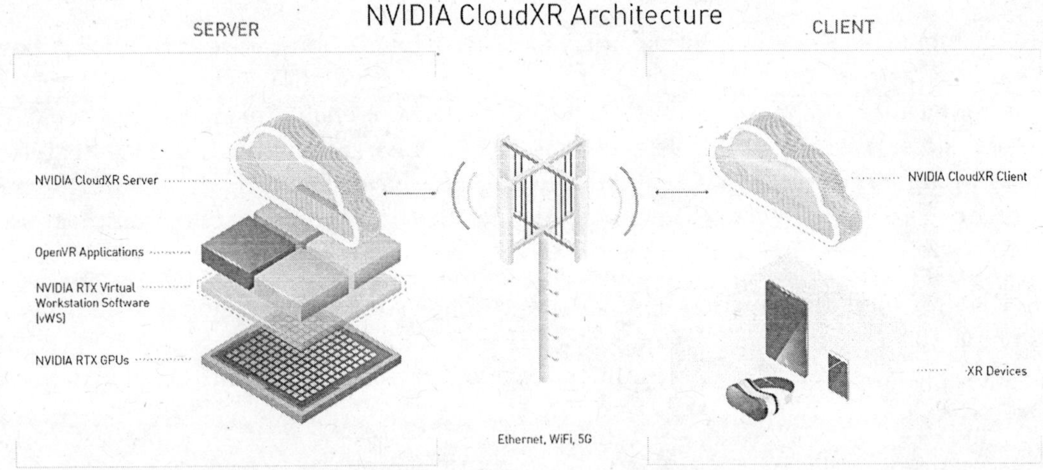

Figure 5.6: *NVIDIA CloudXR Architecture*[7]

By leveraging cloud rendering, XR experiences can benefit from the computational power and scalability of the cloud, allowing for more realistic graphics, complex simulations, and seamless interactivity. Users can experience immersive XR content without being constrained by their device's processing capabilities, resulting in improved overall quality and realism of the virtual world.

Cloud anchors for shared XR content

Cloud anchors are a fundamental component for enabling shared XR experiences. XR devices, equipped with advanced scanning and mapping capabilities, can analyze the spatial environment and identify distinct feature points that characterize it. These feature points serve as reference anchors, representing specific locations or objects in the 3D environment.

Cloud anchors allow these identified feature points to be securely stored and shared. By leveraging cloud-based solutions, such as *Google Cloud Anchors*[8] or Microsoft Azure's *Spatial Anchors*[9], users can access and interact with these shared XR experiences in real time, regardless of their physical location. This means multiple users can virtually gather and collaborate within the same shared space, perceiving and interacting with the same digital content.

For example, imagine a group of friends exploring a virtual art gallery using XR devices. With cloud anchors, each user can view and interact with the same virtual art pieces, experiencing a synchronized and shared XR environment. They can walk around the gallery, discuss the artwork, and even leave virtual messages or annotations that are visible to others. In *Figure 5.7*, we see a user immersed in the virtual art gallery concept.

Figure 5.7: Virtual art gallery experience at a booth in a conference by Thoughtworks

Cloud-based solutions not only enable shared XR experiences but also streamline the distribution and storage of XR content and updates. Instead of manually installing or updating applications or experiences on each individual XR device, the cloud allows for centralized content management and seamless content delivery. Users can access the latest XR experiences without the hassle of manual installations or updates, ensuring they are always immersed in the up-to-date, engaging XR environments.

Geospatial services

Solutions like Geospatial APIs[10] have the potential to take the open AR experience to the next level in the metaverse. It provides developers with access to geolocation data and services, allowing them to create AR experiences that are deeply integrated with the physical world.

By leveraging Geospatial APIs, developers can overlay digital information, objects, or virtual experiences onto specific geolocations in real-time. This enables users to interact with the virtual content in a contextually relevant and location-based manner.

For example, Geospatial APIs can be used to create AR navigation applications that guide users through cities, pointing out landmarks and providing directions in real-time. It can also be utilized to enhance tourism experiences by offering interactive AR content at specific tourist attractions or historical sites. Furthermore, Geospatial APIs can enable collaborative AR experiences, where multiple users can interact with shared virtual content in a specific location. This opens up possibilities for shared gaming experiences, virtual events, or collaborative design projects.

Overall, Geospatial APIs have the potential to enhance the open AR experience in the metaverse by integrating digital content seamlessly into the physical world based on geolocation data. This enables an immersive, context-aware, and interactive AR experiences that blur the boundaries between the virtual and real worlds.

Cloud-based metaverse solutions in nutshell

Cloud-based solutions offer scaling the XR solutions to meet metaverse needs and addressing the limitations of XR devices. These solutions offer efficient infrastructure management, scalability, and cost-effectiveness. Cloud-based XR solutions offload intensive computational tasks to the cloud, allowing for longer and more immersive experiences.

Cloud technologies also enable the sharing of XR content and experiences through features like cloud anchors, where multiple users can interact and collaborate in real-time regardless of their physical location. Cloud-based XR content and device management services streamline the distribution of XR content, updates, and installations. Users can access the latest XR experiences seamlessly, ensuring they are always immersed in the most up-to-date virtual worlds, ultimately enhancing the accessibility and immersive potential of the metaverse.

Accelerating the metaverse with next-generation networks

In this chapter, we discuss the crucial role of next-gen networks in advancing the metaverse. While the metaverse is often referred to as the next Internet, the current stage of development still has a long way to go. However, the next generation of internet technologies is bringing us closer to the envisioned metaverse.

In the previous section, we explored how cloud technologies enable lightweight XR devices that can be worn like everyday accessories. These devices offload the computational load to the cloud, but to achieve real-time and realistic experiences, high network speeds are essential. Rendering XR or metaverse content is like rendering high-quality videos, with each frame being several megabytes in size. To provide a seamless and immersive experience, it is necessary to render at least 60 frames per second. This level of performance requires a high-speed network infrastructure with low latency.

The section highlights the evolution of network speeds and lower latency as crucial factors in pushing the boundaries of the metaverse. Advancements in network technologies, such as 5G and beyond, are instrumental in delivering the necessary bandwidth and responsiveness for the metaverse to thrive.

5G/6G network

This section emphasizes the role of high-speed networks in supporting the metaverse's real-time environment sharing and live collaborations. With the increasing demand for data transfer, a network with exceptionally high speed is required.

Currently, the **Fifth Generation** (**5G**) mobile network is being deployed as the latest global wireless standard, succeeding 1G, 2G, 3G, and 4G networks. 5G introduces a revolutionary network design aimed at connecting everything and everyone, including machines, objects, and devices. It offers significantly higher peak data speeds in the multi-Gbps range, ultra-low latency, improved reliability, massive network capacity, increased availability, and a more consistent user experience. These advancements in performance and efficiency unlock new user experiences and drive the ever-connected world towards the metaverse. Major telecom providers are evolving their offerings to include technologies such as **Multi-Access Edge Computing** (**MEC**) combined with 5G, as seen with Verizon's initiatives[11].

While 5G brings substantial capabilities and standardization, it may not fully meet the future requirements beyond 2030. Therefore, the development of **Sixth Generation** (**6G**) wireless communication networks is already on the horizon. 6G networks are expected to provide global coverage with peak data speeds in the **TeraBits Per Second** (**TBps**) range, enhanced efficiency in terms of spectrum, energy, and cost, improved intelligence, and heightened security. Achieving these ambitious goals will involve leveraging emerging technologies like quantum computing.

The deployment of 5G networks is a significant step towards meeting the high-speed and low latency demands of the metaverse. However, the future will likely necessitate the development of even more advanced **sixth-generation networks** (**6G**) to provide the global coverage and capabilities required for the metaverse's continued evolution.

Quantum computing

Quantum computing is an emerging field of technology that holds immense potential for advancing the capabilities of networks and enabling the evolution of the metaverse. Traditional computing relies on binary bits, represented as 0s and 1s, to process and store information. Quantum computing, on the other hand, utilizes quantum bits or qubits, which can exist in multiple states simultaneously, due to a phenomenon called **superposition**. This inherent ability of qubits allows quantum computers to perform complex calculations and process vast amount of data in parallel, providing a tremendous boost in computational power. As a result, quantum computing has the potential to revolutionize various aspects of the metaverse. *Figure 5.8* depicts a quantum computing multi-layer processor.

Figure 5.8: Quantum computing

One area where quantum computing can significantly impact the metaverse is in network optimization. Quantum algorithms can help to solve complex optimization problems more efficiently, leading to faster data transmission, reduced latency, and improved network performance. This can enable seamless real-time interactions and collaboration within the metaverse, enhancing the overall user experience. Moreover, quantum computing can synergize with other advanced networking technologies to further enhance the metaverse experience. For example, **Light Fidelity** (**LiFi**) technology, which uses light signals to transmit data, can provide high-speed and secure wireless communication within confined spaces, complementing quantum computing's capabilities. The combination of LiFi and quantum computing can enable faster and more reliable data transfer, ensuring smooth and immersive metaverse experiences.

Satellite internet is another technology that can benefit from the advancements in quantum computing. Quantum algorithms can optimize satellite communication systems, improving the efficiency and reliability of data transmission between satellites and ground stations. This can expand the reach of metaverse, making it accessible to users in remote areas or regions with limited infrastructure.

However, it is important to note that quantum computing is still in its early stages of development and faces significant technical challenges. The creation and maintenance of stable qubits, as well as minimizing errors caused by quantum decoherence, remain key areas of focus for researchers and scientists. As quantum computing technology continues to advance, it has the potential to reshape the way we experience and interact with the metaverse, unlocking new levels of immersion, collaboration, and innovation.

Network security

As the network speed and complexity increase, so do the security threats that can compromise the metaverse. Network security has become an integral part of network design, considering the challenges posed by extreme data rates and the need for efficient traffic processing for security purposes.

To address these challenges, distributed security solutions are being adopted which involve processing network traffic locally and on-the-fly in different segments of the network. By doing so, potential security breaches can be detected and mitigated effectively, ensuring a more secure metaverse environment. This approach also enables the incorporation of technologies like attack detection, AI/ML pipelines, traffic analysis, and pervasive encryption to enhance network security. *Figure 5.9* illustrates the security consideration at the core of the metaverse.

***Figure 5.9:** Security by design in the metaverse*

Future 6G systems are expected to incorporate novel aspects such as integrated sensing, artificial intelligence, local compute-and-storage, and embedded devices. These advancements will not only enhance existing **Key Performance Indicators (KPIs)** of security but also introduce new metrics that are not traditionally associated with mobile networks. These metrics include sensing accuracy, computational round-trip time, and AI model convergence time. The focus on these metrics aligns with the goals of sustainability, security, inclusiveness, and trustworthiness.

In terms of network infrastructure, proprietary networks may provide enhanced security through sub-networks. These sub-networks ensure that privacy data is maintained within the control of owners, promoting secure data handling and protection. Additionally, trusted execution environments within the network infrastructure will be defined more strictly, providing an added layer of security. As the metaverse becomes more intertwined with our daily lives, ensuring robust network security measures will be crucial to protect user data, privacy, and overall trust in the ecosystem.

Conclusion

IoT, Cloud, and Next-Gen Networks have significant impact on shaping the future of the digital landscape. The IoT has revolutionized the way we interact with our physical environment, connecting devices and enabling seamless data exchange. The integration of IoT with cloud computing has further accelerated innovation by providing scalable and cost-effective solutions, empowering industries, and individuals to leverage the power of data and analytics. Additionally, next-generation networks, such as 5G and the future promise of 6G, have opened new possibilities for real-time communication, low-latency applications, and enhanced user experiences.

We termed XR devices as evolved IoT devices, and delve into the transformative potential of these various sectors, from smart cities and industrial automation to healthcare and agriculture. We learned how IoT devices, interconnected through cloud infrastructure, can drive efficiency, productivity, and informed decision-making. Cloud-based solutions further scaling the metaverse by enabling lightweight XR devices and facilitating collaborative experiences through shared environments and content rendering. Cloud-based services also ensure efficient management of XR content and device updates, simplifying user experiences.

The chapter also covers the vital importance of next-generation networks. The rise of 5G networks unlocks unprecedented speed, capacity, and reliability, enabling real-time environment sharing, live collaborations, and immersive experiences within the metaverse. The anticipated emergence of 6G networks, supported by technologies like quantum computing and LiFi, holds the promise of even higher data speeds, enhanced efficiency, and novel applications. However, as network speeds increase, network security becomes critical, necessitating distributed security solutions and stringent privacy measures to safeguard the metaverse and ensure user trust.

In essence, this chapter encapsulates the transformative journey of these technologies, highlighting their pivotal role in reshaping industries, empowering individuals, and paving the way for a connected, immersive future.

In the next chapter, we will delve into the imperative for decentralization and the pivotal role of blockchain within the metaverse ecosystem.

Points to remember

Here are the key points to remember from this chapter:

- XR devices, which encompass AR, VR, and MR, are advanced IoT devices that can sense and interact with the environment.
- Digital twins combine IoT and XR technologies to simulate and replicate the behaviour of real-world objects or environments.

- Drones, often referred to as flying IoT devices, have the potential to create large-scale 3D displays.
- IoT devices are becoming increasingly compact, some even being small enough to be ingested or implanted in the human body for direct communication.
- Cloud-based solutions are essential for handling the spatial computing requirements of XR, providing capabilities such as persistent anchors, geospatial logic, and more.
- The next generation of networks, such as 5G and 6G, will further enhance the capabilities of XR devices by enabling offloading of computational tasks to nearby supercomputing machines.

References

1. **https://www.computer.org/csdl/magazine/mi/2017/06/mmi2017060040/13rRUIJuxu9**
2. **https://neuralink.com/**
3. **https://blackrockneurotech.com/**
4. **https://www.techgoing.com/new-apple-airpods-patent-can-monitor-the-wearers-brainwaves-and-other-biosignals/**
5. **https://developer.apple.com/streaming/**
6. **https://azure.microsoft.com/en-au/products/remote-rendering/**
7. **https://developer.nvidia.com/cloudxr-sdk**
8. **https://developers.google.com/ar/develop/cloud-anchors**
9. **https://azure.microsoft.com/en-in/products/spatial-anchors**
10. **https://developers.google.com/ar/develop/geospatial**
11. **https://www.verizon.com/business/solutions/5g/edge-computing/public-mec/**

CHAPTER 6
Decentralization and the Role of Blockchain

Introduction

As explained in the metaverse characteristics in *Chapter 2, Metaverse - Various Forms and Interpretations,* metaverse needs to be open, interoperable, and accessible to everyone. It prompts the idea of a decentralized metaverse and has gained significant traction in recent times due to the need to avoid central ownership or control. Instead, it is believed that the metaverse should be driven by communities and people. This led to the development of decentralized architectures for metaverse solutions. Blockchain distributed app architecture is one such solution that closely aligns with this vision. It also discusses the rise of the creator's economy.

Structure

In this chapter, we will discuss the following topics:

- Rise of decentralization
- Understanding blockchain
- The evolution of blockchain
- Understanding tokens and NFTs
- Rise of creator economy
- A path to decentralized metaverse

Objectives

The objective of this chapter is to provide readers with a comprehensive understanding of decentralization in building metaverse applications and the role of blockchain technology in enabling it. By exploring the principles of decentralization and its significance in the context of the metaverse, readers will gain insights into how blockchain technology can contribute to creating a more open, transparent, and user-centric virtual environment. This chapter aims to highlight the potential of blockchain for enabling secure peer-to-peer transactions, ownership of digital assets, and decentralized governance models within the metaverse. Through a detailed examination of blockchain-based solutions, readers will develop a deeper understanding of the decentralized nature of the metaverse and its implications for the future of immersive digital experiences.

Rise of decentralization

Decentralization refers to the distribution of authority, control, and decision-making across a network rather than having a central authority or a single point of control. It involves the redistribution of power and responsibilities to multiple participants in a system, enabling greater transparency, resilience, and autonomy. In the context of Web 3.0 and the evolving digital landscape, decentralized architectures are playing a crucial role in shaping the future.

The evolution of decentralized architectures can be observed over time as technologies and concepts have emerged to challenge traditional centralized models. These decentralized architectures are revolutionizing various industries and digital ecosystems, offering several benefits.

Let us explore some key aspects of decentralization:

- **Distributed infrastructure:** Envisions the use of *distributed ledger technology*, such as blockchain, to facilitate transparent and secure transactions. This distributed infrastructure eliminates the need for a centralized authority to oversee and verify transactions, ensuring greater trust and immutability. It also leverages *peer-to-peer networks*, where nodes in the network interact directly with each other, enabling direct communication and data sharing without relying on centralized servers.

- **Interoperability**: Emphasize interoperability, allowing different platforms and service providers to seamlessly interact and share data. This interoperability fosters competition, innovation, and choice for consumers and enterprise, while enabling service providers to reach a broader customer base and collaborate more effectively.

- **Data ownership and privacy:** Focuses on empowering users by giving them control over their data. It emphasizes user consent, data protection, and privacy, ensuring that individuals have the authority to decide how their information is shared and used within the digital ecosystem.

- **Collaborative governance:** Promotes collaborative governance involving multiple stakeholders in decision-making processes. It encourages the participation of industry experts, governing agencies, administrations, and technology providers to collectively shape the rules, standards, and policies governing the digital ecosystems.
- **Trust and security:** Decentralized systems enhance trust and security by eliminating the need for users to rely on third parties for verification and validation. The use of cryptographic techniques ensures data integrity, immutability, and protection against unauthorized access.

The rise of decentralized architectures is exemplified by initiatives like the **Open Network for Digital Commerce** (**ONDC**)[1] (*Figure 6.1*) and the VAKT platform[2]. ONDC is an initiative by the Government of India aimed at building a decentralized architecture for e-commerce platforms, creating an open, inclusive, and interoperable digital commerce ecosystem. VAKT, on the other hand comes from the private and enterprise side, focuses on distributed platforms for commodity trading ensuring trade bilateral transactions are accessible only to the partners involved. VAKT was formed by a group of oil majors, traders, and trade finance providers.

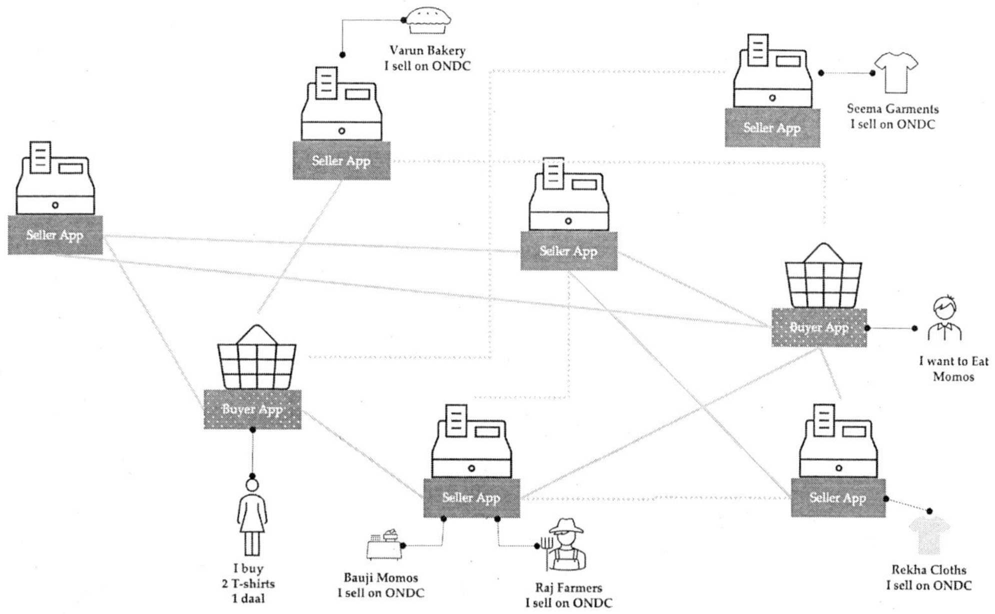

Figure 6.1: *Open Network for Digital Commerce*

Additionally, the evolution of **distributed finance** (**DeFi**) and the success of Bitcoin demonstrates the potential of decentralized architectures. DeFi promotes self-sustainability, allowing individuals to earn and survive within the digital ecosystem with blockchain-based technologies at its core.

In the next section, we will delve deeper into blockchain technology, its evolution over the years, and why it is crucial for the development of a distributed metaverse.

Understanding blockchain

In this section, we will cover the basics of blockchain technology and how it works; the interest in which has grown along with the popularity of cryptocurrencies. Today it is widely discussed not only in the world of finance but is already used for storing and processing personal data and identification in marketing and computer games.

The book analogy

The ledger book analogy provides a simple way to understand the concept of blockchain. Just as a physical ledger in the form of a book maintains a record of transactions, blockchain is a digital ledger that tracks the transactions of digital assets in a decentralized manner.

Drawing parallels to a physical book, imagine each page of the book as a block in the blockchain. Pages are connected to one another through page numbers, representing the order of the blocks in the blockchain. If someone tampers with or removes a specific page, it becomes evident because the sequence is disrupted. Similarly, changing or removing a block in the blockchain can be easily identified due to its interconnected structure. The following figure is an illustration of blockchain as a ledger book:

Figure 6.2: Blockchain as a ledger book

Here are the key aspects of the blockchain:

- **Ledger:** The blockchain is like a complete ledger that records all the credit and debit transactions of a digital asset, whether it is a physical object or something digital like virtual currency or data. It acts as a transparent and immutable record of these transactions.

- **Distributed nature:** Instead of being stored in a single location, the blockchain is distributed across hundreds or thousands of computers or servers. Each computer, also known as a node, maintains a complete copy of the ledger. This decentralized nature ensures that no single entity has control over the entire blockchain.

- **Peer-to-Peer network:** The computers or nodes in the blockchain network are connected in a **peer-to-peer** (**P2P**) fashion, meaning they communicate directly with each other. This network allows the verification of individual transactions without relying on a central authority.

- **Blocks:** In the blockchain, transactions are grouped into blocks. Each block contains digital pieces of information, such as the date, time, and amount involved in the transaction. Additionally, blocks include information that distinguishes them from other blocks, such as a unique code known as a hash.

- **Hashes and cryptographic codes:** Hashes are cryptographic codes generated by special algorithms. They serve as unique identifiers for each block and allows it to be differentiated from other blocks. These hashes ensure the integrity and security of the blockchain.

- **Relationship with cryptocurrencies:** Blockchain and cryptocurrencies are related but distinct concepts. Cryptocurrencies, such as Bitcoin, are digital tokens represented as numbers in the blockchain. The blockchain ledger tracks the ownership and transactions of these digital tokens from the beginning.

By representing blockchain as a book, the analogy highlights the importance of maintaining the integrity and completeness of the ledger. Any alteration or removal of a page or block can have significant consequences, potentially compromising the entire record. The interconnectedness of blocks ensures that any changes made to a block would affect all subsequent blocks, making it difficult to tamper with the data without detection.

Overall, the book analogy simplifies the understanding of blockchain as a decentralized ledger system that records and secures transactions in a transparent and immutable manner.

Working of a blockchain

Blockchain is a system that enables a group of connected computers to maintain a secure and up-to-date ledger. Transactions on the blockchain are performed using *wallets*, which store and exchange cryptocurrencies like Bitcoin. Each wallet is protected by a cryptographic method that uses a unique pair of keys: a private key and a public key.

When a user creates a *transaction*, a block is generated to represent that transaction. These blocks are secured and linked together using cryptographic principles. The created block is then broadcasted to a peer-to-peer network of computers known as nodes which validate the transaction. Once verified, the transaction is combined with other blocks to form a new block that is added to the blockchain. This process can involve cryptocurrencies, contracts, records, or other types of information.

A *block* in a blockchain consists of a block header and a block body. The block header contains components such as:

- **Version number**: Indicates the protocol decisions supported by the miner.
- **Previous block hash**: Establishes the connection and chronology between blocks.
- **Merkle Tree[3] root hash**: Encodes the blockchain data efficiently and securely. It enables quick verification and movement of data within the blockchain network.
- **nBits**: Represents the threshold below which a block header hash must be considered valid.
- **Nonce**: A variable increment used in the **Proof of Work (PoW)** process, where miners try to find a valid hash by guessing numbers.
- **Timestamp**: Serves as a source of variation for the block hash and makes it difficult for adversaries to manipulate the blockchain. It needs to be greater than the median timestamp of the previous 11 or so blocks and less than the network-adjusted time.

Miners play a crucial role in building and adding blocks to the blockchain. They solve the nonce through considerable computation power and effort, a process known as PoW. This proof validates and adds the block to the blockchain. Miners are rewarded for their work with coins or tokens, creating competition among them. As more blocks are added, the blockchain grows, making it challenging to tamper with the data without detection. **Proof of Stake (PoS)** is an alternative to proof of work, where miners' reputation or status in the market determines their ability to add new blocks to the blockchain. *Figure 6.3* depicts computing environment for mining the blockchain:

Figure 6.3: *Depiction of blockchain mining*

The blockchain itself is a chain of data blocks, with the first block called the *Genesis block*. It serves as the foundation of the entire blockchain system. Each block contains a signature, often generated through hashing algorithms like SHA-256, which ensures the integrity of the block's data. The signature of the previous block is included in the header of the new block, forming a linked chain.

What makes blockchain different is the absence of a central authority or third-party intermediation. Transactions are verified by distributed nodes in the network, and anyone can join or leave the network without affecting its consensus mechanism. Blockchain provides verifiability and auditability, as records of transactions can be openly accessed and verified. It enables disintermediation, eliminating the need for trusted third parties. The blockchain also offers confidentiality and integrity through encryption and permission settings. Additionally, the inherent redundancy and decentralization of blockchain makes it robust and fault tolerant.

Smart contracts as the executable web

Smart contracts represent executable nature of the evolving Web 3.0 ecosystem. Web 3.0 aims to create a decentralized and user-centric internet by leveraging blockchain technology and other decentralized protocols. A smart contract, in this context, is a computer program that facilitates, enforces, and executes the logic of an agreement or business process using blockchain technology. It enables parties to exchange value, such as currency, assets, or other valuable items, in a transparent and trustless manner, without the need for intermediaries.

Smart contracts offer several capabilities and benefits within a blockchain framework. They can be used to encode and automate the conditions and actions of various types of transactions. For example, the terms and conditions of a service agreement between two parties, as well as the process of transferring the agreed-upon value, can be programmed into a smart contract, and deployed on the blockchain. Once deployed, *a smart contract becomes immutable*, meaning its contents cannot be altered or taken down.

Smart contracts have a wide range of use cases, ranging from simple tasks like interest distribution to complex functions in multiparty supply chain processes. They are typically written in programming languages specific to blockchain platforms, such as Solidity for Ethereum. Each smart contract has a unique address on the blockchain, separate from regular account addresses. This address serves as the contract host, and contains information such as the code hash and storage route.

To interact with a smart contract, a user needs to connect and transact with it. For instance, a **Decentralized Autonomous Organization** (**DAO**) can utilize smart contracts to collect funds from participants and enable them to vote on projects using native tokens. Smart contracts provide trust and security as they operate within a decentralized system, where the execution of agreements is governed by the code itself, minimizing the need for intermediaries.

Smart contracts are transparent and visible on the blockchain, making them open for validation by all concerned parties. Once an agreement is established through a smart contract, disputes become difficult to file as *the code is considered the law*. This enhances trust and authentication within the metaverse and establishes a system where parties can engage in transactions without concerns about the other party's trustworthiness.

Smart contracts leverage the speed and accuracy provided by blockchain technology, as all transaction details are recorded explicitly on the blockchain, enabling accurate and instant execution from anywhere. However, being on the blockchain also introduces challenges, such as the need to pay **gas fees** for every function or action executed within a smart contract. Gas fees can be high, posing scalability issues for complex contracts.

Overall, smart contracts represent a significant innovation in the blockchain space, expanding the use cases beyond cryptocurrencies and transforming it into a comprehensive network with diverse applications. In the context of the metaverse, smart contracts offer opportunities to automate and secure various operations, including asset transfers, games, and trading procedures. The ecosystem for smart contracts is open and permissionless, allowing anyone to create and deploy their own smart contracts on the blockchain, fostering innovation and development.

The evolution of blockchain

Blockchain technology has evolved through different generations, each introducing new advancements and capabilities.

Here is a breakdown of the blockchain evolution:

- **Blockchain 1.0**: The first generation of blockchain technology was initiated with the development of Bitcoin in 2009 that introduced the concept of a decentralized cryptocurrency, enabling peer-to-peer transfers of assets. It leveraged a PoW consensus system and provided transparency, immutability, and security through cryptographic principles. However, it faced challenges related to scalability, interoperability, sustainability, and speed.
- **Blockchain 2.0**: The second generation of blockchain systems emerged after bitcoin. Ethereum played a crucial role by introducing smart contracts and a Turing-complete programming language. Smart contracts enabled programmable flexibility and expanded the use cases of blockchain technology. Ethereum's platform, **Ethereum Virtual Machine** (**EVM**), facilitated complex transactions and the deployment of **decentralized applications** (**DApps**). Ethereum became a foundation for **decentralized finance** (**DeFi**) and supported the tokenization of assets and DAOs.
- **Blockchain 3.0**: As Ethereum gained popularity, scalability became a significant concern. Scaling solutions, such as *Polygon*[4] and *Arbitrum*[5], were developed to address the complexity and improve transaction speed and cost-effectiveness.

Solution like this ran parallel to the ethereum main chain, providing a better user experience while maintaining blockchain security. Private blockchain solutions like *Hyperledge*[6] also comes into play for enterprises that cannot use bitcoin and Ethereum blockchain.

- **Blockchain 4.0:** The fourth generation of blockchain technology aimed to solve major issues seen in earlier generations. It focused on high transaction processing efficiency, enhanced scalability at lower costs, improved security against attacks, and easier integration with business applications. Blockchain 4.0 also introduced identity and access management solutions and found relevance in the context of Industry 4.0, complementing automation and execution frameworks. Additionally, this generation witnessed the rise of the metaverse, where blockchain technology would provide a framework for user-centric and persisted digital experiences. Blockchain and AI is becoming popular and continues to be, the contribution from the likes of *Matrix AI*[7], *DeepBrain Chain*[8], and *Singularity Net*[9], are shaping into decentralized AI systems.

It is important to note that different projects and platforms contribute to each generation of blockchain technology with each blockchain generation bringing incremental advancements, innovations, and new use cases, shaping the ongoing development of the technology.

Understanding tokens and NFTs

Tokens are digital assets that exist on a blockchain, representing various forms of value. They can represent ownership of physical or digital assets, access to services or platforms, or even represent unique digital collectibles. Tokens are an integral part of blockchain ecosystems and enable a wide range of functionalities.

There are two primary types of tokens: fungible tokens and **non-fungible tokens** (**NFTs**).

- **Fungible Tokens:** Fungible tokens are interchangeable and identical to each other; this means that each token holds the same value and can be exchanged on a one-to-one basis. A common example of fungible tokens is cryptocurrencies like **Bitcoin** (**BTC**) or **Ethereum** (**ETH**). Every unit of these cryptocurrencies are identical and can be used for transactions or as a store of value. Fungible tokens are divisible, meaning they can be divided into smaller units, such as fractions of a token.

- **Non-Fungible Tokens (NFTs)**: Unlike fungible tokens, NFTs are unique and indivisible. Each NFT has distinct properties that makes it different from any other token. These properties can include metadata, such as the token's name, description, and other characteristics. NFTs are commonly used to represent digital art, collectibles, virtual real estate, or ownership rights to physical assets. Each NFT is associated with a specific identifier, often stored on a blockchain, that verifies its authenticity and ownership. *Figure 6.4* depicts an example of NFT block in a blockchain.

NFTs have gained significant popularity because they provide digital scarcity and verifiable ownership of unique items. They enable creators to tokenize and sell their digital creations directly to buyers, eliminating the need for intermediaries. NFTs can be bought, sold, and traded on various online platforms and marketplaces, often using cryptocurrencies as the medium of exchange.

Figure 6.4: Example of NFT block from a smart contract[10]

The concept of tokens extends beyond fungible and non-fungible tokens. There are also utility tokens, which provide access to a specific service or platform, and security tokens, which represent ownership in a company or asset and may have legal obligations attached to them.

Tokens are created and managed through smart contracts, which are self-executing contracts with predefined rules and conditions. Smart contracts enable the issuance, transfer, and tracking of tokens on the blockchain. The transparency and immutability of blockchain technology ensures the authenticity and integrity of token transactions.

Overall, tokens play a vital role in enabling various digital transactions, creating new business models, and empowering decentralized ecosystems. They provide a flexible and programmable way to represent, transfer, and exchange value in the digital world.

Rise of creator economy

The rise of the content economy on the internet is a significant development that highlights the increasing importance of content creation and distribution. In today's digital landscape, communities are actively creating and sharing content on social media platforms such as YouTube, Instagram, Snapchat, and others. However, the distribution and monetization of digital content is often controlled by platform owners, limiting the autonomy, and earning potential of content creators.

The metaverse, as the next internet, evolves in various directions, and community participation as content producer and consumer would play a pivotal role in the success and widespread adoption of metaverse applications. Communities are distributed around the world, and may not be served via traditional centralized ways of content management. *Figure 6.5* depicts the conversance of the content creators communities and decentralized blockchain.

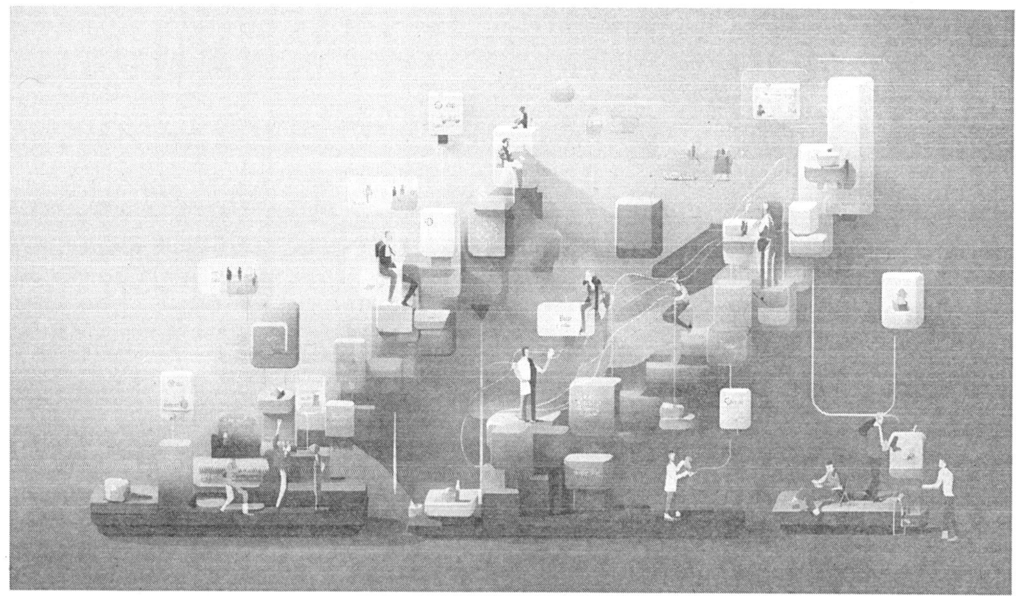

Figure 6.5: *Communities as the content creator, and blockchain*

One of the key drivers of the content economy in the metaverse is the emergence of NFTs. They represent a new form of digital asset ownership and enables creators to monetize their unique digital creations, for example, *Nyan Cat*[11] attracted millions of views and 600k USD equivalent. Although there is still some uncertainty surrounding this field, there has been a significant surge in NFT-based marketplaces, such as Cryptopunks, Hashmasks, SuperRare, Rarible, Sandbox, NFTically, and WazirX.

Metaverse needs a decentralized architecture to thrive upon the open and community-driven initiatives, and it is not controlled and owned centrally by a single entity. Blockchain technology, with its decentralized architecture aligns closely with this vision. It is also the key factor of shaping up the NFT based marketplaces, and the rise of the content economy. Projects like *Decentraland*[12] are building marketplaces on blockchain technology, and even industry giants like Samsung are embracing these concepts by opening stores on the virtual land.

As the content economy within the metaverse expands, traditional payment methods are also evolving to include NFT and cryptocurrency-based payment modes. This shift opens new opportunities for content creators and paves the way for a unique era of advertising and virtual real estate businesses within the metaverse.

A path to decentralized metaverse

We have discussed the importance of decentralization in the development of the metaverse and the role that blockchain technology plays in achieving this vision. While the current stage of blockchain-based architecture may not fully meet the speed and scalability requirements of the metaverse, continuous usage and adoption will drive its natural evolution.

Throughout the chapter, we explored various aspects of decentralization, including the rise of decentralized applications and platforms, the evolution of blockchain technology, the significance of tokens and NFTs, and the emergence of the content economy driven by creators.

The metaverse thrives on community participation and the ability to create, distribute, and monetize digital content. The introduction of NFTs has opened new possibilities for content creators to assert ownership and monetize their creations, while decentralized architectures like blockchain provide the foundation for community-driven initiatives and open ecosystems.

However, the future of the metaverse is shaped by a constant tug-of-war between centralizing forces, such as governments, enterprises, authorities and auditors, and decentralizing forces, represented by communities, individuals, and open ecosystems. This ongoing struggle will likely continue to influence the development and direction of the metaverse for years to come.

Conclusion

In conclusion, the decentralized metaverse is a dynamic and evolving landscape. While blockchain-based architecture may still have challenges to overcome in terms of speed and scalability, the continuous usage and adoption of decentralized technologies will fuel its natural evolution to a more optimal, eco-friendly, and sustainable version. The metaverse's future will be shaped by the delicate balance between centralizing and decentralizing forces, ultimately unlocking its full potential as a vibrant and community-driven virtual realm.

Points to remember

Here are the key points to remember from this chapter:

- Decentralized architecture is essential for achieving the scale and characteristics of a true metaverse, including openness, accessibility, interoperability, and trustworthiness.

- Blockchain technology provides a secure and up-to-date ledger that enables decentralized architectures.
- Blockchain is one implementation of decentralized architecture, but there are other approaches as well.
- Smart contracts play a key role in the execution of transactions and represent the vision of the "executable web" in Web 3.0.
- Tokens, including NFTs are digital assets stored on the blockchain.
- NFTs have emerged to monetize content within the metaverse, but they are not the only means to build the content economy.
- The evolution of decentralized architectures and blockchain technology will continue to meet the evolving needs of the metaverse.

"The Metaverse: The evolution of various technologies shaping the next generation of the internet—an interconnected, accessible, and collectively owned world. It fosters trust, security, and revolutionizes our interactions, creations, and explorations."

In this *Part* 2 of the book, we discussed the evolutionary advancements of various technologies that serve as the building blocks of the metaverse. The rapid pace of these advancements propels us towards a future state of the internet, the metaverse. It is crucial to recognize that evolution is an inherent and ongoing process, irrespective of our preferences. Often, we embrace technological advancements without fully comprehending their potential benefits and drawbacks. Therefore, it becomes paramount to stay informed about these advancements and employ them responsibly. Blind adoption can lead to unintended consequences.

In *Part* 3 of the book, we will explore the vast opportunities that the metaverse presents to the world, followed by an examination of the challenges that accompany its development.

References

1. **https://ondc.org/**
2. **https://www.vakt.com/**
3. **https://brilliant.org/wiki/merkle-tree/**
4. **https://polygon.technology/polygon-zkevm**
5. **https://arbitrum.io/**
6. **https://www.hyperledger.org/**
7. **https://www.matrix.io/**
8. **https://www.deepbrainchain.org/**

9. **https://singularitynet.io/**
10. **Picture Credit: https://en.wikipedia.org/wiki/Non-fungible_token#/media/File:NFT_diagram.svg**
11. **https://gizmodo.com/one-of-a-kind-nyan-cat-gif-sold-in-crypto-art-auction-t-1846312536**
12. **https://decentraland.org/**

Join our book's Discord space

Join the book's Discord Workspace for Latest updates, Offers, Tech happenings around the world, New Release and Sessions with the Authors:

https://discord.bpbonline.com

Part - 3
Metaverse: An Opportunity to Extend the Beliefs

In this part, we will explore boundless potential of the metaverse, a virtual realm that presents us with endless opportunities to reshape our interactions, perceptions, and experiences pushing the boundaries of what we thought was possible. The metaverse opens new avenues for 3D design and visualization, allowing us to interact with products and environments before they even exist in the physical world. Through immersive technologies such as **Augmented Reality** (AR) and **Virtual Reality** (VR), we can explore and manipulate virtual objects with a level of detail and realism that was once unimaginable.

The metaverse is not just about escaping physical constraints. It revolutionizes the way we work, breaking down barriers of location and enabling virtual presence, *Chapter 7, Gaming Redefined: The Metaverse Revolution,* will cover use cases in gaming and entertainment. With remote collaboration and communication tools, physical travel becomes less necessary as we embrace the power of virtual interactions, and *Chapter 8, Connecting and Engaging in the Metaverse* would cover the relevant use cases in this space. *Chapter 9, Revolutionizing Healthcare and Fitness* would focus on health and fitness use cases, and next we will take a deep dive into metaverse economy by cover retail X-commerce, real-state and content economy use cases in *Chapter 10, Exploring the Metaverse Economy*. Education and learning also undergo a profound transformation in the metaverse. Imagine immersive classrooms, where students can engage with interactive content, simulations, and virtual field trips. The metaverse opens a new era of learning, enabling us to acquire knowledge in ways that were once unimaginable. This topic will be covered in *Chapter 11, Skilling and Reskilling in the Enterprise Metaverse.*

The metaverse is not just a concept; it is a paradigm shift, and a stage of internet that redefines our approach to survival and offers innovative ways to thrive. It challenges traditional beliefs and invites us to extend our thought beyond the confines of the physical world.

CHAPTER 7

Gaming Redefined: The Metaverse Revolution

Introduction

Enter the metaverse, where the digital gaming and entertainment industry undergoes a profound transformation. While the metaverse is often associated with gaming, it offers more than immersive gameplay. Explore how the metaverse challenges traditional gaming beliefs and expands the possibilities of interactive experiences. From the early days of Pokémon Go to the advent of real-world gaming, discover how the metaverse is reshaping the gaming landscape. Dive into the evolution of gaming in the metaverse, uncovering the shifts in gameplay, social interactions, and AR experiences. The chapter highlights the extraordinary potential of this emerging realm and its impact on the gaming and entertainment industry.

Structure

In this chapter, we will discuss the following topics:

- Importance of gaming and entertainment
- Types of games
- Transforming gaming studios and amusement parks
- Transforming museums

- Expanding gaming and entertainment beyond confinement
- Decentralized gaming and world building
- Transforming the sports viewing experience
- Revolutionizing film making and viewing

Objectives

The objective of this chapter is to provide readers with an understanding of the evolution of gaming and entertainment in the metaverse, leveraging advancements in technologies such as **Extended Reality** (**XR**) and **Artificial Intelligence** (**AI**). Readers will gain insights into the role of gaming and entertainment in driving technology adoption and explore use cases within confined spaces, as well as the potential for immersive experiences beyond physical boundaries and traditional physical spaces.

Importance of gaming and entertainment

Games serve as a vital aspect of redefining the user experience and driving the adoption of new technologies. Through gaming, complex concepts and skills can be easily understood and learned, making the path of learning enjoyable and engaging. Entertainment goes beyond mere amusement; it encompasses the thrill of being challenged and encourages creative thinking.

Gaming provides a platform where users can experience a sense of achievement and rewards. Just like in physical sports, where athletes strive to achieve greatness and earn recognition, digital gaming offers virtual awards and scores that allow players to stand out on leader-boards and compete with others. This fosters a sense of community and healthy competition. Game rewards can be provided in the form of scores, digital tokens, or even currency, creating an ecosystem where players can earn and spend within the gaming world.

Entertainment extends beyond gaming and encompasses the realm of movie-making. Movies allow us to transcend physical limitations and experience the boundless realms of imagination and creativity. Movie-making and game development share common aspects such as audio-visual elements, scene definition, script writing, storytelling, action and direction. While digital gaming is interactive, movies are not at this stage. However, both mediums rely on engaging the audience or player throughout the experience. Actors in movies bring scripted roles to life, aiming to create an emotional connection with the audience. In the best movies, viewers become so engrossed that they momentarily forget the reality around them.

Games, too, have the power to immerse players in virtual worlds, captivating their attention and making them forget about their surroundings. This sense of immersion from games and entertainment creates an alternate reality where players/viewer can truly escape and explore. The concept of altering reality beliefs is at the core of building XR experiences. It encompasses technologies such as AR, VR, and **Mixed Reality** (**MR**) that blend digital content with the real world or create entirely virtual environments. By merging the physical and virtual realities, XR experiences aim to provide users with seamless and immersive interactions. *Figure 7.1* depicts importance of gaming and entertainment in technology adoption.

***Figure 7.1**: Importance of gaming and entertainment in technology adoption*

As technology continues to advance, the boundaries between physical and virtual realities are becoming increasingly blurred. The metaverse, with its interconnected virtual realm, is an example of how the concept of altering reality beliefs is being realized. In the metaverse, individuals can engage in a wide range of experiences that feel real and transformative, transcending traditional boundaries and offering new possibilities for exploration, creation, and interaction.

Types of games

There are various types of games that exist within the metaverse, catering to different interests and preferences of users. Here are some common types of games:

- **Role-Playing Games (RPGs)**: RPGs allow players to assume the roles of characters within a fictional world and embark on quests, adventures, and character development. These games often involve storytelling, exploration, and strategic decision-making. For example, *The Witcher 3: Wild Hunt*[1], and *Monster Hunter: World*[2].

- **First-Person Shooters (FPS):** FPS games put players in the perspective of a character within the game world, typically armed with weapons, and involve combat against enemies or other players. The focus is on fast-paced action and reflexes. For example, *Half-Life*[3], and *PUBG*[4].
- **Massively Multiplayer Online games (MMOs):** MMOs are vast online worlds where thousands of players can interact with each other simultaneously. These games often feature persistent virtual environments, cooperative gameplay, and various activities such as quests, exploration, and player-versus-player battles. For example, *World of Warcraft*[5].
- **Strategy games:** Strategy games emphasize tactical thinking, resource management, and long-term planning. They can range from **Real-Time Strategy (RTS)** games that require quick decision-making, to turn-based strategy games that allow players to carefully plan their moves. For example, *StarCraft*[6].
- **Simulation games:** Simulation games aim to replicate real-life activities or situations. These can include life simulations, city-building games, vehicle simulations[7], or even specialized simulations like flight simulators[8] or farming simulations.
- **Puzzle games:** Puzzle games challenge players with various puzzles, riddles, or problem-solving tasks. These games often require logical thinking, pattern recognition, and creativity to overcome the challenges presented.
- **Sports and racing games:** Sports and racing games replicate real-world sports or racing events, allowing players to compete against each other or AI opponents. These games often focus on skill-based gameplay, realistic physics, and strategic decision-making. Gamified workout equipment like *Peloton Lanebreak*[9] are also on the rise.
- **Casual and mobile games:** Casual and mobile games are designed for quick and accessible gameplay experiences. These games are often easy to learn and play, and can range from simple puzzle games to endless runners, card games, or social simulation games.

These are just a few examples, and the gaming landscape within the metaverse is diverse and constantly evolving. The wide range of game genres caters to different preferences, offering engaging and immersive experiences for users within the metaverse. In the upcoming sections, we will explore captivating use cases that illustrate the gradual integration of physical gaming and entertainment with the digital world, including the future stage of the internet known as the metaverse. These use cases will showcase the seamless blending of traditional physical experiences with the possibilities offered by digital technologies and the immersive potential of the metaverse. Prepare yourself to witness the exciting journey as physical gaming and entertainment transcend boundaries and evolve in harmony with the digital landscape, paving the way for the immersive metaverse of the future.

Transforming gaming studios and amusement parks

The world of gaming has undergone a significant transformation, driven by advancements in XR technologies and fusion with digital web. Gaming studios and entertainment zones are now embracing immersive interactions and cutting-edge display technologies to create truly captivating experiences. What were once simple experience zones have now evolved into full-body, sensorial adventures. The gaming studies and amusement park are transforming.

Integration of XR experiences

Physical activities like paintball games have transitioned into the virtual realm, offering players an exhilarating combat gaming experience through XR platforms. Body tracking technologies enable players to fully engage in the game, bringing a new level of realism and excitement. The possibilities for gaming studios are virtually limitless, allowing individuals to define their identities and explore diverse virtual environments.

One of the remarkable aspects of this evolution is that physical space is no longer a primary concern for setting up a gaming studio. The need for large physical infrastructures and expensive machinery has diminished which creates opportunities for smaller cities and reduces the investment barriers for aspiring game developers. With the integration of digital technology, amusement parks can become lighter in infrastructure while maintaining their appeal. By combining roller coaster rides with XR experiences, amusement parks can offer visitors an unparalleled level of dynamism and immersion. A simple toy train ride can be transformed into an adventurous journey, where riders pass through a virtual world filled with water, fire, and the sensation of soaring through the skies like a bird. Moreover, the same physical space can be repurposed for different games and events, maximizing the utilization of resources. *Figure 7.2* depicts usage of XR devices in a gaming studio.

Figure 7.2: *Game studio equipped with XR devices*

The fusion of physical and online presence

By integrating physical and online elements, game studios can transcend geographical boundaries, offering experiences that go beyond the limitations of a specific location. Physical spaces provide a tangible and immersive environment where players can gather, interact, and engage with the game in a shared physical setting. These spaces can be designed to enhance the gameplay experience, with specialized equipment, themed decor, and interactive installations. At the same time, online presence of game studios bring a new dimension to gaming. Through online platforms and networks, players can connect with others from different parts of the world, transcending time zones and cultural barriers. The online component allows for seamless multiplayer experiences, where players can team up or compete against each other regardless of their physical location. This global connectivity enriches the gaming experience by introducing diverse perspectives, strategies, and challenges.

The combination of physical and online presence also offers scalability and accessibility. Game studios can extend their reach to a wider audience, attracting players from various regions and backgrounds. This expansion opens up new avenues for collaboration, competition, and social interaction. It fosters a sense of community among players who share common interests and passions, bridging distances and creating bonds that transcend physical boundaries. Moreover, the integration of physical and online presence enables game studios to provide continuous engagement and support for their players. Online platforms offer opportunities for update, expansion, and additional content, ensuring that the gaming experience remains fresh and dynamic. It also facilitates the integration of new technologies and innovations, keeping the game studio at the forefront of the industry.

This fusion of physical and online elements enhance the gaming experience, promotes inclusivity, and provides new possibilities for innovation and interaction. As game studios continue to embrace this hybrid approach, the boundaries of the gaming world will continue to expand, offering exciting and immersive experiences to players everywhere. In the next section, we will discuss about transforming museums, many of which are applicable for amusement parks as well.

Transforming museums

Museums[10] serve as repositories of history, culture, science, art, and more, and serves a great source of entertainment. To provide an immersive experience, museums have traditionally relied on physical design elements, such as colours, layouts, and audio/visual guides. However, with the advent of technological advancements, museums are exploring new ways to engage visitors, particularly the younger generation[11] who are well-versed in digital devices.

Today, museums are evolving their user experiences through innovative technologies. Traditional brochures and signage are being replaced by smart touch displays, websites, and sensor-based touchless interactions. Mobile apps and smart devices have replaced audio tapes, allowing for a more interactive and personalized museum visit. As the world embraces virtual experiences, museums are exploring AR/VR technology to revolutionize interactions and prepare for the future. In the metaverse, museums will not only feature digital replicas but also offer immersive experiences that redefine the concept of a museum.

In the following sections, we will explore various use cases where XR technology can extend the capabilities of the museum industry, unlocking new levels of engagement and transforming the way we experience art, history, and culture.

Revolutionize navigation

Museums are vast spaces, often spread across multiple floors and buildings, and effective navigation has always been crucial to the visitor experience. The journey through a museum begins from the moment a visitor enters the premises, parks their vehicle, and enters the museum to explore different artifacts before eventually leaving. Traditionally, museums have relied on paper-based brochures, maps, signage, and audio guides in various languages to assist visitors. However, these methods present challenge for individuals with disabilities or those who do not understand the supported languages. Additionally, it can be difficult to maintain and update.

In response to these challenges, indoor navigation solutions have emerged, similar to the way outdoor navigation is facilitated by digital maps. Now, AR applications are being developed specifically for indoor navigation as depicted in *Figure 7.3*. Visitors can use their smartphones, tablets, or smart glasses to access an AR-based navigation application. These applications overlay digital information onto the visitor's real-world environment, guiding them along the desired path.

***Figure 7.3:** Indoor navigation on a mobile phone*

Alternatively, a digital character can appear as an assistant, interacting with the visitor and providing guidance to areas of interest or specific points of attraction. Visitors can even choose their preferred language for the navigation instructions. This digital approach eliminates the need for maintaining fixed audio tapes, devices, and paper manuals. Museums can now digitally manage and control the navigation paths, adjusting them dynamically based on the crowd and visitor preferences. They can monitor visitor behaviour, track exploration patterns, identify underexplored areas, and make improvements to enhance the visitor experience.

The navigation application can offer different paths to the visitors with estimated waiting time, points of attraction, and other relevant information, allowing them to choose the path. Furthermore, museums can configure dedicated navigation paths for individuals with disabilities or those requiring special attention. Visitors also have the option to pre-download the navigation app and even pre-book specific navigation routes, providing a personalized and enjoyable experience.

Museums of metaverse will leverage AR technology and personalise navigation paths, enhance the visitor experience, empower accessibility, and optimize exploration for all visitors.

Enhance the museum artifacts

At the heart of any museum lies a collection of precious artifacts that tell stories of history, science, art, and culture. Traditionally, visitors relied on brochures, printed boards, audio guides, or digital tag reader apps/devices to access information about these artifacts. The methods have served their purpose, but often come with limitations and lack flexibility.

With advancements in computer vision and cloud technology, discussed in *Part 2* of the book, a new era of artifact enhancement has emerged. By leveraging XR applications, artifacts can be tagged and anchored within the environment, allowing for augmented information to be seamlessly displayed directly on the physical objects. Imagine looking at an artifact and instantly seeing its rating, views, tags, and comments from visitors, all overlaid onto the artifact. An XR app can be pre-equipped to recognize and augment information for all the physical artifacts in a museum. This means that audio, video, images, text, documents, websites, and more can be strategically positioned and associated with specific artifacts. *Figure 7.4* depicts usage of XR smart glasses in enhancing the museum experience.

Figure 7.4: *Enhance the artifacts with augmented reality using smart glasses*

This revolutionary approach significantly improves the visitor experience by providing contextual information effortlessly and according to individual preferences. Moreover, it streamlines the editing and configuration of the museum, making it easier to introduce new artifacts. By analysing telemetry data, museums can gain insights into visitor behaviour, understanding which artifacts attract the most interest and the specific types of information visitors seek. This valuable data allows museums to update and tailor content accordingly, creating a engaging and personalized experience for all. Additionally, the technology reduces the resources required to manage artifacts, allowing museums to allocate their efforts where needed.

The power of artifact enhancement goes beyond just providing information—it breathes new life into the museum experience. Visitors can delve deeper into the significance of each artifact, uncover hidden stories, and explore different perspectives. Through this innovative approach, museums can capture the imagination of visitors and ensure that the historical and cultural significance of each artifact is fully appreciated.

Gamify visitor experience

In the ever-evolving landscape of visitor expectations, traditional methods of engaging museum-goers are becoming outdated. To captivate the modern crowd, museums need innovative solutions that resonate with today's tech-savvy and socially connected generation.

XR technologies offer exciting possibilities to enhance visitor engagement by gamifying the museum experience. Imagine introducing treasure hunts or Pokémon Go-style games where visitors can sign up, join groups, and compete to uncover hidden treasures or complete challenges throughout the museum. This gamified approach not only adds an element of excitement but also encourages exploration of specific areas within the museum. By strategically placing digital goodies and rewards, museums can guide visitors to discover lesser-known exhibits or hidden gems.

Furthermore, XR apps can empower visitors to provide reviews, feedback, and ratings directly on the artifacts they encounter, and as explained in previous section, this can enhance the artifacts' visualization by overlaying digital interfaces. Visitors can easily share their thoughts and experiences, allowing others to benefit from their insights. These reviews and ratings can be showcased within the XR app, enabling visitors to make informed decisions about which exhibits to explore. Moreover, visitors can seamlessly share their experiences and recommendations on social media platforms, amplifying the museum's reach and attracting new audiences.

Beyond the exhibits, museums can provide value-added services within their XR apps, guiding visitors to nearby food joints, offering exclusive deals and discounts, or featuring relevant advertisements. These additional features enhance the overall visitor experience, creating a holistic and memorable outing. *Figure 7.5* shows a game being playing by the visitors.

Figure 7.5: *Gamified visitor experience in a museum*

By embracing technologies and leveraging the power of engagement, museums can ignite the curiosity and imagination of their visitors. This modern approach transforms the museum experience into an interactive journey, encouraging exploration, collaboration, and sharing knowledge. With visitor engagement at the forefront, museums can foster a deep appreciation for art, culture, history, and science, leaving an indelible impression on all who enter their doors.

Time travel simulation and virtual encounters

Museums can embrace interactive XR booths that push the boundaries of traditional displays. These booths serve as gateways to extraordinary encounters, offering simulations of time travel or virtual interactions with historical figures. Through the integration of XR technologies, museums can transport visitors to different eras, enabling them to immerse themselves in captivating narratives and forge a profound connection with the past.

Imagine wearing smart glasses and gazing at an artifact. Suddenly, the environment transforms around you, transporting you to a bygone era. People adorned in period clothing, architectural designs representative of that time, and the ambiance of that historical period immerse you in an unparalleled experience. This transformative journey through time offers visitors a unique perspective and a deeper appreciation for the artifacts and their historical significance. For example, transport the individuals back to the age of dinosaurs, as they observe dinosaur exhibits, the environment seamlessly transitions into a virtual jungle, complete with lifelike sounds and animated dinosaurs, as shown in *Figure 7.6*. The immersive nature of this experience allows visitors to witness these ancient creatures in their natural habitat, sparking awe and wonder.

***Figure 7.6:** Get into the dinosaur world in metaverse museum*

Similarly, in a car museum, visitors can interact with virtual representations of cars. They can step inside the vehicle, experience the sensation of driving through different landscapes, eras, or even futuristic scenarios. This interactive engagement invites visitors to go beyond observation, enabling them to actively participate in the museum experience.

Multi-user collaboration takes the XR experience to another level, allowing groups of visitors to participate in shared sessions. Visitors can choose and try on clothing from different eras, capturing the moment with a selfie in their virtual attire and sharing it with others. This collaborative engagement amplifies the sense of connection and fosters a shared exploration of history.

Zero museum

The concept of zero museum introduces a paradigm shift in the traditional museum model by eliminating the need for physical artifacts. Instead, the museum space itself becomes a blank canvas, ready to be transformed through virtual representations. Artifacts are presented in a virtual form, either through 3D projections or via smart headsets and AR/VR-enabled devices.

This concept opens up a world of possibilities and flexibility. The same physical space can be utilized to create multiple museum experiences, catering to diverse themes and interests. Visitors can explore different virtual exhibitions within the same space, providing a customized and personalized museum visit for each individual. This dynamic approach breaks the boundaries of a static museum and encourages continuous innovation and variety.

The zero museum concept challenge traditional notions of museums, embracing technology and creative thinking to redefine the museum experience. By leveraging virtual representations and utilizing the urban environment, these concepts blur the lines between physical and virtual realities, fostering new connections between art, culture, and the community. The possibilities for exploration, collaboration, and artistic expression are limitless, creating a truly immersive and inclusive museum experience for all.

Virtual museum

One exciting aspect of metaverse museums would be, the creation of virtual museums, where the entire museum experience can be replicated in a digital environment. There are multiple ways to achieve this. Visitors can access the virtual museum directly through a web browser, immersing themselves in a 360-degree tour of the museum[12]. This allows them to navigate through different galleries and exhibits, exploring the artifacts and gaining insights just as they would in a physical museum.

Alternatively, users can experience the museum in VR headsets. By donning the headset and using a controller or natural movements, users can walk through the virtual museum, interacting with the artifacts and environments in a highly immersive manner. This technology opens up possibilities for educational purposes as well. Museums can create VR training and educational materials that can be used in schools or in dedicated studio setups within the museum premises, offering additional services and engagement opportunities.

The metaverse museums with use of XR extends the reach and accessibility of the museum experience. It caters to both physical visitors who can come to the museum and those who prefer to experience it remotely. XR provides a touchless and safe experience for physical visitors, reducing the need for contact with artifacts and surfaces. Additionally, it offers an immersive virtual museum experience for individuals who are unable to visit in person due to various reasons, such as medical conditions. The metaverse, with its evolving nature, will further introduce new ways of experiencing museums and their collections.

The transformations we discussed for museums, gaming studios, and amusement parks above will also be applied to other use cases confined to physical spaces like conferences, events, social gatherings, and education. In the upcoming sections, we will delve into the enhancement of experiences beyond confined spaces, embracing more virtual, digital gaming and entertainment experiences.

Expanding gaming and entertainment beyond confinement

The concept of metaverse transcends the limitations of confined spaces, opening up a world of possibilities for gaming and entertainment. One fascinating aspect is the ability to create games at a much larger scale, spanning cities, countries, or even regions. Games like *Pokémon Go*[13] have demonstrated that gaming experiences can extend beyond a single location, captivating players on a global scale.

Similarly, the concept of museum parks and events can be expanded to a city-wide scale as depicted in *Figure 7.7:*

***Figure 7.7:** City scale gaming experience*

Rather than confining the museum within a single building, the entire city becomes an open gallery, with public spaces transformed into immersive art installations. Visitors can explore the city, stumbling upon open-air museums and art galleries, experiencing art and culture in unexpected places. This not only enriches the cultural landscape but also encourages community involvement and participation, as individuals can contribute their creation and content.

Niantic Labs[14], for instance, has envisioned a real-world metaverse where the entire world becomes a game, incorporating contextual data tied to geo-locations, time, and local environmental conditions. This concept not only revolutionizes gaming but also offers business solutions. It takes gaming to a whole new level, allowing people to explore uncharted territories. Within cities, multiple hubs or community groups can be formed to compete with each other, fostering a sense of engagement and friendly competition.

The user experience enhancements we discussed earlier, such as artifact enhancement, navigation, time travel, and virtual encounters, can all be scaled to a wider level with a geo-location-aware approach. Imagine concerts, conferences, or social events taking place throughout the city, seamlessly integrated with XR technology, offering immersive experiences without physically altering the city's infrastructure.

Decentralized gaming and world building

As we explore the expansion of gaming experiences beyond confined spaces, it is crucial to acknowledge the significant role that decentralized and distributed architectures play in meeting the demands of scalability, personalization, and trust within the online gaming realm. Blockchain technology, as discussed in *Chapter 6, Decentralization and the Role of Blockchain*, has emerged as a key enabler for these advancements, allowing online gaming accounts to be linked to blockchain wallets and facilitating transactions with digital currencies.

Online gaming has evolved beyond mere entertainment, transforming into immersive experiences that can be accessed through XR devices. Games like *Fortnite*[15] have evolved into digital event spaces, where users can attend dance parties, virtual music concerts, and engage in gameplay of their choice. Platforms like *Roblox*[16] have gained popularity as game hosting offers a multitude of games within a shared virtual space. *Minecraft*[17], known for its world-building capabilities, has also captured the imagination of millions of players, a still from the game is shown in *Figure 7.8*:

Figure 7.8: World making games

Decentraland[18] has emerged as a virtual real estate gaming platform, where users can create and trade virtual properties. Similarly, the *Sandbox*[19] provides a platform for users to create avatars, vehicles, animals, tools, and other objects, which can be traded as **Non-Fungible Tokens** (**NFTs**) on the marketplace or utilized to build games and experiences. These platforms leverage decentralized architectures, allowing users to have ownership and control over their virtual assets. In *Chapter 10, Exploring the Metaverse Economy*, we will delve deeper into the trading and earning aspects of these metaverse games, exploring how users can participate in economy of the metaverse, earning rewards, trading virtual assets, and harnessing the potential of blockchain technology.

The convergence of decentralized architectures, immersive XR experiences, and blockchain technology is shaping the future of online gaming, offering new avenues for creativity, social interaction, and economic opportunities within the metaverse.

Transforming the sports viewing experience

Emergence of the metaverse is set to revolutionize the way we watch and engage with sporting events. Whether we are inside the stadium or watching the live broadcast, the advancements in XR technology are poised to enhance our sports viewing experience.

Watching our favourite teams and athletes in person can be a thrilling experience, but large sport arenas and expansive playing fields often make it challenging to see every detail with the naked eye. XR technology comes to the rescue by augmenting the information on players and the field.

Figure 7.9: *Watching sports on a 3D display*

We can access up-to-date statistics, replays in 3D, and additional insights, just like we see while watching a broadcast, *Figure 7.9* shows experience of watching sport in 3D volumetric displays. Imagine being able to relive a critical shot or analyse the performance of individual players with enhanced visual overlays. XR can also transform the stadium space, bringing imagination to life during opening ceremonies or grand finales.

Moreover, the technology extends beyond physical viewing to enhance live streaming experiences. Augmented contextual information can be seamlessly integrated into the live stream, providing features such as detailed replays, predictions, and physics simulations that aid referees in making crucial decisions. Watching sporting events on television has become more engaging, and with XR devices and 360-degree streaming, the experience is taken even closer to reality. As 5G/6G networks continue to advance, we are on the cusp of experiencing realistic spatial broadcasts, where we can feel as if we are in midst of the action.

The transformation of the sports viewing experience through technology opens a world of possibilities, allowing fans to dive deeper into the game, access real-time information, and engage with the sporting event in unprecedented ways. Metaverse holds potential to bridge the gap between physical and virtual sport experiences, creating immersive and interactive environments that bring fans closer to the game.

Revolutionizing film making and viewing

Films have always captivated us with visual storytelling, pushing the boundaries of immersion from 2D screens to the latest visual effects. However, with technological advancements, the future of filmmaking holds even greater possibilities.

- **Immersive 3D movie experiences:** Imagine stepping into a 3D movie where you can walk within the environment and witness actors' performances as if they were right beside you. 3D scanning technology allows scene to be recorded in three dimensions, enabling interactive and dynamic movie experiences. Specialized devices and walkable spaces are essential to fully recreate this immersive cinematic journey. Studios can design spatial visualizations, transporting viewers into virtual worlds where they can explore and interact with the movie environment. As explained in *Chapter 5, IoT, cloud, and next-gen networks*, drone-swarming light shows add volume and depth to the experience or 3D visualization[20], and another way exemplified by the futuristic entertainment venue of *MSG Sphere*[21] in Las Vegas with spatial sound.
- **AI impact in filmmaking:** AI is revolutionizing the film industry, with virtual characters and enhanced special effects. AI-driven news anchors, such as *Sana* from *Aajtak*[22], deliver news with lifelike authenticity. Lip-syncing technologies like iClone[23] ensure accurate portrayal of virtual characters. Generative AI simplifies the creation of animated stories, eliminating the need for body doubles and enhancing performer safety.
- **Profound implications:** These advancements redefine filmmaking, blurring the lines between the physical and virtual realms. Viewers can engage with films on a new level, experiencing narratives from different perspectives and immersing themselves in rich cinematic worlds.

- **Active participation and exploration:** The future of film is not limited to a passive viewing experience but invites active participation and exploration.

The combination of advanced technology and artistic storytelling will redefine the film industry, ushering in a new era of immersive entertainment. The advancements in technology are revolutionizing film making and viewing. The ability to step into a 3D movie environment and experience film from different angles open up endless possibilities for both filmmakers and audience. As we look towards the future, the boundary between reality and cinematic world will continue to blur, creating transformative and unforgettable movie experiences.

Conclusion

In this chapter, we have explored the transformative impact of metaverse on gaming and entertainment. We began by discussing the importance of gaming and entertainment as drivers of innovation and user adoption of technology. Gaming studios and amusement parks have embraced immersive interactions and cutting-edge technologies, creating captivating experiences that go beyond physical constraints. The museums have also undergone a significant transformation, with XR technologies enhancing artifact displays and visitor engagement.

We then delved into the concept of expanding gaming and entertainment beyond confined spaces. The metaverse has opened up new possibilities for scaling experiences to city-wide or even global levels. VR, AR, and MR technologies have enabled users to explore virtual worlds, participate in decentralized gaming platforms, and create their own content. We discussed the potential of decentralized architectures and blockchain integration in online gaming, allowing for secure transactions and digital ownership.

Furthermore, we explored how the metaverse is transforming the sports viewing experience. XR technologies provide enhanced information, replay options, and immersive experiences for sports fans, whether they are watching games in person or through live streams. The potential for spatial broadcasts and interactive features bring viewers closer to the action than ever before.

Lastly, we examined the impact of metaverse on film making and viewing. Advancement in technology have revolutionized the cinematic experience, allowing for interactive 3D movies and immersive environments. Filmmakers have the opportunity to create futuristic narratives, while viewers can engage with movies in a whole new way.

Overall, this chapter has highlighted the significant role of the metaverse technologies in redefining gaming and entertainment. From gaming studios to museums, from sports event to film making, the metaverse revolutionizes user experience, expands possibilities, and blurs the boundaries between physical and virtual realities. As we continue to explore the metaverse, the potential for innovation, creativity, and community engagement is boundless.

In the next chapter, we will draw insights from gamification and explore the metaverse's profound influence on social interactions, uncovering its transformative power in connecting and engaging people.

Points to remember

Here are some points to remember from this chapter:

- Gamification and entertainment are crucial for driving technology adoption and enhancing user experiences.
- XR technology can transform confined spaces such as game studios, amusement parks, museums, and theaters, creating larger-than-life experiences.
- Integration of entertainment zone with online platform allows for transcending physical boundaries and reaching global audience.
- Technological advancements enable high-quality gaming and entertainment experiences to be accessible in smaller cities and remote areas, promoting equality and equity.
- Gaming and entertainment experiences can extend beyond confined spaces, scaling up to the level of cities, regions, or even global audiences.
- AI advancements blur the line between physical and virtual, enabling AI-generated co-actors in films and immersive 3D movie experiences where viewers can feel and sense the performances.
- The future of gaming and entertainment holds exciting possibilities for immersive and interactive experiences that engages audience in unprecedented ways.

References

1. **https://www.thewitcher.com/us/en/witcher3**
2. **https://store.steampowered.com/app/582010/Monster_Hunter_World/**
3. **https://store.steampowered.com/app/70/HalfLife/**
4. **https://pubg.com/en/**
5. **https://worldofwarcraft.blizzard.com/en-gb/**
6. **https://starcraft2.blizzard.com/en-us/**
7. **https://www.crazygames.com/game/vehicles-simulator**
8. **https://www.flightsimulator.com/**
9. **https://www.onepeloton.com/bike/lanebreak**

10. **https://thinkuldeep.com/post/extending-reality-of-museum-wtih-xr/**
11. **https://www.nytimes.com/2015/03/19/arts/artsspecial/museums-turn-to-technology-to-boost-attendance-by-millennials.html**
12. **https://vila360.com.br/tour/mrciusp/**
13. **https://pokemongolive.com/?hl=en**
14. **https://lightship.dev/blog/designing-real-world-metaverse/**
15. **https://www.fortnite.com/**
16. **https://www.roblox.com/**
17. **https://www.minecraft.net/en-us**
18. **https://decentraland.org/**
19. **https://www.sandbox.game/en/**
20. **https://en.hg-fly.com/lightShow_about.html**
21. **https://edition.cnn.com/2023/07/05/travel/msg-sphere-las-vegas-venue-cec/index.html**
22. **https://www.aajtak.in/anchor/ai-sana**
23. **https://www.reallusion.com/iclone/**

Chapter 8
Connecting and Engaging in the Metaverse

Introduction

This chapter discusses the realm of social interactions and the transformative impact of the metaverse on connecting people. It explores the importance of social connection and engagement in the metaverse, as well as the redefinition of social interactions through virtual meetings and collaboration. This chapter also examines how language and cultural barriers can be overcome in virtual spaces, leading to new forms of social identities and connections. It delves into the emotional and psychological aspects of social interactions in the metaverse and explores the empowering nature of virtual collaboration tools.

Additionally, the chapter explores the role of travel and tourism in exploring and scaling social connections and keeping people engaged with the world. It further explores the role of metaverse technologies in revolutionizing the travel and tourism industry. It highlights the significance of virtual travel experiences, allowing individuals to explore and access virtual destinations. This chapter discusses the planning and preparation involved in virtual travel, as well as the limitless possibilities and enhanced experiences offered through **eXtended Reality** (**XR**) and navigation features. It also addresses the management of crowds and attractions in virtual tourism environments and discusses potential advancements in virtual travel experiences.

Structure

In this chapter, we will discuss the following topics:

- Importance of social connection and engagements
- Types of social connections and engagements
- Social identity in the metaverse
- Direct communication in the metaverse
- Indirect communication in the metaverse
- Travel and tourism scaling the social reach
- Revolutionize travel and tourism in the metaverse

Objectives

The objective of this chapter is to provide readers with a comprehensive understanding of how people can connect and engage with each other in the metaverse. The chapter also aims to understand of role of travel and tourism in expanding the boundaries of social interactions, the evolving nature of social interactions, and the transformative impact of metaverse technologies on the way we connect, communicate, and explore the world.

Importance of social connection and engagement

This section will discuss the fundamental role that social interactions play in human existence. Connecting with others is deeply ingrained in human nature, as we naturally form relationships, remember one another, communicate, help, talk, fight, like, hate, and love each other. These social connections shape the fabric of society, which is composed of various relationships and interactions. Throughout history, humans have sought to engage with the world and with each other through the means of communication they have discovered over time.

In the early stages of human evolution, social boundaries were limited to close-knit groups. However, as humans have progressed technologically, these boundaries have expanded to encompass broader societal identities. This evolution has been driven by the innate human desire to expand influence, presence, and resources. It has resulted in the formation of groups, regions, and countries and has led to activities such as trade, travel, tourism, sports, and even wars. These endeavors have fuelled the exploration of social connections beyond traditional boundaries.

As societies have developed, they have established their own rules, regulations, assets, and cultural aspects that they claim ownership of. Engaging with others on a social level has involved understanding and respecting these differences. Communication and cultural understanding have been key to fostering meaningful social connections globally.

In essence, social connection and engagement are essential for social existence. They enable individuals to earn a living, spend time with others, nourish themselves, live fulfilling lives, and grow personally. Engaging with people and the world around us is necessary for survival and for building a sense of community and interconnectedness. *Figure 8.1* depicts the social connection and engagement in society:

Figure 8.1: Depiction of social connection and engagement in society

Types of social connections and engagement

This section explores the different ways in which people connect and engage with each other in social interactions. Some of the types of social connections are as follows:

- **Family relationships:** These connections are based on blood relations and include close family members such as parents, siblings, and relatives. Family relationships are formed from birth or through individuals who have cared for us since childhood. The concept of marriage has evolved as a form of relationship rooted in love. We do have relations with people who are no more with us.
- **Friendships:** Friendships are formed with individuals we encounter in various aspects of life, such as school, work, or travel. These connections are based on mutual affection and shared interests.
- **Work and business:** Connections in the work and business realm are formed through professional interactions. These relationships are based on shared goals, collaboration, and mutual benefit.

- **Negative relationships:** In contrast to positive connections, there are also negative connections. These involve individuals we dislike, have conflicts with, or consider as enemies. Communication with such individuals can take different forms.
- **Short-term relationships:** These are with people we do not have personal relationships with but interact with in various settings, such as co-passengers during travel or shopkeepers we purchase goods from. *Figure 8.2* below is a depiction of different social connections:

Figure 8.2: Depiction of social connection

Each type of relationship has its own ways of engagement and communication. Societies have defined rituals and events that cater to different types of relationships. There are specific events for family and friends, professional engagements, trade and shopping, and places like markets and malls designed for social interactions. Additionally, travel and tourism provide opportunities to connect with others and explore different relationships and engagements.

With the evolution of technology, social connections have been further enhanced and extended beyond the boundaries of traditional societies. Cultural overlap has increased, and technology has facilitated faster understanding and adaptation to the differences across societies. In the section ahead, we will explore how metaverse technologies can further enhance these social connections and engagements.

Social identity in the metaverse

The concept of social identity in the metaverse encompasses various aspects of our personal and professional lives. It goes beyond just our name and includes metadata such as our address, birthdate, email address, and more. Legally acceptable identities like passports, SSNs, AADHAR, and PANs, which are linked to our physical identities like biometrics, facial recognition, or fingerprints, play a role in shaping our global social identity. Social identities have more things to consider, like the way we look, speak, and behave, things we like and dislike, our status, our friend circle, our habits, our influence and respect, and so on. Social identities are turning into virtual social identities in the metaverse.

Social media platforms have become prominent in shaping our social identities. Today's platforms are evolved versions of what we started with chat rooms from *Yahoo! Messenger*[1], or *Orkut*[2] of the world. Platforms like Facebook, Snapchat, Instagram, X, and now Threads provide spaces for us to represent ourselves digitally and connect with others. Professional networks like LinkedIn have even become essential for showcasing our professional identities and seeking job opportunities. As online gaming platforms continue to evolve, they create new avenues for identity creation and representation. Gamers' profiles and accomplishments on these platforms are becoming symbols of status, and avatars serve as digital recreations of ourselves in the metaverse.

Social identities are now getting verified by some legally acceptable identities. For example, LinkedIn now can be verified by AADHAR[3]. These developments would lead to the wider acceptance of virtual social identities. There will be a time when the Internet will reach the stage of metaverse, the avatars will also be verified legally and accepted as a global identity. It is just a start. Some effort in this direction can be seen from the leading avatar creation platforms, such as *RealPlayerMe*[4]. An avatar, once created here, can be accessed by multiple metaverse applications.

With the advent of **Artificial Intelligence** (**AI**), avatars can mimic human behaviour[5], learning from us, listening to us, and replicating our actions in the virtual world. This opens up possibilities for realistic interaction and communication. For instance, an avatar can realistically wish someone a happy birthday or extend a personal invitation to an event. Eventually, the avatar would be considered as our companion and our personal identity, and would be acceptable as us. It would not replace us for sure, but would do things on our behalf, with our consent and permission. Think of it as personally inviting hundreds of friends and family members for an event with our personal avatar visiting them at their home or personal space, and people accepting it. However, with all this, regulations and guidelines will likely emerge to define the boundaries and behaviors of avatars in the metaverse. *Figure 8.3* depicts some avatars who come to wish a happy birthday:

***Figure 8.3**: Virtual avatars wishing birthday in a metaverse party*

Direct communication in the metaverse

Communication is a fundamental human need that allows us to connect and engage with others. It relies on having a common and understandable medium through which information can be shared and understood. Humans have evolved across different regions of the world, each with their own unique languages and communication systems. However, at the core, human communication remains the same, allowing for translation and communication across regions. Over time, people have learned about cultural similarities and differences, leading to the establishment of a medium for global communication that continues to evolve.

Throughout history, various forms of communication have emerged, each catering to different abilities, needs, and situations. Face to face communication is a direct and personal form of interaction where individuals need to be present in-person at a physical or virtual location or on common medium.

Breaking the communication barriers of physical meetings

Physical in-person meeting is a direct and personal form of interaction where individuals meet in person at some physical location. During such encounters, effective communication relies on a shared understanding of each other's language and culture. In cases where individuals have speech disabilities, sign language can be used as an alternative means of communication. Additionally, people can exchange greetings, presents, and written messages to convey their thoughts and ideas.

However, face-to-face communication can be challenging when there is no common language or when individuals are unfamiliar with one another. When multiple people are meeting face-to-face, challenges are multi-fold. Advancements in technology, particularly as we move towards the metaverse, can address these barriers. With the metaverse, we will have augmented information about the people we interact with, breaking down language barriers with inline translations and enabling seamless communication across different languages and regions, as depicted in *Figure 8.4*. Furthermore, individuals with speech, hearing, or vision disabilities will have access to tools and techniques within the metaverse that facilitate effective communication for all. Refer to the XRAI glasses[6] breaking the communication barrier. If we go even further with advancements in **Brain Computer Interface** (**BCI**), it would be possible to communicate just by thinking:

Figure 8.4: *Breaking the communication barrier in metaverse*

Teleporting in virtual meetings

Virtual in-person meeting is a direct and personal form of interaction, but unlike physical meeting, here individuals do not meet at a physical location but at a virtual medium. The invention of the telephone eliminated physical barriers, allowing people to speak to one another as if they were right beside each other, without physically meeting. With the advent of video conferencing, it is now possible to see and hear the person we are communicating with, creating a sense of proximity, but it still falls short of true face-to-face connection. These transnational communications also help communicate in case of language barriers and culture, and still far from people with speech, vision, and hearing disabilities.

The emergence of metaverse technologies holds the potential to revolutionize communication. These technologies enable the teleportation of a person's 3D representation, allowing others to sense their presence and engage in immersive interactions. Users can shake hands and get the touch-and-feel experience, which is very similar to a physical meeting. We have discussed the evolution of technology in *Part 2* of the book, and concepts like *Google Starline*[7] and *Varjo Teleport*[8] are advancing the development of 3D calling experiences, enabling users to have virtual face-to-face conversations without language or cultural barriers. With advancements in 3D scanning, entire environments can be ported, providing users with the option to choose a common virtual space for their discussions.

Multiple users can join these calls, transforming them into conference calls. Most conferencing tools today have the ability to change backgrounds and apply filters to alter one's virtual face. In the metaverse, these conference calls can take place in virtual meeting rooms, classrooms, or even picturesque locations like beaches. Participants can enter the conversation with the identity they prefer, based on the context and setup of the meeting. This evolving technology is making communication more engaging and immersive, pushing the boundaries of virtual interactions.

Indirect communication in the metaverse

Indirect communication refers to modes of communication where all participants do not need to be physically present in the same location or on the same medium. Traditionally, this form of communication involved methods like mail and telegrams, which required physical delivery. With the advent of technologies like SMS and email, communication shifted to digital platforms. Evolution continued, and the metaverse will transform traditional indirect communication further as follows.

Social interactions on the recreated scene

A simple text message can often convey a message effectively, and nowadays, instant messaging apps like WhatsApp have become popular for indirect communication, replacing SMS or traditional modes. Social media platforms like Facebook, X, Snapchat, and more become a significant medium for sharing life moments, updates, and media content in both textual and visual forms. *Figure 8.5* depicts the social media mapped in the metaverse:

Figure 8.5: *Depiction of social media in metaverse*

Social media, initially a form of indirect communication like mail and email, has evolved into a more synchronous form. We can now see others typing and interacting, even if we cannot hear or see them directly. People use these platform so frequently that it also gives an illusion of it as a direct communication. This shift in communication behavior has led to an influx of information on social media platform, with people actively engaging with people they know or do not know.

In the metaverse, this communication can become even more engaging and immersive. People will have access to a wealth of contextual information alongside their updates, including 3D recordings and recreations of scenes. This means that even those who could not physically attend a meeting or gathering can enter the virtual environment and experience a recreation of what transpired. Not just that, they can go inside those scenes and provide audio-visual comments and share feelings, and notes delivered in that recorded scene.

AI social media organizer

With the abundance of information on social media, AI-powered systems in the metaverse can summarize and fast-forward updates, delivering them in an engaging manner through AI avatars. Not just that, AI avatars would respond on our behalf in some defined constraints. They automatically like or dislike things on social media as they learned from our interests. It would show us the things that really need our attention and discard or auto-process the rest.

This would also inform us which meeting we really need to attend in-person or virtual which can just be an indirect communication. Only the key stakeholders would participate directly or indirectly in meetings, and updates can be disseminated through indirect communication channels or even delivered directly to the brain using BCI. *Figure 8.6* below is a depiction of a conversation with an AI-generated virtual avatar.

Interactions beyond life

A mother reunites with her deceased daughter through a virtual recreation[9], showcasing the powerful impact of immersive technology. Through the metaverse, individuals may have the opportunity to connect with loved ones who are no longer physically present, creating a sense of presence and interaction that was previously unimaginable.

The ability to touch and interact with virtual recreations of loved ones can provide immense comfort and emotional healing to those who have experienced loss. It demonstrates how the metaverse can transcend physical boundaries and bridge the gap between the real and virtual worlds. Such experiences have the potential to offer solace and closure to individuals longing for connection with departed loved ones.

Figure 8.6: *Conversation with AI generated avatar*

Overall, the metaverse can enhance the communication by providing more immersive and engaging ways to share information and experiences. People can participate in virtual environments where they can explore, collaborate, and communicate with others in ways that closely resemble face-to-face interactions. The metaverse can offer a seamless and interactive platform for sharing memories, ideas, and experiences, making communication more meaningful and impactful.

Travel and tourism scaling the social reach

Travel and tourism play a pivotal role in scaling the social reach and connecting people across different regions and cultures. Throughout history, traveling has been an essential means for expanding social connections and fostering cultural exchange. As humans journeyed across lands, they encountered diverse communities, traditions, and languages, leading to the enrichment of their social experiences. Whether for trade, exploration, pilgrimage, or leisure, travel has been a catalyst for building bridges between societies.

In the modern era, advancements in transportation and communication technology have revolutionized the travel and tourism industry. With the advent of airplanes, trains, and other efficient modes of transport, geographical distances have become more manageable, and people can traverse continents in hours. This ease of travel has facilitated face-to-face interactions, enabling individuals to meet and engage with others from different parts of the world.

Tourism, on the other hand, serves as a means of leisurely exploration and discovery. People visit new destinations, cultural landmarks, and natural wonders, embracing the beauty and diversity of the world. Tourism not only encourages interpersonal connections but also fosters an appreciation for the customs and heritage of others. Through travel and tourism, individuals gain a broader understanding of the global community, promoting empathy and cross-cultural communication. *Figure 8.7* below depicts the European sailor Vasco de Gama discovering India:

Figure 8.7: *Depiction of travel, tourism, trade and social evolution*

The metaverse presents unprecedented opportunities for scaling social interactions. By blending the physical and virtual realms, individuals can connect with others beyond geographical limitations. The metaverse's potential for providing realistic and interactive virtual travel experiences will further strengthen social connections, as people from different backgrounds come together to explore and engage in shared virtual spaces. Embracing travel and tourism in the metaverse opens up a new era of social interaction, where people can connect, learn, and grow together on a global scale. The next section describes it in detail.

Revolutionizing travel and tourism in metaverse

In the dynamic realm of the metaverse, travel and tourism are experiencing a profound transformation. eXtended Reality technologies, such as **Virtual Reality** (**VR**) and **Augmented Reality** (**AR**), are providing individuals with captivating, immersive experiences that enable them to virtually *visit* and explore distant locations without the need for physical presence. As we explored in *Chapter 7, Gaming Redefined: The Metaverse Revolution*, the metaverse is revolutionizing the way we interact with museums. Similarly, tourism is also becoming virtual and connected. Online tourism platforms allow users to delve into famous landmarks, historical sites, and even fictional worlds. These experiences open up new avenues for engaging with diverse cultures and environments, transcending physical boundaries, and fostering connections between people across the globe.

In the upcoming sections, we will delve into various compelling use cases where metaverse technologies extend the capabilities of travel and enhance the tourism industry. Moreover, we will venture into the realm of collaborative online travel engagement, where people from different corners of the world can come together virtually and embark on shared adventures. These engaging experiences foster a sense of camaraderie and promote social connection, irrespective of geographical barriers.

Travel beyond destinations

The future of travel is not just about reaching a destination; it is about transforming the entire journey into an engaging and captivating experience. Currently, travel businesses are primarily focused on optimizing routes and reaching destinations efficiently. However, the landscape is rapidly evolving, and disruptions powered by metaverse technologies (discussed in *Part* 2) are set to shift the paradigm.

Imagine a journey where every moment is filled with delightful surprises and interactive encounters. With the use of XR technology, travel experiences can be elevated to a new level of immersion. By tagging sharable cloud AR anchors with GPS coordinates, these augmented elements can be seamlessly integrated into the environment when viewed through AR-enabled devices. Users can interact with virtual objects, access relevant information, and even participate in social AR networks based on their position in the journey.

The potential for businesses to leverage AR anchor storage is immense. Monetization opportunities through advertising and sponsored content could further enhance the travel experience for users. Instead of relying solely on traditional entertainment options like FM radio or video streaming, travelers can immerse themselves in personalized virtual experiences. Future vehicles will be equipped with embedded VR studios, where travel from one location to another becomes a thrilling adventure. It has already started with BMW ConnectedRide smart glasses[10] and Toyota's AR driving glasses[11], as shown in *Figure 8.8* below. We are not far to imagine a journey from your home to the airport transformed into a virtual theme park ride, a scenic helicopter tour, or even an expedition on the surface of Mars. Companies like *Holoride*[12] are already exploring concepts that integrate smart glasses into vehicles, providing passengers with unparalleled immersive experiences. The use of technologies like eye tracking and face detection would make it possible to detect drivers fatigue and sleep or other heath parameters, and vehicle can automatically adjust to what is appropriate in emergency situations.

***Figure 8.8**: Driving glasses and connected car experience*

As advancements in technology continue to progress, we are on the brink of a transformative era where travel becomes an exciting and interactive journey, enriched with context-specific information and immersive entertainment. The metaverse is poised to revolutionize the way we travel, opening up boundless possibilities for unforgettable experiences along the way.

Redefine location and navigation

Traditionally, when people travelled, they relied on physical paper maps and had to frequently stop and ask for directions to ensure they were on the right track. With the evolution of road systems and digital maps like Google Maps, navigation became more seamless, providing real-time updates and localized information. GPS technology played a pivotal role in mapping the world and enabling us to locate connected devices and share live locations with others through social apps.

As technology progresses, we are entering an era of self-driving cars and autonomous vehicles that utilize techniques like **Simultaneous Localization and Mapping (SLAM)** to build virtual maps and locate objects in the environment. This wealth of data generated by moving vehicles will be contextually available to users in the metaverse, enhancing their travel experiences through spatial computing.

Imagine hailing a ride-share service and, through AR maps, easily locating your car in a crowded space with intuitive visual cues. You can virtually step inside the car, adjusting the lighting, ambiance, and entertainment preferences even before it arrives to pick you up. The integration of AR services with map and location data opens doors to various use-cases, such as finding the nearest charging stations, service centres, and fuel stations. **Visual Positioning System (VPS)** and GPS technologies in future vehicles will enable automated actions, making navigation more efficient and seamless. It would step into the future of location-based services that would reshape our understanding of the world around us.

Group travel and tourism

Group travel has always been a rich experience filled with social interactions, where we get to explore the world alongside our companions. Whether traveling with familiar faces or venturing with strangers, group trips offer opportunities to forge new connections and delve deeper into each other's personalities while discovering the world together. Moreover, group travel often proves to be not only economical but also environmentally friendly, as it allows us to save fuel and reduce carbon emissions per person.

In the metaverse, where the lines between physical and virtual realities blur, group travel takes on a new dimension. While not everyone may be physically present, individuals will have the option to embark on journeys with virtual representations of their friends and loved ones. Avatars, as acceptable identities in the metaverse, will enable users to invite their friends along on trips, even if they cannot be there in person. Picture yourself exploring a scenic destination while some of your friends join you through their avatars, creating a unique blend of physical and virtual experiences. Group travel and tourism can also use the use cases we discussed in the last chapter.

Moreover, as autonomous vehicles become more prevalent, the idea of traveling with a virtual driver offers a sense of safety and security. With a virtual driver, travel becomes engaging and anxiety-free, as there is no need to worry about unpredictable human behavior. Similarly, traveling with virtual friends and family in the metaverse may offer novel and engaging adventures without the demands and complexities of real-world dynamics.

However, as we embrace this exciting future, there will undoubtedly be considerations regarding regulations, costs, and personal preferences. Stricter rules may govern the use of virtual avatars, and users may choose how much of their presence they wish to replicate virtually. It will be essential to have clear indications distinguishing real individuals from virtual ones, giving users control over their experiences in the metaverse.

Virtual travel and tourism

Virtual travel, also known as zero-travel tourism, is an emerging concept in the metaverse that offers a whole new dimension to our travel experiences. With virtual travel, there is no need to physically journey to a location; instead, we can explore and experience it from the comfort of our own space or specialised travel studios. This can prove to be an economical and environmentally friendly alternative to traditional travel, allowing multiple individuals to join in these virtual travels. Additionally, virtual travel experiences may serve as powerful sales tools, offering pre-attraction previews that entice travellers before their real journeys.

Imagine a breath-taking virtual travel experience like the one created by *ImaginateXR*[13], showcasing the city of Vishakhapatnam. Refer to *Figure 8.9* below. This digital tour provides a drone's-eye view, top view, and even a bird's-eye view, allowing users to witness the location from various perspectives. The virtual experience is rich with details, such as people flying and moving about, making it an incredibly immersive encounter. While this is just the beginning, the potential for virtual travel to evolve into photo-realistic experiences is enormous. In fact, such virtual experiences can be further utilized to enhance the reality of travel at the actual location. After experiencing the beauty of a place physically, one can now take a virtual tour to explore areas that might otherwise remain unseen:

***Figure 8.9**: Virtual tour to Vishakhapatnam*[14]

In conclusion, the metaverse is revolutionizing the world of travel and tourism. From transforming museums into interactive spaces to offering virtual tours of distant locations, the metaverse technologies are redefining the way we explore the world. Group travel becomes a blend of physical and virtual experiences, with avatars allowing us to connect and embark on journeys together. With virtual travel, we can indulge in remarkable destinations without leaving our homes, making travel accessible and environment-friendly. As the metaverse evolves, so will the limitless possibilities of immersive travel experiences, bridging the gap between reality and the virtual realm.

Conclusion

This chapter has taken us on a journey exploring the dynamic world of virtual interactions and social engagements. We delved into the significance of social connections, an inherent aspect of human existence that spans across cultures and boundaries. The metaverse has the potential to amplify these connections, transcending physical limitations and opening doors to a new era of communication.

We explored the various types of social connections and engagements in the metaverse, from face-to-face interactions to virtual direct and indirect communication. With the aid of cutting-edge technologies, the metaverse offers a plethora of immersive experiences that redefine how we connect with others and the world around us.

Social identity in the metaverse has become a crucial component, with avatars acting as our digital representations in this virtual realm. These avatars hold the potential to replicate human behavior, bridging the gap between physical and virtual interactions. As the metaverse evolves, we can anticipate a future where virtual identities are legally verified, expanding the scope of social connections.

Moreover, the metaverse's impact on travel and tourism is profound, revolutionizing how we experience new destinations. Virtual travel offers a compelling alternative to traditional travel, providing economical and environmentally friendly options to explore distant places. With advanced AR technologies, virtual tourists can immerse themselves in breathtaking locations, enhancing their connection to the world in unprecedented ways.

In essence, this chapter is a glimpse into the transformative power of technology-induced social interactions. As we journey further into the metaverse, we can anticipate the boundaries between physical and virtual worlds to blur even more, ushering in a new era of social connectivity and engagement. The metaverse holds boundless potential to reshape how we interact, collaborate, and connect, promising a future where social experiences transcend time and space. As technology continues to evolve, the metaverse will remain a fascinating landscape where the possibilities for human connection are truly limitless.

In the upcoming chapter, we delve into the revolutionary impact of the metaverse on physical fitness, sports, and the healthcare industry.

Points to remember

Here are some points to remember from this chapter:

- Social connection and engagements will be a focal point in the next Internet metaverse.

- Avatars, as virtual social identities, will become widely accepted, replicating our behaviors and personalities with our consent.
- Rules and regulations will evolve around the usage of avatars, and their presence will be legally recognized.
- Recorded scenes will become common artifacts, enabling the recreation, joining, and updating of experiences, leading to new forms of social media.
- Interactions beyond life will be possible, allowing for reunions and connections with loved ones who are no longer physically present.
- Travel and tourism will play a crucial role in scaling social reach and creating meaningful connections across the globe.
- Travel experiences will focus on the journey itself, providing immersive and entertaining experiences during the travel process.
- Zero travel tourism will emerge as a popular alternative, enabling individuals to explore distant places and attractions without physically traveling.

References

1. **https://www.lifewire.com/yahoo-messenger-1949913**
2. **https://www.orkut.com/**
3. **https://www.linkedin.com/help/linkedin/answer/a1504420/id-verification-on-your-profile-with-aadhaar?lang=en**
4. **https://readyplayer.me/**
5. **https://www.move.ai/**
6. **https://xrai.glass/**
7. **https://techcrunch.com/2022/10/13/googles-3d-video-calling-booths-project-starline-will-now-be-tested-in-the-real-world/**
8. **https://varjo.com/blog/varjo-teleport/**
9. **https://www.youtube.com/watch?v=MU38axHhzxM&t=3s**
10. **https://www.press.bmwgroup.com/global/article/detail/T0422306EN/bmw-motorrad-presents-connectedride-smartglasses**
11. **https://carbuzz.com/news/toyotas-ar-goggles-are-way-better-than-a-head-up-display**
12. **https://www.holoride.com/en**
13. **https://www.imaginate.in/**
14. **https://vizagtourism.org.in/kailasagiri-park-vizag**

Chapter 9
Revolutionizing Fitness and Healthcare

Introduction

In this chapter, we embark on a transformative journey into the world of fitness and healthcare in the metaverse. As technology continues to reshape our lives, the metaverse technologies are considered as the powerful tool with immense potential to revolutionize these vital domains. The metaverse not only offers exciting opportunities for gamifying fitness and wellness but also paves the way for reimagining physical sports in virtual spaces, where immersive and engaging experiences would promote healthy living and active lifestyles. We will witness how metaverse fosters a new era of sports, transcending physical limitations and unlocking endless possibilities for athletes and enthusiasts alike.

Additionally, we investigate the role of digitalization in healthcare, where cutting-edge simulations and medical visualizations empower medical professionals to improve patient care and enhance their training.

While exploring these exciting advancements, we remain mindful of building equity and inclusivity in the metaverse. We examine the accessibility considerations for individuals with disabilities, ensuring that metaverse becomes an inclusive space for everyone, regardless of physical abilities.

Structure

In this chapter, we will discuss the following topics:

- Fitness and health consciousness
- Gamify fitness and wellness in the metaverse
- Transforming physical sports in the metaverse
- Role of digitalization and internet in healthcare
- Transforming healthcare in metaverse
- Building equity in the metaverse

Objectives

The objective of this chapter is to provide readers with a comprehensive understanding of the use cases of metaverse in fitness and healthcare domain. Readers will explore how virtual reality, augmented reality, and digitalization are revolutionizing fitness experiences, sports and healthcare practices. The chapter emphasizes the potential of the metaverse in enhancing well-being and also explains how it promotes equity and inclusivity in these fields.

Fitness and health consciousness

Over the years, the growth of social platforms and the increasing emphasis on collaboration and social connections have led to a rise in fitness and health consciousness. Joining gyms, cycling groups, or health clubs has become a trend and a status symbol for many. People share their fitness journeys, and social media platforms have become a powerful tool in influencing and motivating individuals towards healthier lifestyles. Author *James Clear*'s concept of *Powerful*, *Close*, and *Many* groups of people who can influence behaviour change is evident in the fitness and health community, where people follow powerful influencers, form close-knit support groups, and join communities of like-minded individuals. Digital transformation and educational efforts have further contributed to raising awareness about fitness and health, leading to positive growth in the health and wellness industry[1] despite challenging economic situations.

Various developments in the fitness and health industry include:

- Fitness, health awareness programs, dance, and sports integrated into school curriculums to instil healthy habits from an early age.
- Health clubs offering diverse activities like yoga, dance, zumba, etc., providing options for people with varied fitness preferences.

- Corporate fitness programs becoming part of remuneration packages to promote employee well-being and productivity.
- Mental well-being programs gaining importance to address the psychological aspect of overall health and fitness.
- Fitness and wellness camps gaining popularity as a means of advertising and fostering healthy lifestyles.
- Specialized groups such as cyclist clubs and mountaineers clubs forming around shared fitness interests.
- Events like Marathons, Walkathons, and Community races being organized for social causes, promoting fitness and community engagement.
- Focus on sports and increasing sports followings and events.
- Eating heathy, leading to start-ups and growing business of healthy diets.

With the growing use of technology, fitness tracking devices, such as smartwatches and mobile apps, have become ubiquitous, allowing individuals to monitor their fitness metrics and stay committed to their health goals. Technology is acting as a constant nudge to follow physical routines and encourages healthier choices. Additionally, advancements in food and nutrition tracking technology have contributed to a growing focus on healthy eating habits. The fitness and health industry is witnessing a demand for more experts, trainers, assistants, physicians, dietitians, coaches, and personalized services, as people seek to follow health routines within their personal boundaries. *Figure 9.1* shows a cyclist using fitness tracker:

Figure 9.1: *A cyclist using tracking devices to measure the fitness data*

As we explore the potential of the metaverse in the next section, we will discuss how it has the power to revolutionize fitness and wellness practices, providing more innovative, immersive, and personalized experiences for individuals to enhance their overall well-being.

Gamify fitness and wellness in the metaverse

In the thrilling realm of the metaverse, fitness and wellness have found a new dimension through gamification. Just as completing tasks within a game keeps us immersed and engaged, the rise of fitness and wellness games allows us to embark on physical adventures and play within the virtual space. The concept of gamifying experience has already been explored in earlier chapters, where we discovered how gaming and entertainment will be revolutionized within the metaverse (*Chapter 7, Gaming Redefined: The Metaverse Revolution*), and how social collaboration and engagement will reshape our interactions (*Chapter 8, Connecting and Engaging in the Metaverse*). Drawing inspiration from these insights, the following sections delve into the captivating use cases that extend into the metaverse.

Fitness and wellness studios

Fitness and wellness centers are undergoing a transformation, leading towards the metaverse that is helping transform these centers into captivating experience zones that gamify exercise and well-being. Just as physical spaces for gaming and entertainment have evolved into gaming studios and immersive museums, fitness centers, gyms, clinics, physiotherapy joints, and dance classes are adopting metaverse technologies to provide unparalleled immersive experiences. These futuristic studios are equipped with advanced sensors and connected equipment that constantly track our actions and postures, offering real-time personalized feedback and guidance. AI-powered smart mirrors, VR as exercise gadgets[2], equipment embedded with games[3] are already making their way into these centers, to enhance the fitness journey with intelligent insights.

Within the metaverse, specialized fitness centers would offer innovative exercises and games that engage users without feeling fatigued. Users can burn more calories and achieve their fitness goals more effectively through tailored routines targeting specific body parts. Dance and entertainment studios within the metaverse create exhilarating fitness experiences, allowing users to dance with virtual crowds and even iconic personalities virtually like *Amitabh Bachchan, Emma Watson* or *Sachin Tendulkar*. This social and immersive aspect of dance sessions makes fitness routines more enjoyable and motivating.

Future fitness and wellness studios in the metaverse may not require heavy physical equipment; virtual extended equipment will appear, enabling users to perform exercises with ease. Activities like yoga and meditation become even more beneficial in the metaverse, offering magical and immersive experiences that empower the mind, body, and soul. Users can transport themselves to historical settings, join sessions in ancient gurukuls, and learn from legendary figures of that time like Maharishi Patanjali. The preceding *Figure 9.2* depicts a virtual mediation theme at a fitness studio. The studios will be equipped with cutting-edge technology, such as wearable devices or specialized body suits, to create a seamless and life-like experience.

***Figure 9.2:** Depiction of meditation theme of a fitness studio, blending real and virtual*

Fitness and wellness studios in the metaverse would also have the ability to extend their experiences beyond physical spaces. Users can bring elements of these studios into their personal settings, such as their homes, and seamlessly continue their fitness routines even while traveling. This unparalleled convenience ensures that individuals can stay committed to their health and well-being goals, no matter where they are or what circumstances they face. By blending the virtual and physical worlds, metaverse empowers users to maintain consistent and engaging fitness experiences, making overall wellness a seamless and integrated part of their lives. As the internet reaches the metaverse stage, fitness and wellness studios will become dynamic hubs for personal growth, mental serenity, and immersive fitness adventures, enriching the lives of millions across the globe.

Social fitness and wellness

Social fitness and wellness in the metaverse are a dynamic fusion of social connectivity and gamification, creating a thriving ecosystem that encourages individuals to adopt healthier lifestyles while fostering a sense of community and belonging. As discussed earlier, the rise of social platforms has significantly influenced how we engage and collaborate online, and this influence extends to the realm of fitness and wellness. Fitness-conscious individuals can now join online communities, fitness clubs, and health challenges, allowing them to share their fitness journeys, achievements, and goals with like-minded enthusiasts.

Platforms like *Strava*[4] exemplify the power of social fitness by providing users with the ability to record and share their physical activities, compete in challenges, and interact with other members. These platforms harness the concepts of gamification, competition, and social interaction that motivates individuals to stay committed to their fitness routines. As a result, individuals are not only held accountable for their own progress but also inspired by the achievements of others in their community.

With the emergence of metaverse, social fitness and wellness experiences will reach unprecedented levels of immersion and interactivity beyond the confined spaces, or physical boundaries. It would enable friends and fitness enthusiasts from different locations to come together for shared fitness experiences. We would not have to leave the change behind when our location and situation changes[5]. Virtual meetups will become the norm, allowing individuals to cycle, walk, or exercise with friends and loved ones despite being miles apart. AI algorithms will create immersive virtual routes that simulate real-time companionship, fostering a sense of camaraderie and motivation among participants. *Figure 9.3* depicts a morning walk, with friends joining virtually and physically:

***Figure 9.3:** A morning walk in metaverse. The left-most two are the 3D avatars joining virtually*

One exciting aspect of social fitness in the metaverse is the concept of world or spatial anchors. Physical spaces we visit for cycling, walking, or exercise will become spatial anchors, enabling us to time travel and witness previous visits from friends and groups. We can tag our future schedules to these locations, socialize them with friends and loved ones, and create immersive metaverse experiences even before physically visiting. The frequency of visits to certain places will turn them into hotspots, attracting renowned personalities in fitness and wellness to organize virtual events and conduct fitness sessions.

The metaverse's ability to connect individuals based on common interests just by thinking about it will play a pivotal role in promoting fitness and wellness. Users will automatically find themselves in communities that share similar health goals, interests, and routines. For example, if someone is tracking our health metrics, such as cholesterol levels or blood pressure, and considering following a specific health routine, the metaverse will intuitively guide them to communities and resources aligned with their aspirations, offering support and motivation.

However, it is essential to recognize that with the enhanced immersive capabilities of the metaverse, individuals must have complete control over their interactions and experiences. Privacy consent and user autonomy will be fundamental principles governing social fitness and wellness in the metaverse. Users will have the freedom to choose the level of immersion they are comfortable with and have the power to control who can interact with them, whether virtual or real.

Personal fitness buddy

The digitization era has brought a focus on personalization, tailoring experiences to suit individual preferences and needs. In the metaverse journey, personalization evolves into individualization, catering to unique needs and preferences, ensuring a significant advancement in tailored experiences for each individual. The metaverse will have a deep understanding of our preferences and requirements; anticipating our needs before we do. Fitness and wellness, being inherently personal, are not left untouched by this transformation. Fitness apps like *WowFit*[6], *Cult.fit*[7] and *HealthifyMe*[8] are already redefining personal fitness, with technologies like smart mirrors[9] and AI-based XR apps such as *Zyoga*[10], *Proyoga*[11] and *Insane*[12]. These tools track body postures, joint movements, and provide real-time guidance for targeted workouts.

Not everyone enjoys public workouts or being in social fitness environments while prioritizing their fitness and wellness. Metaverse technologies cater to everyone, offering a personal fitness trainer in the form of a physical or virtual avatar, or even an AI-generated companion. This fitness buddy can come to our personal space, observe us during workouts, and provide real-time guidance, just like a trainer in a physical setup. *Figure 9.4* depicts a virtual personal trainer. The beauty of metaverse is that individuals can follow their healthy routines safely within their personal environments, without the fear of judgment.

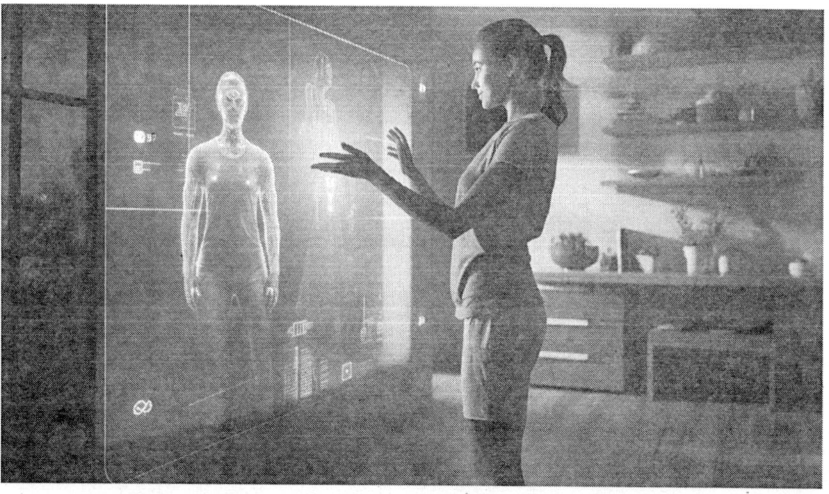

Figure 9.4: *Virtual personal fitness trainer in the metaverse*

As physical fitness and wellness studios evolve into virtual experience zones, individuals can bring these experiences to their homes. The gamified and entertaining fitness experiences can seamlessly transition from the studio to personal setups, ensuring continuity and convenience. The metaverse's ubiquitous nature allows these experiences to be accessible from anywhere, anytime, just like the internet today.

With individualization at its core, metaverse empowers individuals to prioritize their fitness and wellness needs without compromising on privacy or convenience. The personal fitness buddy in the metaverse becomes a trusted companion, offering personalized guidance and support on our journey to a healthier and fitter lifestyle.

Eat, drink, and smell in the metaverse

Healthy eating habits and nutritious diets go hand in hand with fitness and wellness, as people become increasingly conscious of their well-being. Social influences play a pivotal role in shaping eating habits, with social clubs and specialized businesses promoting healthy eating practices[13]. In the metaverse, where individuals are always connected, technology will be adept at tracking our dietary choices and providing real-time feedback. Personalized fitness assistants will keep a close eye on our food intake, offering tailored nudges and adjustments to maintain a balanced diet.

Figure 9.5: Depiction of augmented food information in metaverse

As depicted in *Figure 9.5*, with seamless integration of XR devices, food information such as calories, fats, and ingredients will be augmented onto the actual food, helping individuals make informed and health-conscious choices. Moreover, the metaverse's interconnected nature will enable a deeper understanding of individual preferences, enabling it to guide us away from unhealthy temptations and towards better dietary decisions. Imagine seeing a glimpse of our future selves based on our current eating habits, that can serve as a powerful motivator to adopt healthier choices.

Metaverse will extend its impact to the senses, enabling individuals to experience smell and taste without actual consumption. For instance, it will facilitate de-addiction efforts by providing smokers and alcoholics with a means to fulfil cravings without harmful substances. By customizing environments, metaverse will have the capability to alter food tastes or create desired flavours from healthy ingredients[14].

In conclusion, social fitness and wellness in the metaverse offer incredible potential for transforming health habits and overall well-being. Through social connectivity, gamification, and immersive experiences, the metaverse will establish a vibrant ecosystem that inspires individuals to embrace healthier lifestyles and fosters meaningful connections. As the metaverse continues to unfold, it will undoubtedly revolutionize how we approach fitness and wellness, leading to better health outcomes and a stronger sense of community. Next, we will see metaverse extending the fitness and wellness in a more professional setup - sports.

Transforming physical sports in the metaverse

In the ever-evolving landscape of the metaverse, the transformative potential does not stop at gamifying fitness and wellness; it extends to revolutionizing the realm of physical sports as well. The metaverse use-cases we discussed for fitness and wellness in last section also applies to physical sports. The very arenas where athletes showcase their prowess will transform into immersive sports studios, offering enhanced experiences that transcend the boundaries of traditional training grounds. Athletes, both amateur and professional, will have the privilege of training with a precision that caters to their specific needs while staying motivated by engaging with fellow sports enthusiasts within the metaverse's social framework. In *Chapter 7, Gaming Redefined: The Metaverse Revolution*, we explored the enhancement of sports-watching experiences. This section delves into how the metaverse can revolutionize the sport itself.

Measure and enhance the performance

In the metaverse-driven evolution of physical sports, the very fabric of performance measurement is undergoing a profound transformation. Beyond traditional metrics, cutting-edge sensors are now seamlessly integrated into sports venues and equipment, from balls and bats to gloves and helmets. These sensors, in conjunction with metaverse technologies, meticulously record each movement, each play, and each nuanced action. The result is comprehensive tracking of an athlete's every spatial manoeuvre and physical exertion.

The implications of this meticulous monitoring are profound. Performances and trials are captured in immersive 3D detail, providing a holistic view of an athlete's engagement with the sport. This wealth of data is not just for show; it serves as a springboard for informed analysis. Athletes, their coaches, or AI-powered systems can dissect the recorded performances, identifying gaps and pinpointing actionable insights. These insights extend beyond generalities, delving into specialized training requirements based on individual strengths and weaknesses.

Picture an athlete delving into a metaverse-powered interface, meticulously scrutinizing their 3D-rendered actions. They can assess the torque of their swings, precision of their shots, or the economy of their motions. This comprehensive self-examination serves as the foundation for targeted improvements. Whether it is a specific muscle group that needs strengthening or a nuanced technique that demands refinement, the metaverse's insights pave the way for tailored training regimens. *Figure 9.6* depicts 3D measurement during a practice session of an athlete:

Figure 9.6: Depiction of body movement measurement in metaverse

Moreover, metaverse's capabilities do not end at self-improvement. By analysing competitors' movements, athletes gain strategic advantages that can shape their approach to contests. The metaverse becomes an arena for honing skills, anticipating opponents' strategies, and enhancing overall sportsmanship.

In the words of *Peter Drucker, 'If you can't measure it, you can't manage it'* .The metaverse amplifies this sentiment, empowering athletes to manage every facet of their performance. *Lord Kelvin*'s adage, *'If you can't measure it, you can't improve it'*, finds new resonance in the metaverse era, as athletes harness its capabilities to elevate their skills, refine their techniques, and push the boundaries of their physical capabilities.

Redefine coaching

As the metaverse emerges as a transformative force across various domains, the landscape of sports coaching is undergoing a profound redefinition. The metaverse's ability to provide hyper-precise measurements and insights is raising the demand for coaches who can harness its capabilities to hone athletes' skills to unprecedented levels. The result is a realm of specialized coaching that extends far beyond conventional paradigms. This metaverse-driven coaching revolution comes in a variety of compelling flavours, each designed to cater to athletes' unique needs and aspirations:

- **Remote coaching:** The metaverse is breaking geographical barriers, democratizing access to specialized coaching. Athletes can receive guidance from renowned coaches regardless of their location. Remote coaching transcends the limitations of physical distance, bringing expertise to even the remotest corners of the world. This accessibility ensures that talent is nurtured and excellence is cultivated without constraints.

- **Coaching from renowned personalities:** Imagine receiving coaching from a sports legend, either virtually or through an AI-driven avatar. The metaverse enables athletes to learn from their favourite sports personalities, effectively bridging the gap between aspirants and their idols. This not only imparts expert guidance but also serves as a powerful motivational tool, driving athletes to push their limits.

- **Tailored coaching for specialized needs:** Every athlete's journey is unique, often requiring targeted training. The metaverse would empower athletes to easily find coaches who specialize in specific areas. Whether it is enhancing legwork, mastering a particular technique, or addressing individual challenges, the metaverse would track and know the need, and connect athletes with coaches who understand their unique requirements.

- **Pre-professional coaching institutes:** The metaverse is poised to birth a new breed of coaching institutes that cater to pre-professional training. These virtual or hybrid institutes equip athletes with the skills and knowledge they need before they step onto a real field. Using virtual equipment and immersive simulations, athletes can learn the nuances of their sport, perfect their techniques, and practice safety protocols before engaging in real-world scenarios.

In essence, the metaverse catalyses a coaching revolution that transcends conventional limitations. It melds technology, personalization, and expert guidance into an amalgamation that empowers athletes to redefine their limits. As the metaverse-driven coaching landscape evolves, athletes can look forward to a future where the boundaries of their potential are pushed, horizons expanded, and dreams realized.

Immersive safe practices

As the boundaries between virtual and physical realities blur, athletes are set to enter an era of practice that is both immersive and safeguarded. Imagine a world where practicing a sport becomes an immersive experience, free from judgment or limitations. Within the metaverse's virtual expanse, athletes can engage in training sessions with AI players or opponents of their choice. They can hone their skills, strategize, and analyse their gameplay—all within a controlled, virtual environment. The metaverse offers a unique opportunity to observe and learn from the best in the field, allowing athletes to witness excellence first-hand.

In this transformative landscape, athletes can don specialized gloves and clothing embedded with haptic feedback mechanisms. These innovations provide a tangible sense of immersion, enabling athletes to experience the intricacies of their sport on a visceral level. Whether it is the suffocation[15] of deep-water swimming or the impact of an opponent's punch, the metaverse would let users configure their immersive experiences according to their comfort and preferences.

The growing trend of immersive sports training like virtual taekwondo[16], strivr[17], rezzil[18], etc. are already making strides. *Ghost Pacer*[19], for instance as shown in *Figure 9.7*, introduces a virtual running partner that syncs with physical movement, simulating a competitive environment that drives runners to excel. The metaverse amplifies this concept, ushering in an era of training that merges technology, simulation, and personalization into a seamless whole.

Figure 9.7: *Virtual companion for running from Ghost Pacer*

Beyond the allure of immersive training, the metaverse also holds the promise of enhanced safety. Metaverse technologies can proactively guide athletes through their practice routines, minimizing the risk of physical injuries. As athletes engage in virtual matches, they can experiment, refine techniques, and push their limits—all while minimizing the physical strain that accompanies traditional training.

In summary, the metaverse's transformative influence on physical sports would extend far beyond traditional boundaries. It introduces a realm of immersive training, personalized coaching, and injury prevention that transcends the limitations of the physical world. Athletes can practice with unprecedented precision, access specialized coaching, and engage in competition within controlled environments. This metaverse-driven evolution promises not only enhanced performance but also a safer and more dynamic sports landscape, reshaping how athletes approach their training and empowering them to reach new heights of excellence.

Role of digitalization and internet in healthcare

The healthcare industry has undergone a remarkable transformation with the pervasive influence of digitalization and internet, reshaping the way medical care is delivered and received. Unlike the preventive nature of physical fitness and wellness, healthcare pertains to diagnosis, treatment, and managing health conditions. The impact of digitalization has been profound and multifaceted, encompassing various aspects of healthcare, some of them are discussed below:

- **Hospital management systems**: Digitalization and internet has also reached resource-constrained areas through initiatives like *Bahmni*[20], an open-source hospital management platform. Digital solutions have transformed hospital management, and managing healthcare information, appointment scheduling, patient records, tests, queue management, and more. Patient and visitor engagement have been streamlined through digital platforms. Hospitals are focusing on creating patient-centric environments with enhanced user experiences.

- **Electronic medical records:** This digitalization drive ensures that even underserved populations have access to streamlined medical services. It highlights the potential of technology to bridge gaps and improve healthcare equity. The digitization of medical records, reports, and imaging data has significantly enhanced the efficiency of healthcare operations. Patient information is now accessible at the click of a button, enabling quicker diagnoses and informed decision-making by medical practitioners. This transition from paper-based to electronic records has revolutionized the way healthcare providers manage patient information.

- **Telemedicine:** Telemedicine has emerged as a game-changer, especially during the Covid-19 pandemic. Remote consultations through video calls or specialized platforms have enabled patients to seek medical advice over the internet without the need for physical visits. This approach has not only ensured continuity of care but has also minimized the risk of virus transmission.

- **Remote and robotic surgeries:** Advancements in technology have extended into the realm of surgeries. Remote and robotic surgeries have been explored, showcasing the potential for precision and expertise even across geographical barriers. Operation theatres are equipped with state-of-the-art sensors that assist practitioners and monitor vital signs in real-time, enhancing patient safety during surgical procedures. The portability of medical devices is another facet of digitalization. Portable devices, from blood pressure monitors to glucose meters, empower individuals to monitor their health conditions conveniently. This data can be seamlessly integrated into electronic health records, enabling healthcare providers to make well-informed decisions.

- **Focus on mental health:** It is an increasingly critical aspect of well-being that is benefitting from digitalization. Online platforms offer resources, counselling services, and virtual support groups, social connects and internet, catering to the evolving needs of individuals in a fast-paced world.
- **Online and cost effective pharmacy:** The digital shift extends to the availability of medical services over the internet. In India, platforms like *Practo*[21] aggregate information about healthcare professionals, enabling patients to connect with doctors based on their needs. The convenience of accessing medical expertise through digital means is making healthcare more accessible. Furthermore, the process of procuring medicines has been revolutionized through online platforms aggregators like *PharmaEasy*[22] and other platforms, in India. This digitalization enhances the convenience of obtaining prescription medications and over-the-counter drugs both, online and offline. Furthermore, the internet has also provided a boost to cost-effective medical practices, such as the availability of generic medicine options and the emergence of start-ups like *Generic Aadhar*[23].
- **Alternate healthcare:** Additionally, digitalization and connected ecosystem of internet has played a crucial role in creating awareness and accessibility to alternative healthcare practices like homeopathy, ayurveda, acupressure, naturopathy, and various other therapeutic approaches.
- **Vaccine and immunization records:** The digitization of children's immunization charts has enabled doctors to maintain accurate records, leading to parents and guardians receiving timely alerts and reminders for vaccination due dates. This digital approach has also extended to adult and elderly vaccines. Notably, the COWIN app[24] in India has demonstrated the remarkable capability of digitization in managing vaccine records at a nationwide scale.

In the metaverse, the healthcare landscape is positioned for a transformative paradigm shift. The metaverse technologies explored in *Part 2 - Metaverse: A Result of Technological Evolutions* of this book offer significant potential in the realms of medical education, training, and patient consultation. Leveraging the immersive nature and inherent intelligence of these technologies, and medical professionals can benefit from enriched learning experiences, while patients can gain deeper insights into their health conditions.

In conclusion, the role of digitalization and today's internet in healthcare is transformative, creating a dynamic and patient-centric ecosystem. The integration of internet technology has optimized processes, improved accessibility, and elevated patient care. As the world transitions into the next internet - the metaverse, healthcare is likely to witness even more profound changes, revolutionizing medical practice, education, and patient engagement. In the subsequent sections, we will delve deeper into these exciting possibilities.

Transforming healthcare in the metaverse

In our ongoing journey of becoming deeply embedded in the internet, we are not only connecting with fellow living beings but also with every facet of the world around us. This dynamic interaction is reshaping how we perceive and engage with our evolving reality. With the proliferation of advanced technologies, we are now equipped to not only diagnose but also predict potential health issues, enabling us to take proactive measures. This acceleration of progress is propelling us into an era of rapid evolution, promising to transform our understanding of health and medicine at an unprecedented pace. The complexity of the human body and the vastness of the universe remain profound enigmas[25], even as our scanning capabilities delve deeper. However, the metaverse presents an exciting opportunity for further exploration and discovery. In this section, we will delve into the transformative potential of the metaverse in healthcare, exploring use cases in radiology, remote consultations, simulations, 3D scanning of organs, mental health, and virtual drugs.

Radiology and diagnosis

Radiology stands as a cornerstone of medical science, offering a window into the intricate internal landscape of living beings. This indispensable tool unveils what remains hidden to the naked eye, meticulously pinpointing anomalies that might otherwise go unnoticed. Techniques like X-rays, CT scans, and MRIs penetrate the body's veil, necessitating specialized expertise to understand the insights they provide. The advent of digital imaging has revolutionized the accessibility of these scans, rendering the need for cumbersome physical reports obsolete.

The metaverse is poised to redefine the very fabric of radiology, elevating both diagnosis and patient interaction to unprecedented levels. With metaverse technologies, medical professionals can immerse themselves within a patient's body, overlaying radiology scans onto physical anatomical structures. This enables them to navigate and scrutinize minute details, virtually extracting organs and zooming in for like microscopic examinations. Imagine visualizing the intricacies of a beating heart or analyzing brain functions with unprecedented clarity, identifying blockages and clots in real time. AI assistance will empower these professionals with data-driven insights, aiding in more accurate diagnoses and personalized treatment plans. *Figure 9.8* shows a snapshot from Medivis' SurgicalAR solution[26]:

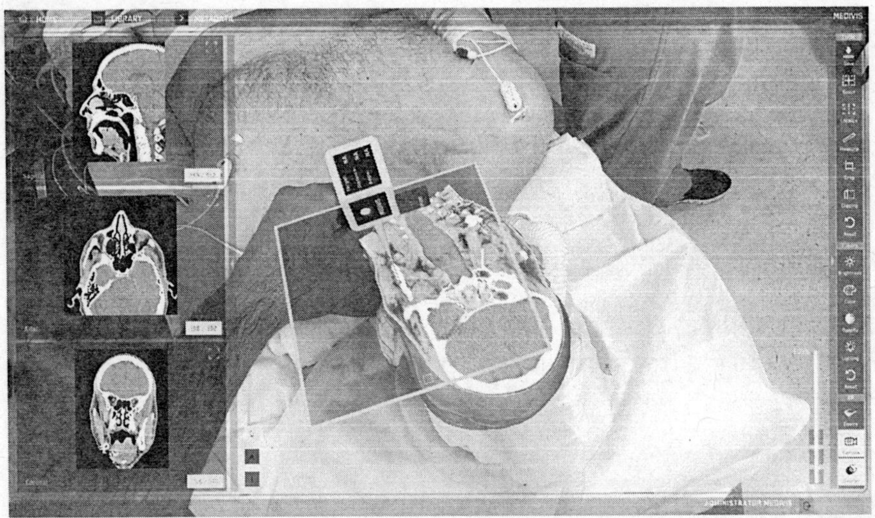

Figure 9.8: Surgical solution superimposing radio imaginary in 3D

Equally transformative is the concept of recording, replaying, and sharing these immersive diagnostic experiences. Collaborative diagnosis, where experts from across the world offer opinions, becomes a seamless reality. Additionally, metaverse-driven diagnosis is set to transcend the traditional boundaries of symptoms and radiological data. By incorporating computer vision and multi-sensory technologies of the metaverse, it can potentially sense early indicators through facial expressions, skin conditions, body movements, vocal patterns, eye behaviour, and even olfactory cues. AI's predictive prowess, based on these multifaceted inputs, could potentially detect health issues long before they manifest as recognizable symptoms, fundamentally altering the trajectory of medical intervention and prevention. Google's Multimodal medical AI[27] is showing the way AI would bring the insights in more interactive ways.

It would also enable use-cases of self-assessment in the personal and private setup. For instance, the case of Peyronie's disease, a fibrous scar tissue within the penis, resulting in curvature and discomfort. With the aid of a specialized app like EndoPharma's self-assessment tool[28] and XR capability, individuals can assess their sexual organs for any anomalies indicative of Peyronie's disease. The metaverse's immersive nature facilitates a comprehensive evaluation, potentially enabling early detection and intervention.

In essence, the synergy between radiology and the metaverse promises to rewrite the narrative of medical diagnosis. This convergence not only enhances the precision of radiological examinations but also introduces a new era of proactive healthcare through multi-sensory input and AI-driven predictions. As we delve further into the potential of the metaverse in healthcare, we will uncover how these advancements can reshape medical practice and patient outcomes.

Remote consultation and assistance

The transformative potential of the metaverse extends to the domain of remote consultation and assistance in healthcare, reshaping the way medical professionals interact with patients and provide essential medical care. Building upon the foundation of existing video consultations, metaverse technologies will introduce a new level of interconnectedness, blending real-time data transmission with immersive experiences. This evolution is anticipated to manifest in several forms:

- **Remote consultation:** Metaverse-enabled remote consultation will revolutionize the traditional doctor-patient interaction. Medical professionals will possess the capability to diagnose patients remotely by leveraging advanced computer vision and AI technologies. Through this approach, doctors can visualize patient data, analyze radiology images, and even conduct virtual examinations without necessitating physical presence. Moreover, the development of remote consultation kits could enhance these interactions by providing haptic feedback, allowing physicians to virtually *touch* patients for more accurate assessments, while continuously tracking and monitoring the patients remotely.

- **Assisted consultation:** In scenarios where physical presence is required for accurate assessment, the metaverse will facilitate assisted consultation. Trained healthcare assistants equipped with specialized devices will visit patients on-site. These devices will enable the remote transmission of sensory data, enabling medical experts to have a real-time understanding of the patient's condition. This approach ensures that critical physical cues are accurately communicated, enhancing diagnostic accuracy.

- **Virtual consultation:** The metaverse will introduce AI-generated virtual medical experts as a viable consultation option. Authenticated by medical authorities, these virtual professionals will provide consultations to patients, especially in underserved regions or situations where physical doctors are unavailable. These virtual experts will not only mimic the expertise of human doctors but also offer more economical and accessible healthcare solutions, bridging gaps in healthcare accessibility. For example *iCliniq*[29] aims to offer such services.

- **Social consultation:** The metaverse's immersive and collaborative nature will give rise to innovative models of community-driven healthcare assistance. **Non-governmental organizations** (**NGOs**) and healthcare communities could leverage the metaverse to offer free consultations and support, particularly for mental health concerns. Renowned medical experts and personalities may back these initiatives, ensuring their credibility and effectiveness in addressing healthcare needs.

As the metaverse transforms remote healthcare consultation and assistance, it promises to bridge geographical barriers, provide expert guidance to underserved populations, and redefine the doctor-patient relationship. This multi-dimensional evolution will leverage technology to deliver a more accessible, efficient, and comprehensive healthcare experience, ultimately benefiting individuals across the spectrum of healthcare needs.

Medical training and practice

The profound impact of the metaverse on education is a topic of extensive exploration, with *Chapter 11, Skilling and Reskilling in the Enterprise Metaverse* delving into its intricate dimensions. However, this section focus on metaverse's influence in the realm of medical education, training and practice. Medical professionals undergo rigorous training and practice before they can apply their skills to real patients. Traditionally, unconventional tools like bananas[30] or preserved specimens are used to simulate procedures, while medical students dissect frogs and study preserved specimens in biology and zoology labs. The metaverse is poised to revolutionize this landscape.

In the metaverse, the concept of training and practice takes on a new dimension. Photo-realistic scans and digital replicas, often referred to as digital twins, will become commonplace. These can be accessed anytime, anywhere, and manipulated within immersive environments for repeated practice. These replicas allow medical students and professionals to learn and hone their skills extensively before applying them to real bodies. The implications are that transformative; intricate procedures, dissections, and simulations can be undertaken without direct interaction with real subjects.

Surgical simulation is one of the most remarkable applications in this context. Surgeons can rehearse entire operations within simulated operating theatres, collaborating with colleagues and support staff in a risk-free environment. Such simulations can be recorded in 3D, serving as invaluable learning resources for others. Furthermore, the metaverse enables surgeons to meticulously plan surgeries, anticipate potential challenges, and refine their approaches through simulations. AI-driven guidance adds another layer of support, offering insights into possible complications and optimal responses. Augmented medical information enhances their decision-making process, exemplified by solutions like Real Response's Varjo mixed reality-based Aeromedical training[31].

The metaverse extends its impact to encompass life-saving training as well. Even those without formal medical training can learn essential skills such as CPR through immersive experiences, as showcased by *Philips*[32]. Additionally, various safety protocols and procedures can be effectively taught using metaverse technologies, enhancing the efficacy and accessibility of training programs.

In essence, the metaverse's influence on medical training and practice transcends conventional boundaries, offering dynamic, immersive, and risk-free platforms for learning and refining critical skills. As metaverse technologies continue to evolve, their integration into medical education and practice is expected to reshape the way medical professionals are trained and equipped to handle complex medical scenarios.

3D scan and bio-print organs

The convergence of radiology advancements with metaverse technology is poised to revolutionize the healthcare landscape, particularly in the realms of 3D scanning and bio-printing of organs, bones, and teeth. The union of these innovative domains is on the precipice of rendering 3D scans of anatomical structures feasible, while the notion of 3D bio-printing is emerging as a compelling possibility within the metaverse. This transformative potential has already been witnessed through experimental implementations in diverse scenarios, underscoring the powerful synergy between advanced radiology and metaverse capabilities.

In the context of medical procedures like dental, bone, and other implant surgeries, the metaverse emerges as an ideal environment for refining and elevating the conventional techniques, and address the challenge of creating appropriately sized implants and dentures. Where conventional moulding techniques have historically prevailed, the metaverse introduces a paradigm shift with intricate 3D models and digital replicas taking center stage. This digital representation serves as a blueprint for the fabrication of physical counterparts through 3D printing. On the other hand, the practice of superimposing 3D organs onto anatomical structures for assessment gains unprecedented depth. Medical professionals can manipulate these virtual constructs, simulating their integration with body postures and joint movements, offering a prelude to the effects of actual implantation. This avant-garde approach empowers surgeons to evaluate potential outcomes in a risk-free environment, refining their strategies and fostering greater precision.

Anticipating the horizon of possibilities, the metaverse's transformative influence is expected to transcend beyond bone and tooth-related procedures. With the rapid evolution of bio-printing technologies, the prospect of artificially producing and printing organs and tissues is approaching viability. This seismic shift holds immense promise for addressing critical medical challenges like organ shortages and enhancing the prospects of successful transplantation.

In essence, harnessing the synergy of 3D scanning and bio-printing capabilities within the metaverse, healthcare professionals can envisage a future marked by enhanced precision, patient-centric solutions, and ground-breaking medical interventions.

Mental health and virtual drugs

The burgeoning awareness surrounding mental health has positioned it as a pivotal focus area, driving the need for innovative solutions to address a range of psychological challenges that were previously often overlooked. The intersection of digitalization and increasing consciousness about mental well-being has catalysed the exploration of metaverse technology as a potential panacea for these modern-day concerns. The profound impact of metaverse immersive technologies on the human psyche has even led Forbes to aptly term it a *drug*[33] for the mind.

Recalling the famous dialogue "*Aye Mamu ... jadoo ki jhappi de daal aur baat khatam*"[34] from the bollywood movie Munna Bhai MBBS, which means, a warm hug can potentially alleviate profound issues. "*chemical locha*", another term used in movie referring to the intricate chemical reactions within our brains that can inadvertently lead to erratic behaviour beyond our control. This concept mirrors the actual complexities of our emotional responses, such as the rush of feelings[35] when connecting with loved ones, which are predominantly governed by the release of specific hormones known as **Dopamine, Oxytocin, Serotonin, and Endorphin** (**DOSE**). These chemical messengers wield the power to induce a spectrum of emotions, with their interplay dictating different feelings.

Interestingly, metaverse environments have been observed to induce similar reactions, prompting a significant question: *Can these digital domains artificially influence brain functions in non-invasive ways*? This query has propelled the development of therapeutic interventions that leverage metaverse technologies to address psychological disorders. Cognitive rehabilitation, for instance, harnesses a gamut of digital methods and serious games to impact impaired brain functions. An exemplary illustration is *MindLenses*[36] by *Restorative Neurotechnologies*, which ingeniously merges non-invasive neuromodulation through specialized glasses and engaging video games to render cognitive rehabilitation more efficacious and enjoyable for patients.

The trajectory towards a fully realized metaverse presents tantalizing prospects for revolutionizing medical practices. Envision a future where anaesthesia might be obsolete during surgeries, as the immersive metaverse environment seamlessly dispels the sensation of pain. This pain-reduction potential is already under exploration by medical professionals[37], underscoring the metaverse's latent role as a virtual analgesic.

In the impending metaverse era, it is not far-fetched to anticipate the emergence of metaverse-driven *virtual drugs* that wield the potency to reshape the way we perceive and manage mental well-being. This progression underscores the metaverse's transformative potential, where technological innovation converges with the delicate intricacies of the human mind to usher in a new era of mental health care.

In the space of healthcare, the metaverse stands as a beacon of unprecedented transformation. From revolutionizing medical training and diagnosis through immersive experiences to enabling remote consultations and augmenting mental health interventions, the metaverse's impact is poised to be profound. The integration of advanced technologies, coupled with the innate potential of the metaverse, holds the promise of redefining how we approach health and well-being.

Building equity in the metaverse

Advancing equity within the metaverse holds a pivotal role in reshaping the landscape of healthcare and wellness. It signifies the transformative power of technology in ensuring inclusivity for individuals with disabilities. *Deepa Mehta*, the first women Paralympian of India, shares how technology makes her life safer and more empowered[38]. From checking her surroundings remotely to monitoring vital signs during training, technology has proved to be a game-changer for athletes and the disabled community alike.

The metaverse extends this promise of equity even further. Innovations like *XRAI glasses*[39] exemplify technology's potential to bridge communication gaps, providing real-time information and enabling seamless interactions across diverse languages. These developments, when coupled with advancements in sign language detection[40], have the potential to transform the way people with disabilities engage with the world, promoting accessibility and understanding. Smart glasses are already being designed for visually impaired[41] and in metaverse it would be closer to real.

Figure 9.9: iGYM[42], an interactive game designed for children with and without disabilities

The integration of AI into the metaverse holds the promise of enhancing equity even further. Initiatives like OpenBCI's *NeuroFly*[43], and *Neuralink Implants*[44] exemplify the synergy of neurology, AI, and perception technology to develop innovative solutions. The emergence of a full-body suit tailored to support individuals with Parkinson's disease[45] is a testament to how advanced technology can be harnessed to address specific healthcare challenges. *Figure 9.9* above underscore the potential of the metaverse to provide inclusive recreational experiences.

Conclusion

This chapter highlights technology's profound impact on human well-being, transforming our approach to fitness and health. From wearable trackers to immersive gamification, technology redefines exercise, fostering community and engagement for healthier lifestyles.

Gamifying fitness within the metaverse merges physical and digital realms, inspiring motivation, and engagement. Augmented reality, AI, and social connectivity create immersive experience zones, turning exercise into addictive and rewarding games.

The exploration of transforming physical sports in the metaverse reveals potential for specialized coaching, precise measurement, and safe immersive practices, reshaping how sports are practiced and experienced.

In healthcare, digitalization and the internet have transformed services, making them more accessible and efficient. The metaverse extends this transformation with advanced radiology, 3D organ scanning, virtual drug therapies, and a focus on inclusivity for individuals with disabilities. The synergy between technology and well-being holds vast possibilities, but it comes with the responsibility to navigate ethical, social, and health-related challenges. With awareness, mindful implementation, and collaboration, we can harness these innovations to revolutionize fitness, healthcare, and equity.

The next chapter will delve into how traditional economic concepts are reshaped to build the metaverse economy, exploring its impact on commerce, property, and value exchange.

Points to remember

Here are some points to remember from this chapter:

- Greater awareness of fitness and health, driven by societal shifts towards well-being.
- The integration of gamification techniques and metaverse motivates individuals to participate in fitness and wellness activities, keep them engaged.
- Metaverse would revolutionize physical sports through enhanced training, performance measurement, and coaching.
- Digitalization and internet integration reshape healthcare practices.
- Remote consultations become more prevalent, ensuring medical access and convenience for patients.
- Rise in alternative therapies and medical practices beyond conventional methods.
- Integration of metaverse technology into medical education offers immersive learning and practice opportunities.
- Possibilities of 3D scanning and bio-printing are explored for creating organ replicas, enhancing medical training and surgery planning.
- Huge potential of AI's potential in medical diagnosis, and prediction.
- Metaverse technology would address mental health concerns through immersive experiences and virtual interventions.
- Metaverse technologies would build and promote equity.

Reference

1. https://www.statista.com/outlook/dmo/app/health-fitness/worldwide
2. https://www.holodia.com/
3. https://www.theverge.com/2022/2/17/22939177/peloton-lanebreak-video-game-fitness-bikes
4. https://www.strava.com/
5. https://thinkuldeep.com/post/habitmatters/
6. https://mywowfit.com/
7. https://www.cult.fit/
8. https://www.healthifyme.com/fitness-trainers/
9. https://www.mirror.co/
10. https://www.zyoga.in/
11. https://www.parjanya.org/prayoga
12. https://insane.ai/
13. https://www.myketokitchen.com/
14. https://medium.com/forwardfooding/virtual-eating-how-vr-can-transform-how-we-eat-drink-and-think-about-food-3ac77ca516fb
15. https://bgr.com/science/horrifying-scientific-study-simulates-suffocation-with-a-special-vr-mask/
16. https://virtual-taekwondo.com/
17. https://www.strivr.com/solutions/industries/sports/
18. https://rezzil.com/
19. https://www.ghostpacer.com/
20. https://www.youtube.com/watch?v=at_iA2aerCY
21. https://www.practo.com/
22. https://pharmeasy.in/#
23. https://genericaadhaar.com/
24. https://app.cowin.gov.in/
25. https://www.livescience.com/new-salivary-gland.html
26. https://www.medivis.com/surgical-ar
27. https://ai.googleblog.com/2023/08/multimodal-medical-ai.html

28. https://www.smsna.org/news/smsna/smsna-collaborates-with-endo-to-launch-peyronie-s-disease-self-assessment-app
29. https://www.icliniq.com/
30. https://pubmed.ncbi.nlm.nih.gov/30135033/
31. https://varjo.com/case-studies/reimagining-aeromedical-training-how-real-response-is-transforming-the-way-we-learn-with-mixed-reality/
32. https://www.linkedin.com/posts/meta-ely_dailyely-metaverse-metaversemarketing-activity-7092513344103870465-gUE0
33. https://www.forbes.com/sites/stevenkotler/2014/01/15/legal-heroin-is-virtual-reality-our-next-hard-drug/?sh=4694f04e1a01
34. Munna Bhai M.B.B.S https://www.imdb.com/title/tt0374887/
35. https://www.linkedin.com/posts/openbci_the-chemistry-or-spark-between-romantic-activity-7092573932863545345-JaXq
36. https://www.restorativeneurotechnologies.com/en/cognitive-rehabilitation-medical-device
37. https://globalnews.ca/news/9034744/virtual-reality-pain-management-canada/
38. https://thinkuldeep.com/event/lenovo-techworld-india-2023/# diversity-and-inclusion-in-tech
39. https://xrai.glass/
40. https://medium.com/xrpractices/sign-language-recognition-in-xr-34bc3a83fd7d
41. https://irisvision.com/electronic-glasses-for-the-blind-and-visually-impaired/
42. https://news.umich.edu/inclusive-play-u-m-art-professor-leads-creation-of-interactive-game-for-kids-with-and-without-disabilities/
43. https://openbci.com/community/assistive-neurotechnology-takes-flight-at-ted2023/
44. https://neuralink.com/
45. https://www.facebook.com/getovertime/videos/a-swedish-engineer-created-a-suit-to-help-people-with-parkinsons-disease-and-str/4032515526809843/

CHAPTER 10
Exploring the Metaverse Economy

Introduction

In the ever-evolving landscape of digital technology, the concept of the metaverse has emerged as a multifaceted realm encompassing diverse aspects of our lives. As we delve into the heart of this virtual universe, it becomes increasingly apparent that its impact goes far beyond mere entertainment and social interaction. An integral dimension of the metaverse's potential lies within its economy—a dynamic ecosystem where traditional notions of commerce, property, and value are being redefined in ways that were once unimaginable.

This chapter delves into the landscape driving metaverse economy, and characterized by innovation, disruption, and boundless opportunities. From the fundamental principles of economics that underpin the creation and exchange of value, to the transformation of real estate and the reinvention of digital commerce, in this chapter, we embark on a journey to unravel the complexities that shape this emerging economic frontier.

We will dissect the metaverse economy's various dimensions, uncovering its potential to redefine how we engage with commerce, value, and property. Understanding the evolution into the digital commerce, the metaverse posed as transformation of real-world businesses to the emergence of novel economic models. Moreover, we aim to provide insights into the transformative role of digital assets within a decentralized and open economic framework. By doing so, we strive to offer a holistic understanding of the economic landscape that the metaverse presents.

Structure

In this chapter, we will discuss the following topics:

- Understanding the property, value and commerce
- Using metaverse technologies in real estate
- Rise of digital commerce
- Extending the digital commerce in the metaverse
- Digital content as the virtual property
- The content creator economy

Objectives

The objective of this chapter is to provide the readers with a comprehensive understanding of the metaverse economy. Readers will gain insights into how traditional economic concepts are being reshaped within the metaverse, exploring its impact on commerce, property, and value exchange. By the end of this chapter, the readers will understand the transformation of real estate, digital commerce, digital content into a decentralized and open content-based economy.

Understanding the property, value and commerce

Before delving into the transformation of the economy within the metaverse, it is essential to grasp the core concepts that underpin it. Economy, as defined in dictionaries, refers to the process or system by which goods and services are produced, sold, and exchanged within a country or region, essentially constituting the method of generating wealth. Simultaneously, comprehending property is crucial. Property signifies items with inherent value, often accompanied by a framework of rights and ownership. The value associated with these items, whether tangible or intangible, drives commerce. Throughout history, commerce has been a vital catalyst that brings together people from different regions, cultures, and countries to forge agreements, trade, and sustain themselves in society.

Ownership rights over property can encompass a range of privileges, such as consumption, modification, sharing, rental, mortgage, sale, exchange, transfer, or destruction, while also entailing the exclusion of others from these activities. Irrespective of the nature of the property, its owner has the right to use it in accordance with the granted property rights. In this chapter, we will primarily focus on the following categories of property and associated services:

- **Real estates:** These encompass immovable properties like land, houses, flats, shops, hotels, factories, buildings, schools, and hospitals. They are further classified as public or private, based on ownership rights. Real estate serves diverse needs and act as hubs for various businesses to generate income.
- **Retail goods:** Goods are transferable items that fulfil human needs, while services are generally attached to goods, and may not be transferable but still provide utility. Goods and services constitute the foundation of the economy, with trade, commerce, and retail forming substantial markets. The advent of digitalization has also significantly transformed the service sector.

As the metaverse is poised to become the next internet with universe-like capabilities, its economy is naturally evolving. Concepts related to real estate, commerce, and assets are being redefined in the metaverse, with digital representations of these entities gaining immense traction and influencing economic dynamics.

Using metaverse technologies in real estate

The concept of real estate business has historically revolved around privately owned properties that cater to both personal and business needs, either on a permanent or temporary basis. Additionally, public properties also play a crucial role in this context. Property is as fundamental as the necessities of food and clothing. Having a roof over one's head has been a cornerstone of human existence since pre-industrial times. The evolution of real estate has paralleled advancements in construction technology, enabling the creation of safer, more efficient, and quicker infrastructure development. The changing landscape has prompted the rise of diverse infrastructure types, leading to the advent of multi-story buildings, shopping malls, shared spaces to live, play, workout, and enjoy, optimizing space and offering cost-effective solutions for communal living.

The digitization wave has profoundly impacted the processes associated with real estate, from construction, sales and purchases to operations and management. However, with the emergence of the metaverse—a reality where living beings seamlessly interact with the tangible and intangible elements of the world—the realm of real estate would be on the turning point of a revolutionary transformation. In this section, we will explore the metaverse's profound impact on real estate, reshaping how properties are constructed, bought, sold, rented, advertised, and serviced. From architectural designs to property transactions, the metaverse is set to reshape the very fabric of real estate practices.

Collaborative spatial designing

The realm of private real estates is characterized by the unique design preferences of individuals—ranging from facilities and colours to styles and comfort. With so many variables to consider, the challenge of creating designs that cater to individual needs has been an ongoing endeavor. Property owners, potential buyers, and stakeholders often seek to visualize the future state of a property before its construction, necessitating the generation of multiple paper designs from various angles. This process, irrespective of whether it involves public or private property, has traditionally been time-consuming, involving meticulous architectural planning and often the creation of miniature physical models. The advent of digitization introduced tools like **computer-aided design** (**CAD**) software that streamlined engineering drawings, allowing greater design flexibility and easier sharing of digital designs over the internet.

As we transition into the metaverse, the next internet, the collaborative design process and spatial design solutions are expected to become commonplace. Architects and stakeholders will convene virtually or in person within the metaverse to personalize designs in a 3D space. *Figure 10.1* depicts the collaborative spatial designing. This process will expedite feedback, revisions, and approvals, leading to faster design production. The metaverse's immersive environment will enable AI-guided structural assessments, facilitating compliance with safety standards and regulations. Additionally, AI-driven simulations will test structures against various disasters, ensuring robustness against earthquakes, floods, thunderstorms, and tsunamis, thus enhancing safety for occupants.

Figure 10.1: *Depiction of the collaborative spatial designing in metaverse*

Leveraging generative AI and technologies like **Generative Adversarial Networks** (**GANs**), as discussed in *Chapter 4, AI Empowering the Metaverse*, creates designs that align with specific requirements, and can be automatically generated. AI can also automate or fast track the design iterations. These AI systems will offer options for city planning, building designs, floor layouts, and bridges based on size and space availability. Tools, such as *ArcGIS engines*[1] and *Modelur*[2] will evolve further and simplify site planning and feasibility studies. Interior design will be similarly revolutionized, with AI adapting styles, sizes, and artifact placements to specific spaces. In the metaverse, the process of generating and selecting designs will be remarkably streamlined, making it a far more efficient and dynamic endeavor.

Construction compliance and 3D printing

Upon selecting and approving an architectural design, the construction process unfolds over time, involving meticulous reviews, audits, and compliance checks against the sanctioned design. On-site architects and experts diligently oversee construction progress. Delays often arise, particularly in areas where uncertainties lie beneath the ground, site—pipelines, cables, sewerage, soil density, and more. Safety remains a paramount concern, as any unsafe practice can result in severe consequences. While technology has brought improvements, manual labor remains essential in construction work.

The emergence of the metaverse offers the potential for a significant upgrade in construction compliance and safety procedures. This includes the integration of intelligent cameras stationed on-site and worn by workers, all connected to AI systems. This real-time connection provides a live map of ongoing construction, constantly validating and assessing safety measures. AI-driven systems can promptly issue warnings and alerts for detected unsafe practices. Noteworthy examples such as *DeepX*[3] and *Painsight*[4] exemplify the application of computer vision technologies to bolster worker safety and extend reality's boundaries within construction. *Figure 10.2* depicts the construction using metaverse technologies:

Figure 10.2: *Depiction usage of metaverse technologies in the construction site*

Additionally, detailed mapping of underground assets—such as gas pipes and sewer lines—within the spatial metaverse will occur. Machinery and tools will offer guided instructions, optimizing resource usage and minimizing waste. Structural components' validation, like beams and construction blocks, can occur seamlessly through XR embedded solutions, reducing the need for extensive physical testing and ensuring their suitability in the virtual world. Analysing and visualizing progress using XR, both remotely and in-person, will become common. The integration of **Building Information Modelling (BIM)** into reality will be routine, with live generation and collaborative sharing with experts.

With digital 3D replicas available for most components and the advancement of 3D printing beyond small objects, the future of construction leans toward assembling blocks and 3D-printing most building parts. This approach ensures compliance, material accuracy, and fewer human errors. It also enables swift design modifications and gradual transitions between different stages. House decoration will involve texturing buildings primarily with reusable materials, facilitating smooth shifts between styles. This transition to advanced construction technologies and 3D printing promises an efficient, sustainable, and adaptable future for the construction industry.

Marketing and trying before buying

Marketing commences long before an idea takes form and continues through indicative design stages. Traditionally, sales and marketing efforts strive to immerse potential buyers in the future through miniature models, sample flats, and sales studios. These platforms leverage videos, images, and 3D displays to explain infrastructure features. However, these methods fall short in representing real-world scenarios, such as sunlight variations during different seasons, airflow dynamics, night views, or the exact balcony scenery. Prospective buyers often need to rely on their imagination, while marketers grapple with the challenge of persuasion using limited means. The decision to purchase is often made solely based on these presentations, despite the inability to experience diverse weather conditions first-hand.

The metaverse is poised to revolutionize this paradigm by introducing "try before buying" experiences. Individuals can inhabit their future spaces virtually before committing to a purchase. This immersive encounter allows them to simulate days, nights, sunlight angles, airflow patterns, rain, summer heat, winter cold, and more, anytime, anywhere and as many times they want. They can even invite friends and family for a virtual gathering within their prospective dwelling. The metaverse thus empowers individuals to make well-informed decisions by providing an enriched understanding of their choices. They can take notes, garner customization insights, and share 3D spatial recordings with architects and designers for tailored adjustments. As a result, confidence in investment decisions grows, and uncertainties diminish, fostering a more streamlined buying process.

Gamifications and people engagement discussed in *Chapters 7, Gaming Redefined: The Metaverse Revolution* and *Chapter 8, Connecting and Engaging in the Metaverse* well extend seamlessly into marketing and sales. By keeping individuals engaged and aligning offerings with their social brand, metaverse-driven marketing strategies thrive. Another aspect of marketing; advertisements, will be explored in the subsequent section.

Personalized advertisement and services

Exploring the economic dimension of property involves avenues such as renting, leasing for personal or commercial use, and the novel concept of *try before buying*, as discussed in the previous section. Within this realm, commercial property utilization takes multifaceted forms, from individuals purchasing or renting space for personal or business ventures to advertising their own or others' enterprises. Traditional advertising methods encompassed fixed areas, walls, signboards, and large physical roadside hoardings, offering limited space for relatively static advertisements. The introduction of digital displays added a layer of dynamism, but the content remained largely generic, targeting a broad audience.

The metaverse is poised to redefine property-based advertising, rendering it highly personalized. As elaborated in *Chapter 7, Gaming Redefined: The Metaverse Revolution*, roadside advertisements will adapt to individual viewers, presenting content tailored to their social profiles and preferences. Property owners stand to generate revenue by leasing their spaces to advertisers, potentially accommodating multiple advertisers concurrently. To safeguard the interests of both lessors and lessees in the metaverse, regulations and laws governing such property usage will emerge. *Figure 10.3* depicts a 3D advertisement in metaverse:

***Figure 10.3:** Depiction of a roadside immersive advertisement space*

The metaverse's impact extends beyond advertising, spawning an array of new services. Community hotspots and avatars of recognizable personalities will merge the virtual and physical realms, engaging people in conversations, events, and performances. This synthesis will rejuvenate community gatherings, concerts, and business interactions, elevating property earnings. Properties proximate to these virtual hotspots will command higher value, attracting investments from property investors aimed at enhancing these burgeoning hubs. The metaverse thus ushers in a new era of economic potential, transforming property into dynamic spaces that not only serve functional purposes but also fuel thriving virtual communities.

Assisted maintenance

Efficient property management involves not only deriving value from tangible and intangible aspects of property, but also addressing the ongoing need for maintenance and operational upkeep. Over time, specialized businesses have emerged to manage property facilities and operations. They oversee a diverse team including plumbers, electricians, masons, carpenters, architects, designers, and more. However, the maintenance process often becomes challenging due to outdated design documentation, leading to increased costs and inefficiencies. For instance, lacking specific building information can cause electricians or plumbers to spend excessive time diagnosing issues or even result in mishaps.

The metaverse introduces transformative solutions to these maintenance challenges. It enables the visualization of concealed infrastructure, superimposing BIM onto real structures and pipelines. Safety practices, compliance checks, and audits within the metaverse echo the principles discussed in the *Construction compliance and 3D printing* section. Furthermore, when repairs or reconstructions are required, the metaverse offers a novel approach. It aids in envisioning property transformations, preserving emotional connections while overcoming traditional hurdles[5]. *Figure 10.4* depicts a plumber using metaverse technologies in fixing issues:

***Figure 10.4:** Depiction of metaverse assisted maintenance*

Metaverse enabled remote assistance and indoor navigation solutions enable the maintenance personnel in the following ways:

- Provide direct and faster access to the sites of interest physically as well remotely.
- Spatial notes anchored to precise world coordinates expedite tasks.
- Circumvent communication barriers of language, time and location accelerate the process.
- Simplified knowledge transfer between team members, and faster onboarding.
- Automated step by step guide from AI, robots, and smart machinery ensure adherence to safety protocols.

Some of the examples are, gates could restrict entry without proper personal protective equipment or masks. In cases of gas leaks or fire hazards, metaverse sensing technology allows real-time visualization, aiding in monitoring gas density and the assurance of safe conditions. Detecting individuals or living entities in distress during emergencies becomes more efficient and accurate within the metaverse enabled environment.

In essence, metaverse is poised to reshape the architectural design process, enabling immersive try-before-buy experiences. It has also introduced personalized advertising and services, leading the real estate landscape to the cusp of a dynamic evolution. Additionally, the metaverse's potential to enhance construction compliance, safety protocols, and assisted maintenance promises a future where property management becomes more efficient and innovative. As the metaverse unfolds, it brings a convergence of technologies and methodologies that redefine traditional real estate practices, offering an enticing glimpse into a more connected, efficient, and immersive future.

Rise of digital commerce

Building upon our exploration of property and value, we now embark on a more comprehensive journey of commerce. While we briefly introduced this concept earlier, our focus now expands beyond real estate to encompass the vast world of goods and services. Goods, the tangible items meeting human needs, span from essential vehicles to everyday utensils, while services, often intricately linked with goods, provide utility even if they lack transferability. Within this landscape, retail emerges as a central form of commerce, serving as a bridge for the exchange of both goods and services. The evolution of retail has undergone remarkable changes, adapting at every step shifts in production, supply chains, delivery mechanisms, marketing strategies, consumption patterns, and post-sales support. Crucially, digitization and the internet, are the catalysts for this transformative change.

What was once confined to local markets has now expanded into a global phenomenon, driven by the strides taken in logistics and transportation. This transformation has led to a profound rethinking of traditional dealer channels, with e-commerce emerging as a challenger to conventional brick-and-mortar establishments. The advent of online platforms not only connects consumers directly with sellers but also weaves in suppliers, producers, and delivery services. Industry giants such as Amazon and Flipkart have disrupted age-old retail practices, ushering in a new era of shopping convenience and accessibility.

With the proliferation of smartphones, a new phase emerged—m-commerce—ushering in a revolution in the way transactions are conducted. As seamless payment gateways and digital wallets gained prominence, the likes of *Paytm*[6], *Google Pay*, and *Amazon Pay* revolutionized financial transactions, instilling trust through initiatives like UPI[7] and making digital payments an integral part of daily life. The mobile app landscape burgeoned, resulting in a seismic shift in the retail paradigm. The intersection of technology, convenience, and commerce became increasingly evident.

The digital commerce story continues to evolve, branching into various sectors with astonishing agility. Aggregation platforms such as *Uber*[8] and *Ola*[9] revolutionized transportation, while *Zomato*[10] and *Swiggy*[11] disrupted the food industry, reimagining delivery and customer experiences. The rise of innovative start-ups like *Blinkit*[12], and *Dunzo*[13] pushed the boundaries of instant deliveries, transforming the very notion of convenience. In India, government initiatives such as ONDC[14] have emerged as strong pillars supporting the digital commerce ecosystem, aiming to connect every entity engaged in buying and selling, thus, promoting efficiency and growth.

However, the journey does not end here. The digital commerce realm is poised for further transformation, and our next section will cast light on how the metaverse, with its immersive possibilities and advanced technologies, will propel the evolution of commerce into uncharted territories, reshaping interactions, personalization, and consumer experiences in unprecedented ways.

Extending the digital commerce in the metaverse

Stepping into the metaverse transcends the contrast between digital and physical commerce. While the rise of e-commerce and m-commerce has reshaped our shopping habits, the allure of traditional experiences like leisurely window shopping and hands-on showroom exploration persists. These experiences continue to hold a distinct place in the fabric of commerce culture. The metaverse introduces an entirely new dimension, seamlessly merging the tangible and the virtual realms. This expansion not only enriches the digital landscape but also amplifies interactions within the physical world. This change would affect every facet of goods and services, spanning the entire lifecycle from creation and distribution to marketing, sales, consumption, post-sale support, training, and operational processes. It is a transformative tide that engulfs diverse industries, from agriculture and manufacturing to fashion, electronics, groceries, and medical supplies.

In this section, we embark on an extensive journey to uncover the diverse categories of use cases within the metaverse. These span across a broad spectrum of industry segments, offering a holistic understanding of how the metaverse is reshaping various sectors.

Productivity booster

Enhancing productivity is a pivotal aspect of any commerce ecosystem as it directly influences the production of goods and related services that underpin economic activities. The metaverse, with its amalgamation of cutting-edge technologies, stands poised to further amplify this productivity drive. The manufacturing landscape is set to benefit significantly as metaverse technologies seamlessly integrate into production processes. Factories, farms, and production facilities will leverage metaverse tools to monitor, measure, and adhere to quality standards while minimizing wastage through AI-driven recommendations in planning and execution. This technological fusion would reduce unnecessary transport and travel, streamline remote support, facilitate smoother onboarding, and elevate the work experience to new dimensions, fostering a harmonious relationship between humans and technology.

The metaverse's transformative power extends beyond human labor to even impact the animal realm, exemplified by XR gadgets that influence cows to produce more milk by providing soothing virtual environment to them[15], *Figure 10.5* depicts the phenomenon. The profound potential of metaverse technologies is akin to a catalyst, elaborated in *Chapter 9, Revolutionizing Fitness and Healthcare,* acting as a driving force that rejuvenates and sustains engagement, akin to a *work drug*. Imagine workspaces evolving into engaging, gamified domains that nurture creativity. Automation systems relieve individuals of repetitive tasks, liberating them to focus on imaginative endeavors. The metaverse's versatility accommodates a range of intelligences—both intellectual and emotional. AI-integrated systems deliver tailored instructions and training, adjusting to each worker's profile, fostering uniform quality across various skill levels and backgrounds.

Figure 10.5: *The metaverse gadgets influencing ability and work productivity*

In this metaverse-driven era, employing people will emerge as a costlier investment, surpassing the significance of machines or virtual counterparts. The metaverse's synergy with machines will empower individuals to achieve more in less time, utilizing fewer people, resources and exerting less effort. This partnership between human ingenuity and technological efficiency will not only elevate production levels but also cultivate a skilled workforce, fostering swift and informed decision-making. The metaverse embodies a future where the potential of human intellect is amplified by AI, propelling industries toward unprecedented heights of productivity and innovation.

Marketing and communal shopping

Marketing and sales are integral components of product adoption, with their significance amplified in the digital era. With the rise of digitization, social media and community-driven marketing has emerged as crucial strategies for reaching and engaging customers. Refer *Chapter 8, Connecting and Engaging in the Metaverse* to redefine how brands would communicate and interact with their audiences. Social media tactics will evolve within the metaverse, necessitating a shift in marketing strategies to encompass both physical and virtual platforms. Building on the insights shared in the section *Redefining Real Estate in the Metaverse,* **hyper-personalized marketing** will extend beyond real estate to encompass retail goods and services. This shift will usher in a future where commerce is intrinsically tied to communities, offering tailored offers and discounts that align with specific community preferences. Consumer choices will carry a heightened social impact, underscoring the metaverse's role in reshaping consumption patterns.

Communal shopping is poised to be a hallmark of both, the physical, and virtual dimensions of the metaverse. Window shopping, a classic activity that allows consumers to explore products before purchase, will undergo a transformation. Concepts such as "try before buying" will flourish, enabling users to experience products virtually before making a decision. Augmented reality will provide consumers with insights into unopened packages, allowing them to assess products without unpacking them. Additionally, augmented information like customer reviews and ratings[16] will empower buyers to make informed choices. Shopping malls and showrooms will take on a new identity within the metaverse, becoming experiential real estate. These spaces will be **gamified and immersive**, enhancing the overall shopping experience and navigation. However, in the metaverse, the focus will extend beyond the products themselves to encompass the strategies employed in selling and marketing.

Metaverse shopping portals are on the brink of reshaping the retail landscape, much like innovative platforms including *YeppAR*[17], *Obsess*[18], and Dell's exploration of explaining computer and data platforms in WebXR[19]. These portal solutions hold the promise of entirely transforming the shopping experience by virtually transporting the showroom directly into each user's personal space. This perpetual accessibility, unrestricted by time zones, will redefine the conventional limitations of shopping in terms of operating hours and physical location. AI-powered systems will act as the driving force for moulding user interactions in alignment with their unique preferences and behaviors in physical and virtual world. These AI systems will possess the foresight to understand potential buyers, creating a trustworthy and secure environment. This personalized approach will undoubtedly contribute to a more enjoyable and immersive shopping journey.

Future shopping[20] signifies a profound transformation in the retail landscape, transcending the boundaries of conventional product offerings and revolutionizing the dynamics of consumer engagement. According to the insights provided by Eclipse Group's report[21], an impressive 71% of shoppers express their willingness to increase their shopping activities if they were able to utilize XR-enabled technologies. This concept will be further examined in the upcoming section, delving into the intricate synergy between digital commerce and the intricate mechanisms of fulfillment within the expansive realm of the metaverse.

Delivery and fulfilments

The process of delivering goods and ensuring order fulfillment holds a crucial position within the supply chain of modern commerce. With the rapid digitization of trade and the surge in online marketplaces, a plethora of aggregation platforms have emerged, effectively bridging the gap between suppliers and consumers and facilitating rapid, often instantaneous, deliveries. This shift towards on-demand delivery services has become a defining feature of the current commercial landscape. However, the advent of the metaverse promises a subtle yet transformative shift in focus – from the simple act of delivering a product to the immersive experience of how the delivery itself unfolds.

Imagine a scenario where the metaverse allows you to witness the recipient of your gift joyfully engaging with it before you make the purchase. This pre-purchase insight not only elevates the shopping experience but also *imparts an emotional dimension* to the act of gifting, even before it occurs. *Figure 10.6* depicts delivering the emotional experience with a product:

Figure 10.6: *Depiction of delivering experience than just a product*

For instance, traditional celebrations like Rakshabandhan[22], where sisters and brothers exchange tokens of affection, could seamlessly transcend physical boundaries within the metaverse. A virtual *rakhi* could be sent and tied across distances, bringing the emotional significance of the tradition into a digital realm.

In the metaverse, the process of order delivery and tracking takes on an entirely novel dimension, enriched by both **speed and safety** enhancements. Delivery methods are diversifying to include options like drones or vehicles equipped with metaverse scanning and environment sensing capabilities. The wait for a package transforms from a simple anticipation to an engaging encounter, shared in real-time with others. Through immersive narratives, consumers can embark on a journey that unveils the story behind the product – from its creators and meticulous craftsmanship to its intricate voyage through the manufacturing and production phases. By the time the awaited product arrives, it carries not only its physical value but also an intricate emotional connection, nurturing a distinctive bond between the consumer and the item. Thus, the act of receiving an order metamorphoses beyond transactional boundaries, evolving into a multi-faceted and captivating engagement.

Additionally, the concepts like the **Open Network for Digital Commerce** (ONDC) are leading the way in revolutionizing how commerce operates, particularly in large economies like India. These platforms decentralize commerce, connecting various stakeholders while building a **sense of trust and transparency**. As the internet converges with the metaverse, these platforms are likely to become the bedrock of the new commerce ecosystem. As the metaverse becomes the hub for enhanced shopping experiences, its intertwined relationship with decentralized commerce platforms will drive a new era of connectivity, empowerment, and economic growth.

Connected and continuous services

Ensuring a seamless onboarding experience for consumers is paramount. This involves the setup and installation of products upon their first encounter. In the realm of retail goods, self-setup and intuitive installation processes prove invaluable, or in traditional scenarios, dedicated installation and training services step in. As the adage goes *You never get a second chance to make a first impression - Will Rogers* - a sentiment that rings true, especially in the context of product introduction.

Within the metaverse, products and services would be connected and embedded, ushering in an experience that commences even before the item is physically in hand. The emotional bond users develop with their products is further heightened through an interactive **Out Of the Box Experiences** (OOBE), akin to a game, guiding users or technicians through the assembly and installation process with contextual instructions anchored and overlayed on the products as depicted in *Figure 10.7*. Users find themselves rewarded with a sense of achievement for successful self-setup, enriched with deeper insights into their products. This approach benefits both those inclined towards self-help and experts seeking efficient solutions, making self-installation the preferred and environmentally conscious choice.

Figure 10.7: Step by step assembly a showpiece using smart glass

While the initial impression carries immense weight, the significance of ongoing services cannot be understated. Continuous maintenance is integral, and in the metaverse's connected environment, products will feature auto-maintenance capabilities that operate at specified intervals to ensure optimal performance and minimal physical servicing. Products will proactively raise alerts and facilitate customer care requests if a physical visit is required. Remote troubleshooting and assisted services will become commonplace, with AI continuously monitoring usage patterns and conditions, anticipating potential issues and offering timely resolutions. This proactive approach not only enhances product longevity but also minimizes wastage. Users will often have the ability to perform self-services and repairs, further contributing to economic and environmentally friendly practices.

These combined initial and continuous impressions of products culminate in shaping the product's social brand, a concept further elucidated in the subsequent section on ratings.

Consumption and ratings

Consumption and the subsequent feedback process forms a crucial phase in the lifecycle of products and services. As we acquire and engage with these offerings, their tangible reality aligns with our expectations, representing the convergence of our choices with real experiences. This process is set to undergo significant transformation due to the ongoing digital revolutions and the emergence of the metaverse.

The ongoing digital revolutions have shown the integration of ratings and reviews marking a significant shift in the landscape of online marketplaces and aggregators. Platforms like Amazon, once a mere product showcasing platform, now prioritize consumer feedback, altering the way products are perceived. This shift from traditional commerce to digital platforms has not only empowered consumers but has also built confidence in the significance of ratings, shaping a more reliable and trustworthy shopping experience. Prioritizing consumer satisfaction has become crucial, as negative ratings can profoundly impact a product's fate. Furthermore, the culture of feedback and shared experiences has become pervasive across various aspects of our interactions with products and services. From rating drivers to evaluating medical practitioners, apps, and even colleagues, feedback has become an integral part of our modern lives. This culture improves decision-making, drives improvements through continuous feedback mechanisms, and aids others in making informed choices.

Looking ahead, the metaverse is poised to revolutionize feedback mechanisms by seamlessly integrating ratings and social feedback into the fabric of products. Going beyond traditional ratings, the metaverse will emphasize the importance of contextual information surrounding the feedback. It will leverage its capabilities to capture consumption behaviors and emotions, enabling feedback through expression or brain interfaces without explicit communication. Artificial intelligence systems will play a crucial role in validating and filtering feedback and ratings, enhancing its authenticity and trustworthiness. Simultaneously, the metaverse will redefine consumption habits, introducing novel experiences such as virtual decorations and the ability to engage with products without disrupting others. This inclusivity and diversity will reshape our interactions with products, encouraging us to celebrate, engage, and immerse ourselves in entirely new ways, extending its influence beyond products to revolutionize various facets of our lives.

The interplay between consumption and ratings is undergoing a transformative shift, powered by digital revolutions and the emergence of the metaverse. *Figure 10.8* depicts augmented social feedback of products in metaverse:

Figure 10.8: *Social feedback and reviews on the product in metaverse*

In summary, the metaverse would serve as an extension to digital commerce, ushering in transformative changes ranging from heightened productivity and personalized marketing approaches to reimagined shopping encounters and ground-breaking delivery methods. The integration of the metaverse within digital commerce would not only facilitate seamless and immersive interactions but also emphasize engaging onboarding experiences and continuous services. This integration would reshape the commerce landscape, erase conventional boundaries, and give rise to an era of interconnected and experiential trade that converges the physical and virtual dimensions. This evolution would enhance consumer engagement and fundamentally shift how we perceive, interact with, and consume products and services. As we move forward, the upcoming sections will delve into the concept of digital goods and services as property, exploring their intrinsic value and the virtual economy they underpin.

Digital content as the virtual property

Digital content stands as a pivotal element in the evolving landscape of commerce, significantly shaped by digitization and the internet's transformative influence. The metaverse, an extension of this digital revolution, aims to mirror and simulate all aspects of existence, creating a parallel universe that coexists harmoniously with the real world, either as an alternate realm or as an enhancement of our physical surroundings. Notable strides have been made in embracing digital content as virtual property, including:

- **Digital identity and legal documents:** An integral part of this transition is the concept of digital identity where even legal documents are gaining acceptance in digital form, demonstrated by initiatives like e-Aadhar[23] and platforms such as *DigiLocker*[24] in India. Innovations like *DigiYatra*[25] are simplifying travel experiences through seamless digital solutions.

- **Emergence of digital asset management platforms:** In the realm of physical content which encompasses various creative expressions like art, crafts, photography, and books, the shift to digitization has given rise to platforms such as *Shutterstock*[26] and *Pixabay*[27]. Similar trends are witnessed in diverse content domains, including *Spotify*[28] for music, *YouTube*[29] for video, *Slideshare*[30] for presentations, and *Sketchfab*[31] for 3D and e-book platforms. The advent of generative AI technology, discussed in *Chapter 4, AI Empowering the Metaverse,* both challenges and enhances these content platforms.

- **Transformation of content-based entertainment:** The landscape of content-based entertainment has witnessed substantial transformation with the emergence of **Over-The-Top (OTT)** applications designed for television and mobile devices. This disruption has reshaped traditional TV broadcasting and cable entertainment, aligning content consumption with the preferences of social communities. The rapid rise of web series within a short timeframe further highlights this shift as content dissemination evolves in sync with modern social engagement and media consumption dynamics.

- **Influence of social media content:** The internet's vast array of content is just a click away, creating commercial opportunities for content-based commerce. Individuals have transitioned from content consumers to content creators, influenced by the social media paradigm. Every like, view, and engagement contributes to a digital footprint that increasingly resembles virtual property. This property is harnessed for commerce, enabling individuals to own, sell, collaborate on advertisements, and generate income from their digital creations.

- **Digital identity-linked wallets:** As paperless processes become more prevalent, traditional currency notes have also transitioned to digital forms. Digital identity-linked wallets have replaced physical wallets, facilitating direct transactions between digital wallets. Some wallets have introduced their digital currencies, akin to past credit card reward programs, embraced by digital commerce platforms and payment gateways.

In essence, digital content's evolution into virtual property introduces inventive revenue generation avenues and novel transaction paradigms. The subsequent section will delve into the convergence of these concepts within the metaverse economy, spotlighting how individuals, as both content creators and economic participants, are driving transformative shifts.

The content creator economy

Having established the significance of digital content, it is crucial to recognize its central role within the metaverse. We have already examined the ascent of social platforms and community-driven content creation as well as innovative revenue streams in previous sections and chapters of this book. In *Chapter 6, Decentralization and the Role of Blockchain*, we delved into the emergence of the creator economy, and this section aims to take that exploration to a deeper level in content generation, distribution, ownership and monetization in content economy.

Content generation and tuning

Content generation is a dynamic process that demands both, creativity and the right tools. Over time, technology has introduced digital editing tools for various forms of content, such as text, images, audio, and video. These tools have revolutionized the creative landscape by offering functionalities like undo/redo, erasing, and enhancing visual elements. While much attention has been given to 2D content generation, the metaverse is set to elevate spatial creativity to new heights. Designing in 3D will become seamless, allowing creators to bring their imaginations to life. The metaverse will usher in a new wave of expert creators, supported by advanced infrastructure and an ecosystem that facilitates content creation, hiring, and compensation. Artists like *Anna Zhilyaeva*[32], who excel in 3D art as shown in *Figure 10.9*, will find even more opportunities for immersive expression in the metaverse:

Figure 10.9: A 3D artist creating an immersive art live

Live editing platforms are poised to revolutionize content creation by enabling collaborative design in both, 2D and 3D. As AI comes into play, the boundary between these dimensions will blur, allowing for the conversion of 2D content into immersive 3D experiences, thereby expanding the creative landscape. As discussed in the start of this chapter, real estate itself will undergo a transformation, becoming digital content that populates virtual environments. Existing 3D content creation tools are evolving to seamlessly integrate with live 360°, VR camera[33] and XR devices, thereby enhancing the potential for innovative 3D designs. Generative AI, often seen as a challenge to conventional content creation practices[34], will, in fact, amplify creativity by offering diverse options and novel approaches. For instance, tasks like background removal and object placement within specific environments can now be accomplished within seconds through generative AI support. Refer to *Chapter 4, AI Empowering the Metaverse* for a comprehensive exploration of AI-driven editing tools that can rapidly translate textual descriptions into intricate 3D scenes.

The metaverse will provide tools and services for converting content into multiple formats and optimizing it for various devices. Universal formats will likely emerge to ensure seamless access across different devices, bolstered by new protocols designed for smooth content accessibility. The subsequent section delves into content management, sharing, and ownership, shedding light on how the metaverse's content ecosystem will function.

Content distribution and ownership

After content creation, the process of distribution and ownership unfolds within the content business landscape. This involves generating revenue through content sales, copyright transactions, and sponsored creations. Creators can either be directly compensated or relinquish their ownership rights to buyers, who then utilize these rights across a variety of distribution channels. The rise of the internet has led to the emergence of both formal and informal distribution channels. Among these, social media platforms have emerged as major hubs for content creators and distributors. However, this proliferation has occurred without stringent enforcement of rules and regulations, resulting in copyright violations and challenges related to content ownership and creator recognition.

Addressing these challenges, the metaverse is poised to introduce measures that foster trust and safeguard content authenticity on social platforms. The metaverse's decentralized nature, as elaborated in *Chapter 6, Decentralization and the Role of Blockchain*, plays a pivotal role in creating a secure content distribution framework. Blockchain technology, particularly in the form of **Non-Fungible Tokens (NFTs)**, has emerged as a ground-breaking solution. NFTs, which are unique units of block data, are pivotal components driving the content economy within the metaverse. They allow creators to monetize their distinct digital creations while ensuring transparency and verification of ownership.

The emergence of NFT-based marketplaces like *Cryptopunks*[35], *Hashmasks*[36], *Rarible*[37], *NFTically*[38], and *WazirX*[39] highlights the growing significance of NFTs in content commerce. These marketplaces are witnessing a substantial surge, underscoring the importance of NFTs as tools for monetizing digital content. Moreover, the decentralized nature of the metaverse reinforces the ascent of NFT-based marketplaces. Unlike centralized platforms, the metaverse thrives on community-driven initiatives and open ecosystems. Noteworthy projects like Decentraland and Sandbox are establishing blockchain-based marketplaces, and industry leaders like Samsung are embracing this concept by establishing virtual stores within the metaverse.

As the metaverse evolves, NFTs are anticipated to assume a pivotal role in maintaining content integrity, facilitating secure transactions, and ensuring that content creators receive rightful recognition and compensation. This section explained how the metaverse's landscape of content distribution and ownership is undergoing a transformation to enhance content trust, ownership, and commercial viability. Next we discuss how content consumption would feed the content cycle.

Content consumption and monetization

The essence of social media revolves around its community of content consumers who actively shape interactions by providing views, likes, and engagement. This consumer-driven approach is set to extend its influence into the metaverse, where the relationship between content creators and consumers remains pivotal. In this ecosystem, content creators will finely tune their offerings to align with the desires, feedback, ratings, and behavioral patterns of consumers. The advent of artificial intelligence further amplifies this dynamic, as AI algorithms analyze consumption behaviors to suggest content that resonates deeply with specific communities and target audiences.

Monetization becomes a driving force for both content producers and consumers in the metaverse. Beyond the creators, users themselves are also incentivized to engage actively within platforms such as; for social media, YouTube, Instagram, X and for content marketplaces, *SketchFab*[40], *Shuttrestock*[41] or NFT market place as discussed in the last section, along with gaming platforms like *Roblox*[42]. The **Play-To-Earn**[43] **(P2E)** concept is a demonstration of this shift, as shown in *Figure 10.10*, where individuals are rewarded for their engagement, viewing, and interaction with specific content types. This concept underscores the value attributed to active participation in the metaverse. Moreover, as these solutions clubbed with AI become proficient at assessing the value of assets and content interactions, content monetization will take on new dimensions.

Figure 10.10: *Depiction of a monetization concept for content consumption*

The metamorphosis of content into virtual property stands as a hallmark of the metaverse's influence on digital commerce. We have explored the trajectory of content distribution and ownership, underlining the transformation from traditional copyright practices to the innovative realm of NFTs. It empowers creators to monetize their distinctive digital creations, ensuring provenance and ownership verification. The metaverse would host not only for immersive experiences but also as a revolutionary space for content creators to secure recognition, compensation, and the longevity of their creations.

Conclusion

In conclusion, the exploration of the metaverse economy through the aforementioned sections has provided a comprehensive understanding of its multifaceted dimensions. Beginning with the fundamental concepts of property, value, and commerce, we delved into the innovative ways the metaverse is reshaping these traditional notions. The metaverse's transformative impact on real estate was a focal point, highlighting how virtual properties have become not only an investment but also a platform for immersive experiences and commerce.

The rise of digital commerce emerged as a driving force, facilitated by the seamless integration of metaverse technologies. This integration promises to revolutionize the shopping experience, redefine order delivery mechanisms, and introduce novel paradigms of consumption. Our exploration extended into the realm of digital content, where the conversion of content into virtual property underscored its pivotal role within the metaverse economy. The burgeoning content creator economy, propelled by the advent of NFTs and decentralized platforms, is ushering in a paradigm shift in the recognition, compensation, and participation of creators within a decentralized content landscape.

As the metaverse assumes a central role, it is fundamentally reshaping how we perceive, interact with, and assign value to both tangible and virtual assets. This chapter offered a glimpse into a future where commerce transcends physical confines, where properties transcend geographical borders, and where ingenuity and engagement emerge as potent economic catalysts. The rapid evolution of the metaverse economy underscores its potential to reshape industries, foster novel opportunities, and redefine the very essence of value, property, and commerce within a connected and immersive digital realm.

In the upcoming chapter, our exploration will pivot towards the enterprise facet of the metaverse, elucidating how industries are poised to reap its benefits and usher in transformative change.

Points to remember

Here are some points to remember from this chapter:

- Commerce within the metaverse thrives on the valuation of property items, driving its economic dynamics.
- The metaverse reshapes real estate, integrating 3D design, secure construction, sales, and maintenance services.
- Metaverse technologies seamlessly merge with digital commerce, revolutionizing shopping, delivery, and consumption.
- Digital commerce experiences a surge propelled by metaverse technologies, transcending physical boundaries.
- Digital content's transformation into virtual property underscores its central role in the metaverse economy.
- Content creators find new empowerment through NFTs and decentralized platforms, redefining recognition and rewards.
- The metaverse alters perceptions of assets, ushering commerce into a realm transcending traditional confines.

References

1. **https://www.esri.com/en-us/arcgis/products/arcgis-cityengine/overview**
2. **https://modelur.com/**

3. https://deepxhub.com/
4. https://plainsight.ai/blog/workplace-health-and-safety-computer-vision/
5. https://thinkuldeep.com/post/xr-enabled-home-renovation/# the-need
6. https://paytm.com/
7. https://www.npci.org.in/what-we-do/upi/product-overview
8. https://www.uber.com/in/en/
9. https://www.olacabs.com/
10. https://www.zomato.com/
11. https://www.swiggy.com/
12. https://blinkit.com/
13. https://www.dunzo.com/
14. https://ondc.org/
15. https://www.thenationalnews.com/business/technology/2022/01/12/how-vr-goggles-sooth-cows-and-help-a-turkish-farmer-produce-more-milk/
16. https://thinkuldeep.com/post/extending_reality_with_ar_and_vr-2/# use-case-4-contextual-experiences
17. https://yeppar.com/
18. https://obsessar.com/
19. https://www.youtube.com/watch?v=DAk1aRgLbaQ&t=20s
20. https://thinkuldeep.com/post/future-of-shoping/
21. https://www.eclipsegroup.co.uk/wp-content/uploads/2020/06/The-Impact-of-Augmented-Reality-on-Retail.pdf
22. https://www.raksha-bandhan.com/
23. https://eaadhaar.uidai.gov.in/
24. https://www.digilocker.gov.in/
25. https://www.india.gov.in/spotlight/digi-yatra-new-digital-experience-air-travellers
26. https://www.shutterstock.com/
27. https://pixabay.com/
28. https://open.spotify.com/
29. https://www.youtube.com/

30. **https://www.slideshare.net/**

31. **https://sketchfab.com/**

32 **https://www.youtube.com/@Annadreambrush**

33. **https://in.canon/en/consumer/announces-its-first-virtual-reality-video-production-system/news**

34. **https://thinkuldeep.com/post/generative-ai-for-3d-content-in-xr-and-beyond/**

35. **https://www.larvalabs.com/cryptopunks**

36. **https://www.thehashmasks.com/**

37. **https://rarible.com/**

38. **https://www.nftically.com/**

39. **https://wazirx.com/**

40. **https://sketchfab.com/**

41. **https://www.shutterstock.com/**

42. **https://www.roblox.com/**

43. **https://www.playtoearn.online/**

Join our book's Discord space

Join the book's Discord Workspace for Latest updates, Offers, Tech happenings around the world, New Release and Sessions with the Authors:

https://discord.bpbonline.com

CHAPTER 11
Skilling and Reskilling in the Enterprise Metaverse

Introduction

Embarking on a transformative journey, this chapter delves into the profound impact of the metaverse on the educational and corporate landscape. It commences by emphasizing the importance of continuous skill development and reskilling, illuminating how the metaverse possesses the potential to revolutionize the paradigms of training, onboarding, and educational institutions themselves. As we venture deeper, our exploration takes us through the realm of virtual universities, digital learning resources, interactive educational experiences, and the hands-on cultivation of skills through virtual laboratories and cutting-edge tools. The amalgamation of art, science, and technology within the metaverse becomes a focal point, unveiling its power to redefine creativity and foster interdisciplinary learning.

Our journey further extends to investigating metaverse applications across industries such as automotive, manufacturing, and beyond, casting a spotlight on innovative training methods, remote assistance, dynamic product design, and the optimization of complex industrial processes. In its final stride, the chapter delves into the concept of location-independent workspaces, unveiling the manifold advantages of remote work facilitated by the metaverse. Moreover, a glimpse into the potential future advancements within the dynamic landscape of the enterprise metaverse is provided, underlining its capacity to reshape workspaces, enhance collaboration, and unlock unprecedented avenues for skill acquisition and professional growth.

Structure

In this chapter, we will discuss the following topics:

- Understanding the dynamics of skill development
- Innovating education in the metaverse
- Importance of reskilling in the corporate sphere
- Understanding the enterprise metaverse
- Navigating the landscape of the enterprise metaverse

Objectives

This chapter aims to offer readers insights into how the metaverse is poised to reshape education, training, and onboarding processes, thereby redefining the landscape of skill development. It delves into the fascinating realm of the enterprise metaverse, explaining how the corporate world is both constructing and leveraging the metaverse. Within these pages, readers will learn the use cases of enterprise metaverse, particularly in the context of revamping workspaces, refining human resource dynamics, and optimizing operational processes.

Understanding the dynamics of skill development

Skill development is an innate and continuous process that starts from birth and adapts to our evolving needs. This process is influenced by both our **Intelligence Quotient** (**IQ**) and **Emotional Quotient** (**EQ**). Traditionally, education has followed a gradual trajectory as we mature, with our IQ/EQ levels adjusting in accordance with age and life experiences. As time has progressed, educational systems have undergone transformations, further catalyzed by the advent of digitization. This evolution has touched every aspect of learning and skill development, redefining schooling approaches. Classrooms have transitioned into more experiential environments through the incorporation of digital boards, projectors, and audio systems. Moreover, education has seamlessly merged with remote learning, digital textbooks, curriculum modules, worksheets, and online assignment submissions, driving a profound shift in educational paradigms. This evolution encompasses not only students but also educators, as evidenced by platforms like *Diksha*[1] that facilitate billions of sessions across India. Before delving into the revolutionary impact of the metaverse on this landscape, it is crucial to comprehend the distinct levels within the learning, training, and upskilling journey. The various stages of education are depicted in *Figure 11.1* and explained as follows. These may vary slightly based on geographical and educational system differences.

Figure 11.1: Stages of education and skill development

- **Early childhood education:** This phase focuses on developing a child's fundamental skills and motor abilities through educational games and interactive plays. It aims to teach children effective communication, emotional awareness, and the basics of expressing their needs. Specialized schools catering to children with disabilities are also present within this stage.
- **Primary education:** Following kindergarten, children enter primary and middle school education systems. Here, they are introduced to foundational concepts in subjects like mathematics, science, and arts while also participating in sports activities. The emphasis is on overall growth, and various education boards, recognized on national and international levels, design the curriculum. The primary education phase provides a common curriculum covering diverse areas, including math, science, arts, culture, and physical activities. This period lays the groundwork for their future education.
- **Secondary education:** In this stage of higher education, individuals delve into subjects that interest them or take them toward a career they want to pursue. They select curricula aligned with their preferences, such as medical studies, scientific or engineering fields, commerce, arts, or social and political culture. Schools and institutes are equipped with labs and resources that align with the educational boards they follow. Supporting institutions dedicated to enhancing skills in specialized areas also exist. During secondary or higher secondary education, students develop a strong foundation in their chosen disciplines, preparing them for further professional studies.

- **Professional education:** This phase involves colleges, universities, or institutes offering professional education and granting relevant certificates, degrees, and diplomas. Many corporate and enterprise positions require these credentials as entry criteria. Professional education spans various levels, from undergraduate to postgraduate, adding specialized skills and value. This education equips individuals with the competence to enter a profession or establish their own.

- **Enterprise onboarding:** In this phase, enterprises, whether government, public, or private, with established processes and regulations, onboard new professionals. Onboarding processes differ based on roles, work environments, shifts, working conditions, tools, safety requirements, and more. While some professionals possess requisite skills and experiences, others need specific onboarding. This stage ensures employees are equipped for their roles and acquainted with the organization's operations.

As discussed, the influence of digitization has reshaped the landscape of education and its content. Similarly, the corporate and enterprise sectors have undergone a similar transformation. Traditional methods of training and onboarding are evolving to embrace digitized approaches. The modern workforce is rapidly adopting advanced technologies, and relying on conventional training methods would not be viable in the future.

In earlier chapters of *Part 3-Metaverse: An Opportunity to Extend the Beliefs*, we explored how the metaverse is reshaping consumer perspectives and erasing the boundaries between the physical and virtual realms. By gamifying user experiences and enhancing connectivity and engagement, the metaverse is altering fundamental beliefs. This impact extends even to areas like personal fitness and healthcare. As individuals increasingly integrate metaverse technologies into their lives, the realms of education and enterprise are also undergoing revolutionary changes. The subsequent sections will delve into these transformations in detail.

Innovating education in the metaverse

In the era of digitization, education has undergone a remarkable transformation, with remote and virtual learning becoming practical alternatives, especially in situations where conventional methods fall short. In *Chapter 9, Revolutionizing Fitness and Healthcare,* we explored the metaverse's impact on medical education, underscoring the heightened connectivity it brings and its potential to become an essential tool in influencing EQ and IQ, thereby shaping skill development across various levels, as outlined in the preceding section.

The essence of the metaverse lies in its ability to amplify experiences, and this is particularly pertinent to the realm of education. This section will delve into how the metaverse is reshaping the landscape of learning experiences, describing how education is innovatively evolving to harness the power of metaverse technologies.

Immersive learning experiences

The metaverse introduces the potential for immersive learning experiences that transport individuals into dynamic learning environments, blurring the boundaries between reality and virtuality. These experiences create a sense of presence and engagement that fosters deeper understanding and retention of knowledge. The transformation of traditional educational resources is evident through the digitization of books and papers, which can be enhanced further with **Extended Reality** (**XR**) assets to create interactive and captivating learning materials. For instance, platforms like *Phibonacci*[2], *ePathshala*[3], and *StartAR*[4] showcase how physical books can now come alive with digital content overlayed on them, providing learners with a holistic and enriched educational journey.

Education in the metaverse extends beyond static learning materials. Classrooms become immersive centers where history can be relived through simulated environments, physics experiments can unfold before students' eyes, and complex biological processes or mathematical data representations[5] can be observed and explored easily. The metaverse enables learners to engage with content that may be risky or unfeasible in real-world settings, such as conducting experiments involving fire or chemical reactions. From arts and culture to socio-political education, the metaverse opens up new dimensions of learning for learners of all ages. *Figure 11.2* depicts a smart book with features of experiential learning.

Figure 11.2: *Smart books with experiential learnings*

Gamification takes center stage, transforming learning into an engaging adventure. Whether it is reading books, completing worksheets, submitting assignments, or taking exams, the metaverse's immersive nature ensures that every learning activity becomes an interactive and stimulating experience. **Perception science**[6] can be well experienced using metaverse technologies. Additionally, concepts like **Metaversity**[7] are emerging, reimagining the very structure of educational institutions. In this virtual realm, universities transcend physical limitations, offering entire campuses complete with walkways, labs, sports facilities, and more. The metaverse empowers learners to choose environments that suit their preferences, fostering personalized and effective learning journeys.

The metaverse's capabilities extend to tracking learners' experiences and responses in real-time. Through sensory input and brain interfaces, immersive environments can gauge individual engagement levels and adapt the learning pace to match learners' needs. Teachers also benefit from tools that enable effective and efficient instruction. As e-learning transforms into experiential learning (X-learning), the adoption of immersive educational interactions drives the evolution of both content and individuals within the metaverse, as elaborated in the subsequent section.

Interactive learning experiences

As traditional learning materials transition into digital formats, interactions are seamlessly integrated into educational content through animations, videos, and responsive behaviors. These materials are delivered through a variety of applications, catering to different devices and accessible over the internet. Online learning has evolved to include step-by-step interactive tutorials and instructor-led sessions, fostering engagement and understanding among learners of all ages.

The metaverse elevates interactive learning to new heights by intertwining the virtual and physical realms. Human interaction with the environment takes unprecedented forms, ranging from hand, head, and body gestures to even utilizing eye movements or vocal commands. Innovations like AlterEgo[8] suggest a future where the metaverse becomes an **extension of our minds**, bridging the gap between the internet and our thoughts. This potential fusion could reshape the landscape of learning and skill development. Just as we no longer rely on memorizing multiplication tables due to the ubiquity of calculators, the metaverse will likely shift the focus away from rote learning, placing greater emphasis on leveraging tools and techniques to solve complex human challenges.

Interactions with educational content in the metaverse will undergo a fundamental shift. Learners can comment, ask questions, and engage directly within the context of materials, whether that's a digital book page, a frame in a video, or within a 3D virtual space. Educators and experts can provide immediate responses, leading to dynamic and engaging exchanges. Moreover, these interactions are recorded, capturing the learning journey comprehensively. Upon course completion, relevant notes, highlights, and key takeaways are automatically generated based on individual usage patterns.

The metaverse would offer diverse pathways to achieve degrees and diplomas, accommodating variations in time, effort, and resources invested. Learning experiences within the metaverse can be customized to align with individual needs and capacities. The subsequent section will delve into how this customization caters to a spectrum of learning styles and preferences, fostering an inclusive and adaptable education ecosystem.

Personalized learning experiences

In the data-rich landscape, the integration of AI has revolutionized the market by recognizing patterns and aligning products and services according to customer segments. This principle of personalization finds a profound application in the metaverse, discussed in *Chapter 1, Metaverse-Various Forms and Interpretations*, the metaverse as the internet of metadata and people, promising hyper-personalized experiences. As the metaverse comprehends individuals, their behaviors, and the surrounding environment, this hyper-personalization extends even to the level of individualization.

Figure 11.3: *A classroom in metaverse*

The metaverse would disrupt conventional education methods that uniformly deliver the same content to all students in a class, irrespective of their unique IQ, EQ, or capabilities. This traditional approach does not provide a level playing field, particularly for learners with varying speeds of comprehension. However, the metaverse would transform this paradigm, offering tailored learning experiences to students within the same educational setting. This approach ensures that each student receives an education aligned with their pace and capacity, while teachers gain insights into providing precise attention where needed. *Figure 11.3* depicts personalised experience in a classroom.

As highlighted in *Chapter 9, Revolutionizing Fitness and Healthcare* the metaverse addresses the needs of individuals with disabilities, providing customized experiences to ensure equity and inclusivity. It can assist those with visual or auditory impairments, would serve as a mental support system, or even offer physical support for mobility. It can well act as a translator for those who struggle with language barriers. In this context, learning and skill development are evaluated within an inclusive framework, accommodating diverse needs.

The metaverse incorporates devices with adaptable modes of interaction, personalized to individual preferences. By offering personalized learning experiences tailored to individual needs and interests, the metaverse enhances learning efficiency and effectiveness. This revolution in personalized education signifies a pivotal step forward in reshaping the landscape of skill acquisition and knowledge dissemination.

Collaborative learning experiences

The rapid evolution of social media and the widespread adoption of digital communication platforms have catalyzed a significant transformation in the realm of education and learning. Collaborative learning experiences have surged in popularity, revolutionizing the way people acquire knowledge and skills. This paradigm shift is driven by the ease with which individuals can now share their learning journeys and follow the progress of others. The concept of the metaverse, an interconnected digital universe, holds the promise of further augmenting collaborative learning experiences.

Here are the key transformations:

- **Rise of social learnings hubs:** Social media online platforms serve as hubs where like-minded individuals converge to engage in group learning, foster meaningful interactions, and even discover employment opportunities that align with their expertise. The metaverse would offer personalized services tailored to specific social communities enhance the learning journey. Recommendations, course offerings, and resources would be curated to match the unique preferences and goals of each individual within a collaborative learning network. The motivational aspect of group learning is amplified in the digital realm, as participants engage in discussions, collaborative projects, and interactive activities that foster a strong sense of community.

- **Social profiles as resumes:** The traditional paper-based resume has gradually yielded ground to dynamic digital representations of professional profiles, with LinkedIn emerging as a prominent platform. These digital profiles not only showcase academic achievements and qualifications but also encapsulate an individual's skill set, certifications, and active involvement in volunteer initiatives. This multifaceted approach to self-presentation provides a more comprehensive overview of a person's capabilities, contributing to a holistic understanding of their potential contributions.

- **Metaverse learnings as status symbols:** As connectivity intensifies, individuals become perpetually immersed on the internet. Within this metaverse, learning would not be limited by physical constraints; instead, individuals from diverse backgrounds can coalesce around shared interests and pursuits. Tagging the context that includes people and environment would become norm. The learning modules will be tagged with context to promote social collaboration. Learners would engage with educational content from virtual avatars of experts. The ability to participate in virtual learning environments becomes a status symbol, offering a futuristic dimension to traditional education.

- **Educational events:** In this digitally mediated landscape, educational milestones and events are also undergoing the change. For example, degree distribution ceremonies, once bound to physical auditoriums, are now transitioning into virtual setups, where avatars representing graduates gather to commemorate their achievements[9]. Learning events such as hackathons, competitions, and challenges would be organized to create a healthy and stimulating competitive environment across various domains, spanning from sciences, arts, and commerce to mathematics, research, culture, and sports.

The dawn of the metaverse heralds a new era of collaborative learning. The upcoming section will delve into the transformative impact of the metaverse on traditional notions of location and presence, redefining the way people interact with their environments and with each other.

Global learning experiences

The pervasive influence of the internet has significantly altered numerous aspects of life, including education and skill development. With the advent of online platforms, individuals now possess the capability to access learning content from across the globe. However, the concept of the metaverse, defined as the evolution of the internet, is poised to elevate this transformation even further. The metaverse seeks to transcend geographical boundaries, making education universally accessible regardless of one's location, region, religion, caste, culture, language, or race.

The propagation of community-driven and collaborative learning has expanded on a global scale. The imminent rise of decentralized architecture promises to serve the vast global audience of the metaverse with a delicate balance between universal appeal and localized optimization. The metaverse intends to aggregate diverse learning content, educators, and providers spanning across the globe. Esteemed educational institutions, renowned schools, and universities are anticipated to extend their offerings beyond physical borders, enabling education without the necessity of relocating to specific locations. The metaverse aims to discourage the need for individuals to physically travel for education, as educational institutions reach out to learners rather than the other way around. This transformative shift will not only facilitate shared learning experiences but also enable individuals to gain insights into different cultures, fostering connections and greater cross-cultural understanding, as depicted in *Figure 11.4*:

***Figure 11.4:** Depiction of global learning experience in metaverse*

Artificial Intelligence (AI) is expected to play a crucial role in shaping these global learning experiences. By analysing user preferences, AI systems can align learners with content that best suits their individual needs and aspirations. As people interact in this dynamic digital realm, they may establish virtual boundaries that are not tied to specific countries or regions. However, as with any technological advancement, challenges and potential biases might emerge. The equitable distribution of resources, the prevention of bias, and the promotion of inclusivity will be critical considerations as the metaverse evolves.

Fundamentally, the evolution of education within the metaverse encapsulates a wide array of revolutionary strategies. It encompasses immersive engagements that fully envelop learners in dynamic surroundings, interactive experiences that actively involve them, personalized journeys meticulously customized to individual requirements, collaborative initiatives that nurture collective inspiration, and worldwide endeavors that transcend geographical confines, uniting learners and experts worldwide. Together, these advancements reshape the educational landscape, heralding an era where learning becomes dynamic, interconnected, and limitless. Subsequently, our exploration will pivot towards the corporate and enterprise dimensions of education within the metaverse, shedding light on its ongoing evolution.

Importance of reskilling in the corporate sphere

Until now, our exploration of the metaverse has primarily delved into its impact on the consumer side of education, encompassing elementary education through schools and extending to professional training within institutions and universities. As we transition into this section and the subsequent ones, our focus will shift towards the corporate domain: how enterprises train and onboard individuals, preparing them for their respective industries. In subsequent sections, we will also delve into how the metaverse influences this sphere, and build **the enterprise metaverse**.

In the face of the digital revolution and the accelerated pace of product development and consumption, the significance of a skilled and adaptable workforce cannot be overstated. The process of skilling and reskilling must evolve in tandem with the changing times. Industry faces the challenge of addressing the shortage of skilled workers and the need to effectively onboard new talent with the right skills. According to the *Global Talent Crunch*[10] report, the retirements of 10,000 baby boomers each day for the next 19 years, expedited by the impact of Covid-19, have further exacerbated these challenges. By 2023, 75% of the global workforce will comprise millennials, rendering traditional onboarding and training methods inadequate for this generation. Furthermore, as enterprises become more complex, the necessity of collaborating with machines and AI emerges, compounded by complicated workforce safety compliance requirements.

Herein lies an opportunity for onboarding and training processes, coupled with remote collaboration within the metaverse, to ease up some of these challenges and enhance operational efficiency. The future of work and the workforce are poised to be more metaverse-ready. Government-led initiatives such as community and open education portals like *Swayam*[11] promotes self-learning scale the industrial education. Within the metaverse, the learning experiences, discussed in the preceding section, will also transform the landscape of skilling and reskilling for enterprises.

In this technologically empowered metaverse, AI-driven capabilities will play a pivotal role. Precise recommendations for required training, optimal duration, contextual on-the-job guidance, co-working harmoniously with machines, and remotely controlling machinery are poised to become reality as depicted in *Figure 11.5*. Individuals will be further empowered by technology to make quicker, informed decisions. They will be able to record their work, rewind, and rectify errors in their tasks. While concerns abound regarding technology potentially displacing human roles and jobs, it is increasingly evident that those adept at utilizing technology will replace those who are not. Therefore, it is imperative for both industries and the workforce to embrace upskilling in technology and collaborate seamlessly with technology to ensure mutual growth and progress.

Figure 11.5: Working with smart machines and robots

Understanding the enterprise metaverse

While our discussions thus far have delved into the realms of the consumer metaverse, encompassing entertainment, gaming, and evolving social interactions, enterprises have unique needs that must be addressed. The metaverse, when tailored to meet these distinctive requirements, takes on a distinct identity known as **the enterprise metaverse.** Industry giants such as *Lenovo*[12], *Qualcomm*[13], *Pico*[14] and more are actively developing devices and metaverse solutions specifically designed to cater to the intricate demands of enterprises.

The journey towards establishing an enterprise metaverse begins with a foundation built on consumer adoption and experiences. Even in the context of enterprise, the key tenets of consumer adaptation and experience remain paramount. However, the enterprise metaverse introduces a set of considerations that are central to its successful implementation and integration.

Key considerations for enterprise metaverse:

- **Enterprise integration:** Metaverse solutions must seamlessly integrate with a multitude of enterprise systems responsible for managing assets, personnel, policies, compliance, and regulations. Features such as single sign-on, which allows access to resources based on permissions and roles, are imperative.
- **Enterprise content and assets management:** Enterprise metaverse solutions should facilitate the end-to-end management of enterprise content, from creation

and publication to distribution and consumption. This interconnectedness ensures collaboration across all organizational departments, streamlining processes from design and development to quality assurance, production, sales, and support.

- **Training and onboarding:** Effective onboarding and training are pivotal requirements for enterprises. The enterprise metaverse must support dynamic task-based guided workflows that self-guide and gauge training effectiveness, with simulations playing a crucial role.
- **Quality assurance and compliance:** Industries often require complex compliance setups, which the metaverse, in conjunction with computer vision technology, can automate and optimize. Quality assurance and safety compliance are vital considerations.
- **Location-agnostic workspace:** The need for a location-agnostic workforce is on the rise in various industries. Common use cases include remote experts assisting from distant locations.
- **Assisted services:** Enterprises seek assistance services that provide workers with the right information to make informed decisions. Real-time guidance and information access are integral to these services.
- **Workforce health and safety:** Maintaining a healthy workforce is paramount for business success. Monitoring workforce well-being, including mental health, and providing adequate rest and assurance before work shifts, are an essential aspect of the enterprise metaverse. Safety and compliance are also central concerns.

As we proceed, we will witness the enterprise metaverse in action across various industries, observing how it revolutionizes processes, enhances efficiency, and reshapes the way enterprises operate in this ever-evolving digital landscape.

Navigating the landscape of the enterprise metaverse

In an era where technology is evolving at an unprecedented pace, enterprises find themselves on the cusp of a transformative revolution. The requirements from infrastructure, work environments, workforce skills, and even environmental considerations are swiftly adapting to the changing technological landscape. With the advent of the next internet, characterized by ultra-high-speed networks, quantum computing chips, in-device processing, and devices powered by sustainable natural resources, coupled with the omnipresence of AI, the corporate world is set for a profound change.

The enterprise metaverse tends to impact all major industries, especially the ones with highly complex processes and practices. In this section, we will explore how the enterprise metaverse is poised to reshape some of these complex industries and domains. We have already covered the education industry in this chapter. Next, we will navigate this ever-evolving landscape for other industries and uncover the opportunities, challenges, and profound impacts that the enterprise metaverse holds for businesses across the globe.

Extending the reality of automotive and manufacturing

The automotive and manufacturing industries, where vehicles are designed, manufactured, and serviced, are undergoing a profound transformation within the enterprise metaverse. These sectors have historically been at the forefront of technological innovation, with assembly lines and factory setups evolving through various industrial revolutions. While robotics and automation have taken center stage for repetitive tasks, human workers continue to be indispensable to these industries. In recent years, significant shifts have occurred to adapt to emerging technologies, enabling humans to co-work seamlessly with machines and necessitating the establishment of distributed factories to tap into skilled resources worldwide. Traditional, outdated training and onboarding methods have already been replaced by digitalized counterparts.

In this context, modern enterprises face the intricate challenge of managing multiple layers of complexity across thousands of assets, workflows, and processes. There is virtually zero tolerance for issues that interrupt operations, compromise profitability, or jeopardize worker safety.

Metaverse technologies offer innovative solutions in several critical ways:[15]

- **Cost effective training and onboarding:** Traditional training methods, relying on books, rote memorization, rudimentary mock-ups, and presentations, struggle to keep pace with the complexities of modern enterprises and meet the evolution needed. Skilled individuals have limited time to train others or reskill themselves, leading to interruptions and increased costs. Metaverse technologies brings the contextual instructions on the job, immersive visualization, accelerating learning and improving decision-making and reduce out of the context interruptions. It enables more efficient, monitored, tracked, and repeatable training. Boeing assembly facility have measured 35% improvement using metaverse.[16]

- **Faster time to market, and product customizations:** Product design and development in these industries are inherently complex and time-consuming. Autonomous vehicle and machines are evolving faster, development of these requires substantial computing resources, time, and cost. Testing such technology in physical environments can be both expensive and risky. Metaverse technologies expedite product design and development, with collaborative and automation simulated environment[17], thus faster to market, and reduced martials wastage. Optimal results are achieved first in the metaverse before validation on real machines and environment. In addition, metaverse technologies also facilitate rapid prototyping, incorporating real-time user feedback to deliver tailored products efficiently. *Figure 11.6* depicts designing a car in metaverse:

Figure 11.6: *Collaborative car designing in the metaverse*

- **Extended sales experiences:** Selling complex products, such as high-end vehicles or remote medical operating theatre equipment, can be challenging without the ability for customers to *try before buy*. Creating immersive experiences through the metaverse simplifies the sales process and boosts conversion rates. Customers can visualize product options in real-time, saving costs and aiding informed decision-making. This approach also creates opportunities for cross-selling accessories, supplies, and supporting products. *TechMVerse*[18], *Nexaverse*[19], and *Arenaverse*[20] are some examples in this direction.

- **Location agnostic expertise and service:** The shortage of skilled workers can significantly impact productivity and safety, leading to costly downtime and hazardous incidents. As experienced employees retire, replacing their knowledge becomes increasingly challenging and expensive. Metaverse technologies offer novel ways to navigate operational complexity and mitigate costs and risks. For instance, *General Electric* saved $1.6 billion using digital twins for remote turbine monitoring[21]. Many are already utilizing evolving metaverse technologies to enhance employee safety, reduce errors, and minimize downtime.

The factory of the future is poised to give rise to the industrial or enterprise-focused metaverse, where factories themselves become metaverse entities, and vehicles or products transform into metaverse devices, ushering in a new era of efficiency and innovation.

Exploring beyond earth and beneath the seas

Unearthing resources, whether on Earth, in the depths of the ocean, or beyond our planet, has always been a formidable challenge. These frontiers are characterized by the unknown, where unpredictability lurks at every turn. Those venturing into these domains require extensive training and compliance with the highest safety standards, as any misstep in these unpredictable environments can have fatal consequences. Extensive trials and meticulous preparations precede any actual actions.

Take, for instance, India's successful landing of *Chandrayaan-3*[22] on the moon, a remarkable achievement that required rigorous research and practice. Multiple landing trials were conducted, with each error analyzed and corrected step by step. Some lessons were learned at the cost of entire missions, while others could be captured and refined within simulated or mock environments.

Metaverse technology is poised to revolutionize this realm. Imagine onboard 3D scanners creating a fully immersive, real-time environment in distant, unpredictable terrains. This environment could also be experienced and tested on virtual humans, accounting for factors like varying gravity and other unique conditions. In the metaverse, AI could further enhance the realism of these simulations, potentially saving valuable time and resources by reducing the need for extensive trials. Drones, equipped with onboarded flight capabilities, could navigate these uncharted territories, performing actions remotely and with precision.

Training and onboarding within these simulated environments would be far more accessible and dynamic than replicating physical environments. As the world races to explore uncharted territories, whether on Earth, beneath the seas, or in the vastness of space, the expansion of the metaverse is poised to be even more monumental than anticipated.

Revolutionizing scientific discovery and precision services

Scientific research and discovery need highly precise engineering and manufacturing practices, and environmental conditions like temperature, moisture, lighting conditions, airflow, dust, or hygiene conditions can have a big impact. Examples of such industries are nano and quantum chip manufacturing, drug discovery, bio-organ implant development, brain implants, heart implants, farming and plant research, atomic science, metal and material, chemical reactions, and radiation industry inventions.

These high-accuracy industries need involved training and onboarding, as well as stringent safety requirements. People work in specific routines and set ways of working. They need to be ready for any negative consciences for experiments. Metaverse technologies aim to improve training and onboarding and are poised to reduce experimentation cycles; for example, generative AI would help in drug discovery, while XR would help visualize complex concepts graphically and simulate some experiments. The work environments would be fitted with metaverse technologies, which provide high-quality depth and density sensors, build digital twins in real time, and monitor for any unwanted situations.

Warn about changing situations like moisture, temperature, chemical, bacterial, or radiation presence, and cease areas that are not favorable for living beings. It would keep monitoring people's actions, warn against any undesired ones, and provide on-demand training and support. Automatic assistance from the environment and wearables like smart glass and smart PPE kits would revolutionize this area in great ways, as depicted in *Figure 11.7*:

Figure 11.7: *Depiction of a scientific research lab in the metaverse*

People will be able to work remotely in such an environment, thereby letting robots and machines take over, while humans focus on actual inventions and decision-making.

Enhancing disaster response and recovery

Training and onboarding for disaster response departments, whether it is for fire, flood, earthquakes, or other crises like cloud bursts, radiation leaks, or gas emergencies, has always been a challenging endeavor. These situations are inherently difficult to replicate in training scenarios, as they often involve unpredictability and real-time decision-making. While the advent of the internet, satellite communication, and digitization has improved training to some extent, there remains a significant gap between training environments and the chaotic reality of disaster response.

However, the metaverse holds the promise of strengthening disaster management in unprecedented ways. It empowers support teams with on-demand instructions and remote guidance, revolutionizing the way they prepare for and respond to disasters. Before deploying personnel into dangerous situations, metaverse technology could dispatch 3D scanner-equipped drones to survey the area. Using 3D satellite imagery it can create highly accurate simulations of the disaster environment. These simulations can be used to plan disaster responses that are not only faster but also safer and more effective. *Figure 11.8* shows fire training in a simulated environment of the metaverse:

Figure 11.8: Depiction of fire training in a simulated environment.

Furthermore, AI tools within the metaverse can provide detailed analyses of the damages inflicted by the disaster, including structural assessments affected by environmental conditions. This data can be instrumental in developing precise disaster recovery strategies, ensuring a more efficient and coordinated response from the authorities. The metaverse, with its immersive and data-driven capabilities, is set to redefine disaster management, making it more effective, efficient, and ultimately saving more lives.

Advancing investigations and analysis

The fields of law enforcement, police work, and forensic science play pivotal roles in maintaining law and order in society. Technology has become a crucial tool in this endeavor, with surveillance systems and visual monitoring aiding in crime prevention and resolution. The justice system relies heavily on concrete evidence and meticulous investigations to build trust and make informed decisions. Traditionally, investigation agencies recreate crime scenes and bring suspects to these locations to document intricate details, comparing imagination with reality to uncover the truth.

The metaverse promises to revolutionize these complex domains by facilitating the recreation of crime scenes and exploring various investigative possibilities through AI and immersive XR environments. This technological leap enables investigators to substantiate their findings with concrete evidence. Forensic experts, like *Gourav Ostwal*[23] explain that metaverse technologies, such as AR/VR, can virtually seal crime scenes, evidence numbering, determine the direction of blood droplets, trace bullet trajectories, identify firearm types, and calculate the distance between victims and perpetrators during the crime. By reducing the physical visits required from forensic experts and investigating officers, metaverse technologies expedite the investigation process and contribute to a swifter justice system. *Figure 11.9* shows a crime scene recreated in the metaverse:

Figure 11.9: *Crime scene recreation in the metaverse*

Generative AI in the metaverse further enhances this capability by recreating various possibilities of crime scenes within the metaverse. For example, car crash / accident analysis using 3D scans can re-create the accident scene with accuracy helping with insurance claims and the judicial trials. It allows judges and court officials to immerse themselves in these environments, gaining a deeper understanding of the events and their accuracy.

The metaverse's inherent connectivity, facilitated by its global network of users, their social identifies connected with detectable biometrics, vehicles, and interconnected devices, ensures that data is readily available. This makes it increasingly challenging for traditional, basic crimes to go undetected.

However, the misuse of technology poses a significant concern for the future, a topic we will delve into in the next part of this book. The metaverse, while offering immense potential for improving investigations and analysis, also presents novel challenges that must be addressed as it continues to evolve.

Empowering security forces and the military

The realm of security forces and military is undeniably complex, responsible for upholding the sovereignty of nations, protecting communities, and ensuring peace through force. While some view the tech-driven advancements in this domain with controversy, it's an indisputable fact that armed forces worldwide are evolving and leveraging technology to enhance their capabilities and capacities. The arms industry itself has become a parallel economy, producing a wide array of sophisticated weaponry.

This evolution extends to the equipment used by security forces, with heavy machinery now equipped with night vision capabilities, remote control functionality, and advanced monitoring systems. Additionally, the integration of drones and robotics has become increasingly prevalent. Metaverse technologies are poised to play a pivotal role in the future of armed forces and security operations, offering extended vision capabilities, heightened safety measures, enhanced environmental awareness, and the ability to remotely control and strategize for future missions. The weaponry would be tested in metaverse well before it would be produced, as depicted in *Figure 11.10*:

Figure 11.10: *Weapon trials in the metaverse*

It is essential to recognize that security forces not only safeguard borders but also contribute significantly to disaster management and peacekeeping efforts. While there are concerns about overreliance on technology, the trajectory of our future suggests that we will be deeply entrenched in the metaverse. Internet access will become an essential part of daily life, and securing cyberspace will be a top priority for security forces. The metaverse itself will become a powerful tool, with its responsible and ethical use being a matter of paramount importance.

In essence, the enterprise metaverse spans multiple industries, offering transformative opportunities and challenges. It extends the reality in automotive and manufacturing, explores uncharted territories on Earth and beneath the seas, revolutionizes scientific research and precision services, enhances disaster response, advances investigations and analysis, and empowers security forces. While it promises optimization, safety, and efficiency, it also requires responsible navigation to address the evolving landscape's unique challenges and responsibilities.

Conclusion

In this chapter, we embarked on a journey through the ever-evolving landscape of skill development, education, and training and onboarding in the enterprise metaverse. We began by understanding the intricate dynamics of skill development in an era where the metaverse is poised to reshape how we learn and adapt. We explored the innovative possibilities within education, from immersive experiences that transport learners to new realms to personalized pathways tailored to individual needs. We delved into the corporate sphere, recognizing the paramount importance of reskilling in a world where technology transforms industries at an unprecedented pace.

The enterprise metaverse, a convergence of virtual and real worlds of industries, presented us with opportunities and challenges while managing the enterprise complexity. From extending the capabilities of the automotive and manufacturing sectors to venturing beyond Earth's boundaries and beneath its seas, from revolutionizing scientific research and precision services to enhancing disaster response and advancing investigations and analysis, the metaverse offers transformative potential.

However, *with great power comes great responsibility*. The metaverse necessitates a thoughtful and responsible approach, especially as it empowers security forces and the military and can go into the hands of criminal minds. Navigating this dynamic landscape requires vigilance, ethical considerations, and a deep understanding of how technology can be harnessed for the greater good while mitigating its potential misuse.

As we conclude this chapter, we stand at the threshold of a new era, one where the metaverse, education, and industry converge. The path ahead is filled with opportunities to shape the future, enhance our capabilities, and push the boundaries of what is possible. Yet, it is a path that requires wisdom and ethical stewardship to ensure that the enterprise metaverse serves humanity's best interests, driving progress, innovation, and security in equal measure. In the chapters to come, we will delve even deeper into this promising yet challenging landscape, exploring the metaverse's impact on society, ethics, and the broader implications for our world.

In this *Part 3 - Metaverse: An Opportunity to Extend the Beliefs*, we delved into the boundless potential of the metaverse, a virtual realm that shattered boundaries and redefined our interactions and experiences. Here are the key highlights:

- **3D Design and visualization:** The metaverse offered opportunities for advanced 3D design and visualization, enabling us to interact with virtual products and environments with unprecedented realism. Metaverse technologies enhanced our ability to explore and manipulate virtual objects.

- **Breaking down physical constraints:** The metaverse transformed the way we worked, erasing the limitations of physical locations and allowing for virtual presence. This shift has redefined gaming and entertainment through metaverse applications.

- **Enhancing connectivity:** Remote collaboration and communication tools reduced the necessity for physical travel as virtual interactions gained prominence. We delved into the ways the metaverse connected and engaged people across distances.

- **Transformation in healthcare and fitness:** We showcased the metaverse's impact on fitness, sports, and healthcare, where it introduced innovative approaches to well-being and treatment.
- **Metaverse economy:** We explored how the metaverse economy was revolutionizing sectors like retail, X-commerce, real estate, and content creation, providing fresh perspectives on economic activities.
- **Education transformation:** Education and learning were significantly transformed within the metaverse, offering immersive classrooms, interactive content, simulations, and virtual field trips. We highlighted the evolution of education in this dynamic environment.
- **A paradigm shift:** The metaverse represented more than just a concept; it is a paradigm shift in the internet's evolution. It would challenge conventional beliefs and encouraged us to extend our thinking beyond the boundaries of the physical world, presenting innovative ways not just to survive but to thrive.

In this part, we explored the diverse ways in which the metaverse has reshaped our world, pushing the boundaries of what was once deemed possible. It invited us to reimagine our interactions, work, learning, and lifestyles within a new digital frontier.

In the next part, we will delve into the critical aspects of the metaverse that raise concerns. Additionally, we will examine various ethical considerations that must be addressed to construct a responsible metaverse, one that fosters thriving and responsible engagement.

Points to remember

Here are some points to remember from this chapter:

- Skill development is evolving rapidly, influenced by the rise of the metaverse and digital transformation.
- The metaverse is poised to revolutionize education, offering immersive, interactive, personalized, collaborative, and global learning experiences.
- Reskilling in the corporate sphere is crucial as industries transform rapidly due to technology.
- The enterprise metaverse extends its influence across various complex industries, from automotive and manufacturing to scientific research and security.
- The enterprise metaverse presents opportunities for optimizing costs, enhancing safety, and transforming security forces.
- Responsible navigation of the enterprise metaverse is essential to harness its potential for the greater good while addressing ethical concerns.

References

1. https://diksha.gov.in/
2. https://phibonacci.com/
3. https://epathshala.nic.in/
4. https://www.startar.co/product/startar-smartbooks-pack/
5. https://www.linkedin.com/posts/fuadd_lifeofkristenc-ai-ar-ugcPost-7090352668094644225-AP8m/
6. https://japan--forward-com.cdn.ampproject.org/c/s/japan-forward.com/how-augmented-reality-can-make-objects-seem-heavier/amp/
7. https://themetaversity.app/
8. https://www.media.mit.edu/projects/alterego/overview/
9. https://www.youtube.com/watch?v=y3Y10ypvm-s
10. https://www.kornferry.com/content/dam/kornferry/docs/pdfs/KF-Future-of-Work-Talent-Crunch-Report.pdf
11. https://swayam.gov.in/
12. https://news.lenovo.com/thinkreality-vrx-road-to-mixed-reality-enterprise-metaverse/
13. https://www.qualcomm.com/products/technology/metaverse
14. https://business.picoxr.com/gb/industryFunction
15. https://thinkuldeep.com/post/managing-enterprise-complexity-xr/
16. https://hbr.org/2017/11/why-every-organization-needs-an-augmented-reality-strategy
17. https://thinkuldeep.com/post/training-autonomous-vehicles-in-xr/
18. https://www.techmahindra.com/en-in/techm-unveils-techmverse/
19. https://nexaverse.nexaexperience.com/
20. https://arenaverse.marutisuzuki.com/
21. https://www.ge.com/digital/industrial-managed-services-remote-monitoring-for-iiot/
22. https://www.isro.gov.in/Chandrayaan3_Details.html
23. https://medium.com/xrpractices/ar-vr-future-of-forensic-science-crime-scene-investigation-55605d0b3b8a

Part - 4
Metaverse: The Concerning Part

This part of the book dives deep into the concerns that accompany the emergence of the metaverse and its profound impact on humanity. As the metaverse continues to integrate our digital identities and metadata with the physical world, our exposure and vulnerability become more apparent. We will explore the mind-blowing impacts of the metaverse on various aspects of society, from social dynamics to mental well-being. *Chapter 12, Identity Preservation and Privacy Protection* will delve into the concerns arising from multiple societal identities and the challenges of safeguarding one's identity in an environment as exposed as the metaverse. We will also scrutinize the legal complexities associated with the metaverse, including matters related to intellectual property rights and jurisdictional challenges. In a way, we will touch on the management of law-and-order issues in this transformative digital realm.

Additionally, we will examine the critical sustainability aspects of the metaverse in *Chapter 13, Metaverse and Sustainability*, addressing its environmental consequences and emphasizing the need for responsible technological development. Awareness of these concerns is as vital as embracing the technology itself. Nothing comes without a cost, whether to the environment, society, or humanity. Moreover, striking a balance between extracting the benefits and preserving the natural equilibrium is of utmost importance for our collective survival.

In essence, this part offers a comprehensive exploration of the intricate ethical and societal considerations that accompany the metaverse's ascent. While the metaverse promises to redefine many aspects of our lives, ensuring it becomes a responsible metaverse is a shared responsibility that we must collectively embrace.

CHAPTER 12
Identity Preservation and Privacy Protection

Introduction

The chapter delves into critical aspects of identity preservation, privacy protection, and mitigation of the potential impacts of the metaverse. It begins by emphasizing the importance of preserving identity in the metaverse and explores the risks associated with identity theft and impersonation. It examines the consequences of compromised identities on individuals and society as a whole. We will learn about the implications of unregulated privacy in the metaverse and highlights the significance of establishing a legal framework to address these concerns. Furthermore, the highly impressive impacts of the metaverse are explored, including its influence on emotions, memory, and societal dynamics, and the potential risks associated with manipulation. This chapter addresses the need to mitigate these risks and ensure trust in metaverse environments. Ethical considerations and responsible usage are emphasized, along with the importance of partnerships and collaborations to create a safer and more responsible metaverse.

Structure

In this chapter, we will discuss the following topics:

- Importance of identity
- Identity preservation challenges in the metaverse

- Significance of privacy in social context
- Implications of unregulated privacy in the metaverse
- Prioritizing safety, security, and ethics in the metaverse

Objectives

The objective of this chapter is to raise readers' awareness regarding the inherent challenges and side effects in the metaverse. It serves as an important reminder that as the metaverse reshapes our beliefs and creates new possibilities, it is not without its drawbacks. Readers will gain insights into the pressing concerns related to safeguarding identity and privacy within the metaverse. By understanding these issues, they can navigate this digital landscape more safely and effectively.

Importance of identity

The concept of identity is fundamental to our existence and how we interact with the world around us. It encompasses a wide range of factors, from our physical attributes and sensory experiences to the societal and environmental influences that shape us. Identity is something that begins even before our birth, and continues to evolve throughout our lives, heavily influenced by the metadata of our existence. *Chapter 2, Metaverse-Various Forms and Interpretations* defined the metaverse as the internet of this metadata. Our identity is also tied to the assets we possess, the societies we belong to, and the cultural norms we follow. Throughout human history, and certainly in the present and future, the quest for identity has been a driving force behind motivation, conflicts, and more.

In a social context, identity holds immense significance, to the extent that many individuals can become highly vulnerable if their identity is threatened. Safeguarding one's identity is of utmost importance, as it represents a culmination of years of personal development, experiences, and emotional investment. With the ongoing digital age, our identities are transitioning into digital formats. We no longer rely solely on physical, paper-based legal identities; instead, our digital personas are becoming increasingly vital. Storing and managing identity information in digital lockers[1] is a commonplace practice.

With the emergence of the metaverse, identities will assume new dimensions. Individuals may possess multiple identities tailored for different purposes or specific groups of people. The vast amount of data interconnected with us will automatically generate artificial identities in the digital realm. As we become more artificially connected within the metaverse, the exchange of data will reach unprecedented levels, potentially extending to the integration of our thoughts and experiences. *Chapter 8, Connecting and Engaging in the Metaverse,* provides insights into the formation of social identities in this digital landscape. In essence, the complex network of identities will underpin the identities of the future, presenting unique challenges for identity protection. The design of the metaverse will need to account for these complexities.

Identity preservation challenges in the metaverse

The preservation of identity in the metaverse presents a significant challenge, given its critical importance in our social lives. We have already begun the process of digitizing our legal identities, aiming to secure them against duplication and impersonation. However, as technology evolves, it exposes new dimensions of our data that may not currently seem concerning but could become instrumental in shaping our identities in the future. Factors such as our preferences, online activities, and social connections—all publicly available—could be used to construct a comprehensive digital identity. The metaverse introduces several key challenges that must be addressed to safeguard these identities:

- **Multiple identities in the metaverse:** The metaverse is likely to give rise to multiple virtual identities based on our interests and activities. These sub-identities will form a complex network, making identity management a daunting task. Keeping track of which avatar has access to what platforms and what permissions will require innovative solutions. Just as managing numerous passwords can be cumbersome, managing these multiple identities efficiently will be crucial. The metaverse needs to provide tools and mechanisms for users to manage, monitor, and secure these identities proactively, helping to prevent any misuse.
- **Risk of identity theft and impersonation:** Identity theft and impersonation are common challenges in the age of social media. With the metaverse, the risk becomes even more substantial. Consider an incident where someone impersonated another user's identity on a platform and began contacting friends and family, potentially leading to financial fraud. As the metaverse adds things like 3D avatars simulating our expression, and voice to our identities, it makes it easier for bad actors to closely observe and pretend to be someone else. Replicating a similar-looking identity will not be a daunting task, whereas distinguishing between an impersonated and an original identity will become increasingly difficult. To combat this, the metaverse must implement robust solutions to make identity theft challenging. The creation of avatars and their use in forming identities needs to be legally regulated. Verification mechanisms should be established to quickly identify whether an identity is verified. Further, public awareness campaigns will

be essential in safeguarding these identities. *Figure 12.1* depicts impersonation of identities in the metaverse:

***Figure 12.1:** Depicts impersonation of identity in the metaverse*

- **Consequences of compromised identities:** The consequences of compromised identities in the metaverse can be severe and far-reaching. It goes beyond a mere security breach, opening gates to unimaginable vulnerabilities. In the metaverse, a compromised identity is equivalent to challenging an individual's existence. All our data, whether public or private, becomes at risk. The implications for social and mental health are profound. Compromised identities can lead to irreversible damage to one's image, work, earnings, and even survival. In the upcoming sections, we will discuss privacy concerns that resulted from compromised identities. All these have a cascading effect on privacy and confidentiality, breaking trust in people, systems, processes, and environments, and potentially may lead to social isolation, depression and more.

Preserving identity in the metaverse is not just a technological challenge but also a societal and ethical one. Addressing these challenges will require a collective effort to ensure that individuals can navigate the metaverse securely and with confidence in their identities.

Significance of privacy in social context

Privacy holds profound significance in various contexts of social living, extending far beyond data protection. It encompasses a fundamental human right that every individual deserves. Privacy manifests itself in different forms, ranging from bodily autonomy and personal thoughts to expressions, associations, data, and the communication of that data. In the digital era, social rights regarding privacy become increasingly complex, varying between different countries and societies. The social landscape of the digital age is interwoven with people and data. The complex networks of this data, and privacy concerns can be categorized as follows:

- **People privacy:** People have the right to navigate the internet freely, choosing the type of information they are exposed to and wish to engage with. No one should be compelled to encounter unwanted information or take actions based on it. Common examples of privacy infringement in this category include unwanted advertisements, unsolicited emails, and intrusive calls.
- **Data privacy:** Individuals should possess the rights to control how and where their associated metadata is collected and used. Legal frameworks like **General Data Protection Regulation** (GDPR) and others[2] have been introduced to define and uphold data privacy laws. Users should be able to categorize their data as personal, private, or public, ensuring its safe handling and usage.
- **Network privacy:** Network privacy is a fundamental right which ensures that data sent over networks like the Internet reaches its intended recipient securely, without unauthorized access and violation of the data's integrity. *Figure 12.2* depicts the complex data network connected with people:

***Figure 12.2:** Relation between people, data and network*

As we immerse ourselves in the metaverse, the significance of these digital privacy aspects grows even more critical. Data is exploding at an unprecedented rate, blurring the lines between what is public and what is private. Generative AI models are built upon vast amounts of publicly available data, potentially allowing them to make predictions about individuals, and generate social bias around them. In the metaverse, as the distinction between physical and virtual realms becomes increasingly blurred, multiple layers of virtual privacy for virtual identity or data come into existence and the digital privacy standards of today would fall short in the future.

The metaverse is evolving rapidly, often with insufficient focus on these privacy aspects, which could have far-reaching implications. The next section delves deeper into these emerging privacy challenges within the metaverse, shedding light on the complexities and consequences of this evolving digital landscape.

Implications of unregulated privacy in the metaverse

The metaverse, a digital realm is shaped by the rapid advancement of diverse technologies discussed in *Part 2, Metaverse: a result of technological evolutions*. However, amidst this rapid innovation, the vital aspect of privacy protection is at times relegated to a secondary position, occasionally overshadowed by the drive for widespread adoption.

As we delve deeper into the consequences of this relatively unregulated approach to privacy within the metaverse, we encounter a complex web of challenges. These challenges possess profound impacts on the adoption of the metaverse and the quality of life within this digital domain. Upcoming sections will cover some of them.

Infringement of natural people privacy

The evolution of technology, from calculators to smartphones, has gradually shifted our reliance on mental arithmetic and memory. Basic calculations, once mentally executed, now often rely on calculators or digital tools. Similarly, the emergence of AI has revolutionized creative endeavors by making it possible to generate various forms of art and content with a simple command.

Enter the metaverse, a space that seeks to challenge and reshape our beliefs and cognitive processes. It has been described as a *digital drug* for its potential to profoundly influence human cognition. This influence extends to various aspects of our mental faculties, including our grasping of information, memorization abilities, and even our intellectual and emotional intelligence (IQ and EQ). It is an infringement of natural people's privacy.

As AI continues to advance and fuels metaverse, it is poised to redefine our traditional notions of innovation and art. The creation of art, literature, and other forms of content may increasingly become automated, blurring the lines between human and machine creativity. This transformation raises questions about the value and authenticity of these creative outputs.

Moreover, the metaverse's impact extends beyond creative realms. It challenges our perceptions of critical thinking and decision-making. In a world where AI can process vast amounts of data and provide insights, distinguishing who possesses genuine critical thinking skills or talent becomes increasingly complex. AI algorithms might even influence decisions about job suitability and allocation of responsibilities, potentially side-lining human judgment.

In this context, human critical thinking may find itself at a crossroads. While the AI-backed metaverse can undoubtedly augment our problem-solving capabilities and decision-making processes, there is a concern that we might become overly reliant on machines, leading to a decline in our innate cognitive abilities. The metaverse's influence on critical thinking thus prompts us to contemplate the future balance between human ingenuity and artificial intelligence.

Intrusions into digital and intellectual properties

Imagine a scenario where unauthorized access to personal data leads to individuals gaining control over virtual properties and assets within the metaverse. In this context, the implications are far-reaching and potentially alarming, and some of them are as follows:

- **Digital trespassing:** This refers to individuals gaining illicit entry into virtual assets, spaces, properties, or platforms, often with malicious intent. These intruders can manipulate, disrupt, or misuse these digital properties in ways that may cause significant distress to their rightful owners.

- **Impact on social interactions:** One of the distressing consequences of such intrusions is the potential for individuals to misbehave within these virtual spaces and society. Friends and family members who share these spaces may find themselves victims of harassment, deception, or even exclusion. This not only affects their experience within the metaverse but can also strain real-world relationships as a result.

- **Financial implications:** Many individuals expected to invest considerable sums of money into acquiring and developing virtual properties, and assets within the metaverse. These properties can hold immense personal or even financial value. Unauthorized access can lead to individuals losing control over these assets, resulting in significant financial losses. This situation is akin to having one's domain name stolen, where years of effort and investment are suddenly wrested out of their control.

- **Forced property takeovers:** In more severe instances, individuals with malicious intent may forcefully seize control of virtual properties, assets and IP rights. This intrusion can lead to not only financial losses but also a profound sense of violation. It is akin to having one's property forcibly taken over in the physical world, with all the accompanying emotional distress and financial repercussions. *Figure 12.3* depicts intrusion and block access in a metaverse property:

Figure 12.3: Depiction of intrusion and access denied in metaverse

These scenarios underscore the troublesome implications of compromised access to digital properties. The violation of privacy and security can have far-reaching consequences, affecting individuals' digital and physical lives. In the evolving landscape of the metaverse, where the boundaries between the digital and physical worlds blur, addressing these challenges becomes paramount. Ensuring the security and integrity of digital data and virtual spaces is not only a technical concern but also a matter of personal safety and well-being.

Emotion and sentiment manipulation

In the absence of adequate regulation and privacy safeguards, the metaverse could become a breeding ground for troubling phenomena, including emotional manipulation and sentiment exploitation. The potential ramifications of such activities are extensive and, some of them are described below:

- **Vulnerability to manipulation:** The metaverse's immersive nature may become a powerful platform for brainwashing and training individuals for harmful activities. Unethical, immoral entities could exploit this environment to teach and desensitize users, pushing them towards unethical or even criminal behaviour. We live in a world already grappling with the influence of social media on extremism, terrorism, and riots. The metaverse's expanded capabilities could worsen these issues, particularly among impressionable and vulnerable populations.

- **Addictive gaming and extreme challenges:** Various reports[3] mention that online games could encourage children and adolescents to undertake extreme challenges, often with life-threatening consequences. The metaverse's immersive nature could amplify such issues, potentially leading young users down dangerous paths. Addictive applications within the metaverse may wield considerable influence over users. These applications could manipulate individuals into distrusting their real-world connections, fostering a belief that virtual influencers understand them better and can solve their problems.
- **Blackmail and manipulation:** Malicious actors gaining access to users' private data within the metaverse may exploit this information for blackmail and manipulation. This could result in victims experiencing financial losses, severed relationships, and potentially engaging in criminal activities. The consequences of such manipulation may be severe, leading individuals down paths of crime that ultimately result in incarceration or lifelong social isolation. Many parents freely share their children's data on social media, often with people they have never met. Innocent moments captured and posted online become a permanent digital footprint accessible to anyone. This poses potential risks to a child's safety, especially considering the impact of artificial intelligence. A video went viral[4] that told the story of a girl explaining how her childhood social media pictures have been manipulated, leading to measurable challenges in her life.
- **Social and political bias and influence:** The metaverse's unregulated landscape may facilitate AI-driven bias that influences individuals' voting behaviour. This, in turn, could have far-reaching consequences for governments and democratic processes, potentially swaying elections and governance in unexpected directions. *Louis Rosenberg*, an AR/VR pioneer, explained the dangerous side effects of AI generated media in a recent paper.[5]

The metaverse's potential to manipulate emotions, exploit sentiments, and manipulate user behaviour carries significant ethical, societal, and political implications. Without stringent safeguards and ethical considerations, it could become a breeding ground for undesirable behaviors and beliefs. As we navigate the evolution of the metaverse, it is crucial to address these concerns and prioritize the responsible development and regulation of this dynamic digital frontier.

Social isolation

One of the profound impacts of the metaverse that warrants its close examination is the potential for social isolation among its users even when everything is interconnected. This concern arises from the contrast between the virtual realm and the physical world, and has the potential to affect individuals in the following ways:

- **Juggling between two lives:** In the metaverse specially gaming and entertainment, users would often create vibrant, influential personas, and they may be kings and queens in that world, but in the real world they might just be perceived as reclusive or even lazy. This difference between their virtual and physical selves can lead to a growing disconnect with reality. The charm of the metaverse, where their desires are immediately gratified, may begin to overshadow the complexities and challenges of the real world. It urges them to stay away from the reality.

- **Escapism and dependency:** Users who find relief, success, and fulfillment in the metaverse may increasingly turn to an escape from the rigors of reality. The metaverse offers an attractive refuge where everything aligns with their desires, potentially causing them to neglect their physical lives. This escapism can create a dependency on the metaverse, wherein users increasingly prioritize their virtual existence over their real-world obligations and relationships. *Figure 12.4* depicts the scene of a lonely and isolated person overconnected with technology:

Figure 12.4: Depiction of technology induced social isolation

- **Mental health implications:** This divergence between virtual and real-world lives may cause mental health concerns. The individuals who grow emotionally attached to their metaverse personas may experience feelings of discontent, isolation, and disillusionment in the real world. Prolonged exposure to the metaverse and the resulting detachment from reality could lead to depression, anxiety, and an overall decline in mental wellbeing. Virtual Reality is being considered as the next hard-drug[6] inducing happy hormones.
- **Strained real-world relationships:** As users invest more time and emotional energy into their virtual personas, real-world relationships may suffer. Neglected family members and friends could feel marginalized and unimportant, straining their bonds with the individual. These strained relationships can further contribute to social isolation, as users find solace in the virtual world, believing it to be more accepting and accommodating than the real one.

Addressing the issue of social isolation in the metaverse requires a balanced approach. Users must be encouraged to reconnect with the real world, maintaining a healthy equilibrium between their physical and digital lives. Ethical concerns surrounding the metaverse's potential to foster social isolation cannot be understated. Responsible development and use of metaverse technologies should incorporate safeguards and guidelines to prevent excessive immersion to the detriment of real-world relationships and well-being.

Unforeseen metaverse crimes

We have delved into the complexities of protecting privacy and ethics within the metaverse, but what happens when something goes wrong? Social media trials are already being considered a threat to the legal system[7], irreversible damage happens well before the legal system can act on it. The metaverse would be more serious than that to today's security concerns. How do we ensure that justice is served in this digital frontier?

Consider scenarios where actions permissible in the metaverse, such as violence in video games, may not align with real-world laws and values. What if someone commits a serious offence within the metaverse? Who will monitor and enforce rules? Will there be a virtual police force, or will the existing justice system evolve to accommodate metaverse-related crimes?

These questions remain largely unanswered as the metaverse continues to evolve. However, one thing is certain: ethical considerations and mechanisms for addressing metaverse-related crimes must be built into its design from the outset.

In the absence of a clear framework, addressing these challenges poses numerous difficulties. The metaverse introduces a paradigm where distinguishing between virtual and physical realities becomes increasingly complex. Crimes that are not offences in the virtual world may still have significant ethical implications in real-world environments.

In the next section, we will explore potential strategies for managing these risks and building trust in the technology underpinning the metaverse.

Prioritizing safety, security, and ethics in the metaverse

In today's rapidly evolving landscape of product development, there is often a strong emphasis on getting a **minimum viable product** (**MVP**) into the hands of users quickly, with the intention of refining it based on user feedback. However, this approach can sometimes lead to essential concerns, like the vulnerabilities we have previously discussed, being overlooked, especially as the metaverse gains widespread adoption. However, if we intend for the metaverse to genuinely evolve into the next stage of the internet, these concerns must be paramount from the very beginning. Following are the crucial considerations for constructing the metaverse with a focus on risk mitigation and the establishment of trust:

- **A secure metaverse:** Security must not be an afterthought in the metaverse; it has to be a foundational principle[8]. From its inception, metaverse applications must be designed with security as a core component. Given that the metaverse is poised to become the future of the internet, it is imperative to address security issues at the network and native level. This entails ensuring that no insecure data can be created, stored, or transmitted over the metaverse's network. The metaverse network should be structured to safeguard identities and privacy, thwarting unauthorized access and impersonation of the metaverse artifacts. This necessitates strict adherence to metaverse standards and regulations. Essentially, the rules and regulations of the metaverse need to be seamlessly integrated into the fabric of the metaverse itself, with a clear connection to the laws of the land.

- **A safe metaverse:** Safety is not confined to physical well-being; it extends to mental and economic well-being within the metaverse. The metaverse that genuinely prioritizes people must consider their safety as a top priority. The design of the metaverse solutions must be rooted in a human-centric and people-oriented approach, enabling users to navigate the metaverse safely. It is not just about protecting users from physical harm; it is also about safeguarding their mental and emotional health. The metaverse devices should encompass safety features that go beyond the virtual realm. These features should include the capacity to detect falls or potential physical or mental harm and promptly alert users. Importantly, if a device identifies vulnerabilities or potential risks, it should have the capability to deter users from further immersive experiences. Every metaverse device should provide comprehensive information concerning its effects, best practices, tips, tricks, and potential side effects. Devices should only be approved for public use if they meet rigorous safety standards and benchmarks.

- **An ethical metaverse:** The metaverse should not be a lawless digital frontier; it must be governed by a strong ethical code. Ethical conduct should be encouraged and upheld within the metaverse. The practices within this virtual realm must align with stringent ethical standards. The metaverse should not endorse any form of harm, whether physical, mental, or economic, to living or non-living entities. It should actively discourage unethical practices, such as extreme violence, illegal activities, addiction, drug abuse, conflicts, war simulations, riots, social harm, or destructive actions for public consumption. Users should be able to engage with the metaverse knowing that it aligns with their own ethical principles and values.

- **A responsible metaverse:** Responsibility, accountability and transparency should constitute foundational principles of the metaverse[9]. While comprehensive laws and robust enforcement mechanisms are vital, every user should shoulder the responsibility of maintaining a safe, secure, and trustworthy metaverse for all. Achieving this objective necessitates a responsible partnership and collaborative efforts involving authorities, governments, academia, industry stakeholders, and the general public. The metaverse should not be a place where users can act without consequences; it should encourage responsible behaviour and a sense of shared responsibility for its well-being. *Figure 12.5* depicts the responsible and carefully planning the metaverse build up:

Figure 12.5: *Plan the metaverse carefully and responsibly*

In summary, the metaverse must place trust-building at the forefront of its development, going beyond technological considerations to include awareness-building and a commitment to responsible use. *Part 5 - Shaping the metaverse: standards and practices* of this book will delve deeper into how these considerations are actively shaping the metaverse and outline further actions required to ensure its secure and ethical evolution.

Conclusion

In this chapter, we embarked on a journey through the fascinating yet complex landscape of identity preservation and privacy protection within the metaverse. We explored the profound importance of identity, tracing its roots from our pre-birth beginnings through the complex web of our societal and environmental influences. Our identity shapes our motivations, our interactions, and our very existence in the world.

However, as we eagerly step into the metaverse, we are faced with a host of challenges. The metaverse would mixup our physical and digital identities, giving rise to a multitude of virtual personas and avatars. While this identity mix-up holds exciting possibilities, it also presents a formidable challenge of safeguarding these identities from theft, impersonation, and misuse in a realm where lines between the real and virtual blur.

Privacy, a cherished cornerstone of our society, finds itself cast in a new light within the metaverse. We've delved into the profound significance of privacy, not just as a shield for our data but as a fundamental human right encompassing our thoughts, expressions, and associations. In a metaverse brimming with interconnected data networks and generative AI, the traditional boundaries of privacy are stretched thin, demanding innovative solutions to protect our digital sanctuaries.

The implications of unregulated privacy within the metaverse are vast and intricate. From exposing personal data to the risk of identity theft and impersonation, the metaverse's rise may also lead to unforeseen consequences, affecting mental health, trust in society, and even economic or political stability. These challenges demand our immediate attention.

As we confront these challenges head-on, it is abundantly clear that the metaverse's development cannot merely follow the path of innovation and adoption. Rather, it must prioritize safety, security, and ethics from its very inception. We must lay a strong foundation, where security is not an afterthought but a core principle, where safety encompasses both physical and mental well-being, where ethics govern our actions within this digital realm, and where responsibility is shared among all its inhabitants.

In the pursuit of a metaverse that truly elevates humanity, trust is not an option; it is an imperative. The metaverse is not merely a creation of its developers; it is a collective endeavor, shaped by the actions and choices of its users.

As we look to the future, the next chapter will cast a critical eye on the metaverse, examining it through the lens of sustainability. In a world where our digital lives increasingly intersect with the physical, where the boundaries of reality blur, we must ensure that the metaverse we shape is not just a technological marvel but a force for good in the world.

Points to remember

Here are some points to remember from this chapter:

- Identity and privacy are fundamental in the digital realm.
- Realistic avatars and multiple identities increase identity theft risks.
- Unregulated privacy can expose personal data.
- Emotional manipulation is a significant concern.
- Immersion in the metaverse may lead to social isolation and distrust.
- Human creativity's value may change in the metaverse.
- Over-reliance on AI and metaverse tech is a real risk.
- Resolving metaverse crimes is complex.
- Unregulated privacy and identity have severe consequences.
- Security and safety by design are crucial for the metaverse.
- Ethical use and responsible behaviour are collective responsibilities.

References

1. https://www.digilocker.gov.in/
2. https://www.meity.gov.in/writereaddata/files/Digital%20Personal%20Data%20Protection%20Act%202023.pdf
3. https://gulfnews.com/lifestyle/11-dangerous-games-on-the-internet-that-could-kill-or-seriously-injure-1.2252866
4. https://www.linkedin.com/posts/sudhanshusaxena26_ai-socialmedia-crime-activity-7089229292865298432-MjzT/
5. https://www.linkedin.com/posts/louis-rosenberg-025851132_generative-ai-as-a-dangerous-new-form-of-ugcPost-7107000831408799744-YjnV/
6. https://www.forbes.com/sites/stevenkotler/2014/01/15/legal-heroin-is-virtual-reality-our-next-hard-drug/?sh=7fdf76ec1a01
7. https://blog.ipleaders.in/social-media-trials-threat-society-legal-system/
8. https://www.mctd.ac.uk/wp-content/uploads/2023/07/MCTD-SecuringTheMetaverse-Report-WEB-1.pdf
9. https://www.xrtoday.com/virtual-reality/responsible-metaverse-meta-platforms/

CHAPTER 13
Metaverse and Sustainability

Introduction

This chapter explores the intersection of the metaverse and sustainability, focusing on its environmental, economic, and socio-political aspects. This chapter will discuss the challenges that the metaverse presents in e-waste generation and the power consumption of generative AI. It also identifies the opportunities for sustainability, including promoting carbon-neutral metaverse operations, reducing e-waste through responsible design and recycling, and developing sustainable business models and technologies. This chapter emphasizes the need to balance sustainability and growth, recognizing the trade-offs involved. Collaboration among stakeholders is emphasized as a crucial aspect in addressing sustainability concerns. By prioritizing sustainability in the metaverse, it is possible to create an environmentally conscious, economically viable, and socially responsible world for the future.

Structure

In this chapter, we will discuss the following topics:

- Understanding sustainable development
- Sustainability challenges in the metaverse
- Sustainability considerations for the metaverse

Objectives

The objective of this chapter is to provide readers with an understanding of sustainable development, an exploration of the sustainability challenges inherent in the metaverse from social, economic, and environmental aspects, and a discussion of crucial sustainability considerations for responsible development in this digital realm.

Understanding sustainable development

In the world of metaverse, the concept of sustainable development is of paramount importance. Sustainable development, as initially defined by the *Brundtland Commission*[1], encapsulates a fundamental principle: *any development that meets the needs of the present without compromising the ability of future generations to meet their own needs* (United Nations 1987; WCED 1987). This definition serves as the cornerstone upon which the metaverse must build its foundations.

To grasp the essence of sustainable development, it can be conveniently divided into three foundational pillars, as illustrated in *Figure 13.1*:

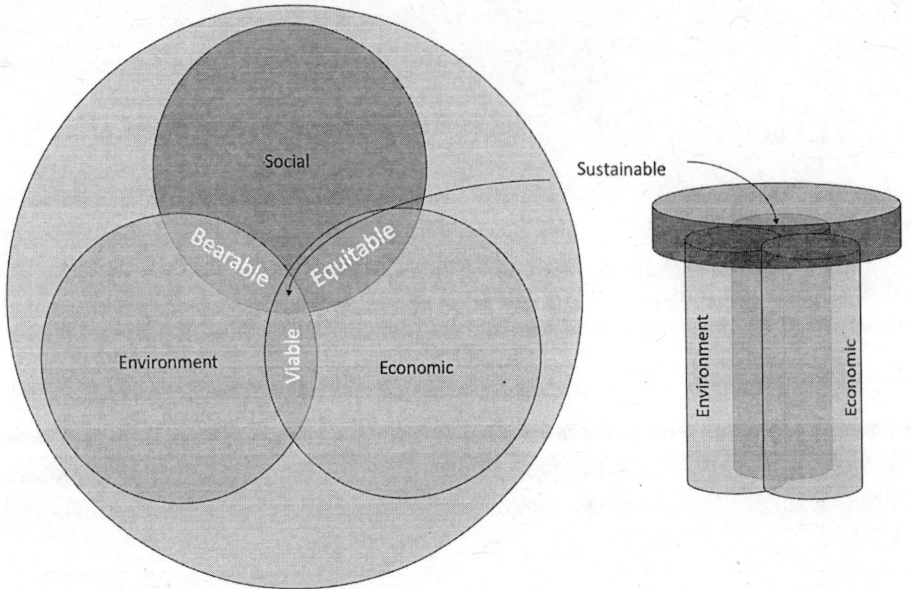

***Figure 13.1:** Three pillars of sustainability*

These three pillars - environmental, economic, and social sustainability - act as the sturdy support for the overarching roof of sustainability. Each pillar is indispensable, and any weakness in one threatens the stability of the entire structure. The synergy among these pillars, both individually and collectively, imbues sustainability with profound meaning[2]. The sustainable development consists of following characteristics:

- **Viable development**: Environmental and economic sustainability converge to ensure the viability of living conditions. However, this viability remains at risk when social unrest prevails.
- **Bearable development:** The intersection of environmental and social sustainability strives to create bearable living conditions for all. Nevertheless, this equilibrium will fall when financial resources are insufficient to sustain it.
- **Equitable development:** Economic and social sustainability intersect to foster equitable living conditions. Yet, this equilibrium breaks when environmental degradation reaches a point where Earth can no longer sustain human life.

Sustainable development necessitates the harmonious intersection of all three facets. It is at this intersection that the three *pillars* converge to craft an equitable economy, making it viable for the environment while ensuring that living conditions remain bearable for society. This convergence encapsulates the very essence of the sustainable development concept[3].

As the metaverse emerges as the next frontier of the internet, it must uphold and balance all aspects of sustainability. The following sections will discuss the challenges and considerations associated with maintaining this equilibrium among the pillars, as the metaverse endeavors to forge a sustainable and prosperous future.

Sustainability challenges in the metaverse

As the metaverse rapidly unfolds, it brings with it a host of sustainability challenges that require our immediate attention. This evolution of internet, while promising limitless possibilities, must also address critical environmental, economic, and social issues. In this section, we will explore these pressing challenges and their implications for the sustainable future of the metaverse.

Economic sustainability in the metaverse

In *Part 3, Metaverse: An Opportunity to Extend the Beliefs*, we explored how the metaverse is poised to reshape our beliefs and introduce innovative ways of working and earning. It is not just about playing to earn; but also about finding new avenues for income within this digital realm. The metaverse has the potential to birth entirely new businesses and job opportunities. In *Chapter 2, Metaverse: Various forms and interpretations* we defined self-sustainability as the key characteristic of this transformative landscape.

At its core, economic sustainability within the metaverse revolves around concepts like currency, trade, and the creation of digital businesses. We have witnessed use cases where the metaverse enhances productivity, streamlines training and onboarding for enterprises, and even harnesses the power of the human mind to deliver personalized skill-building content. As times change, the metaverse will necessitate ongoing learning and adaptation, ensuring that individuals can keep up with its evolving demands.

However, this economic prosperity does not come without costs. While we have discussed the potential for a decentralized metaverse driven by AI, 5G/6G, IoT covered in *Part 2, Metaverse: A Result of Technological Evolutions*. It is essential to recognize the hidden infrastructure and computing resource requirements. Behind the scenes, this means increased energy consumption, which translates into more carbon emissions and directly contributing to global warming. Most countries still burn good amount of coal and fossil fuel to meet their energy consumption needs. In a world increasingly concerned about being eco-friendly, it is important to acknowledge that our journey into the metaverse may inadvertently contribute to rising carbon levels and the depletion of vital resources, thereby impacting our planet's climate and environment.

Moreover, the metaverse is not just about economics; it is also about societal dynamics. Keeping the metaverse open and neutral presents challenges, and there is a risk of socio-political sustainability crumbling under the weight of various influences. The metaverse has the potential to transform nearly 90% of existing jobs, with some being automated by AI, while others requiring substantial reskilling. This shift in the job landscape may exacerbate economic disparities within society, creating a potential divide between those who can thrive in the metaverse and those who struggle to adapt. *Figure 13.2* depicts training and onboarding of the factory workers using metaverse technology, however the living standards will not be improved just by using such technologies.

Figure 13.2: *Training and onboarding factory workers using metaverse technology*

In essence, while the metaverse promises economic opportunities and self-sustainability, it also demands that we grapple with the environmental and societal implications of this digital frontier. Hence, metaverse development may lead to non-viable and non-equitable development. Our actions building metaverse have far-reaching consequences, affecting not only our livelihoods but also the health of our planet and the stability of our societies.

Balancing these competing interests is a challenge that we must address as we navigate the exciting and complex terrain of the metaverse.

Environmental sustainability in the metaverse

The metaverse is also set to revolutionize how we experience travel tourism, and entertainment. It offers us the chance to explore new places and experiences without physically traveling there. This *no-travel* option has a significant environmental upside—it can help reduce the carbon emissions associated with traditional travel methods like planes, trains, and automobiles. It may also save local bio-life balance, especially the coral reef corrosion and disappearance that is mostly attributed to tourism. Think about it: no more long flights, no more traffic jams, and no more boarding and loading that contribute to pollution or wastage. The metaverse might even make commuting to a physical office unnecessary, leading to a decreased need for office spaces and related infrastructure, which can further reduce our carbon footprint.

The metaverse's ability to supercharge productivity means that we can produce more in less time with fewer resources. This means that, per unit of production, we generate relatively fewer carbon emissions. This is done by simulating products and demonstrating them with digital twins. By this, we can save on material wastage and reduce industrial waste. Essentially, we can do more with less, which is great for the environment.

When it comes to learning and education about the environment, the metaverse can offer exciting new possibilities. We have discussed skilling and reskilling in the metaverse in *Chapter 11, Skilling and Reskilling in the Enterprise Metaverse* and the same applies to learning about environmental suitability. The metaverse can make learning more engaging and interactive, helping us better understand and appreciate our natural world. The same goes for making environmental awareness fun through gamification and entertainment. The metaverse can provide eco-friendly options that are both enjoyable and educational.

However, it is important to recognize that the metaverse itself is not without its environmental impact. It requires massive computing resources to deliver the fast and immersive experiences we expect. This means we need robust telecom infrastructure, which is often powered by energy resources that have environmental consequences. Right now, it is challenging to accurately measure the net carbon emissions caused by the metaverse compared to traditional ways of doing things.

Let us say, for a moment, that the metaverse somehow manages to have a net negative carbon impact, meaning it reduces overall carbon emissions. Even then, we cannot ignore the potential negative effects it might have on society and the economy. What happens to people whose livelihoods depend on traditional travel and tourism? Their entire careers and investments might be threatened. Similarly, the metaverse could disrupt existing forms of entertainment, education and the livelihoods of those associated with them. *Figure 13.3* depicts virtual traveling in metaverse affecting the livelihoods of taxi drivers:

***Figure 13.3**: Virtual traveling and impact of it on society*

Moreover, the metaverse has socio-political implications. It could prioritize environmental concerns at the expense of other important aspects of society. This imbalance might lead to a form of pseudo-sustainability where the environment is protected but at the cost of making society less viable and bearable for certain groups and may lead to social unrest in society.

In essence, while the metaverse offers exciting environmental benefits, we must carefully consider its broader impact on society and the economy. Balancing these complex factors is crucial to ensuring that the metaverse contributes to genuine sustainability and does not inadvertently create new challenges for us to tackle.

Social sustainability in the metaverse

The technology behind the metaverse can be a powerful tool for promoting fairness and inclusivity, especially for people with physical disabilities. Imagine a world where the metaverse can influence our brains to react differently, sense things like collisions, sound, temperature, and even emotions. The metaverse has the incredible power to encourage positivity, connectivity, and unity beyond the confines of traditional boundaries. Within the metaverse, people will have more opportunities to connect and be a part of communities that share their interests and values. In these digital realms, they would not face judgments based on their appearance or behaviors. For some, these virtual communities might become a sanctuary where they feel more accepted and comfortable than in the real world. Additionally, the metaverse could then be a valuable tool in helping individuals cope with psychological disorders and phobias.

However, it is essential to recognize that while the metaverse has the potential for positive impact, it could also be used negatively. It could influence people towards harmful activities like terrorism, destruction or criminal training. The metaverse without regulation may lead to a fair amount of abusing and anti-social behaviours in society, and potentially posing a greater threat to society than its advantages. *Figure 13.4* depicts a simulation of destruction planning in the metaverse. Furthermore, the theft of social identities and privacy breaches, as discussed in *Chapter 12, Identity Preservation and Privacy Protection*, could have severe consequences.

Figure 13.4: *Simulation of destruction in the metaverse*

We must strive to build a secure and safe metaverse that prioritizes social well-being. People may need to invest their time and resources into the metaverse, much like they earn to survive in the physical world. For some, this may not be feasible, leading to societal divisions due to economic instability and inequality. The metaverse could also phase out certain skills and jobs, further complicating the employment landscape. Even if the metaverse enhances social well-being, it could come at an environmental cost. The metaverse may require spatial computers and extensive edge/cloud infrastructure, constantly connected to robust telecom networks. This infrastructure demand can have significant environmental consequences. So, while the metaverse may be socially sustainable, it might not necessarily be bearable and equitable. Achieving social sustainability in the metaverse is a complex landscape that offers both, opportunities for positive change and challenges that need to be addressed.

Sustainability trade-off in the metaverse

In the metaverse, the three pillars of sustainability - economic, environmental, and social – are intrinsically interconnected. Achieving a sustainable metaverse hinges on striking a delicate balance among these pillars.

To make the metaverse accessible to the masses and cost-effective, extensive infrastructure, hardware, and services are required at scale. This ubiquitous access, however, comes with an environmental challenge: the proliferation of electronic waste (e-waste). As the metaverse evolves, it relies heavily on physical components. Notably, nearly all electronics depend on Coltan[4], a mineral predominantly mined under harsh conditions in Congo, as depicted in *Figure 13.5*:

***Figure 13.5**: Mining coltan in terrible conditions that makes the electronics*

Nāg[5], a technologist at Thoughtworks, often says *It is no wonder we look up when we think of cloud, but we should actually look down to the earth in the mines!*. The production of more electronics inevitably translates into increased resource extraction, potentially benefiting the economy but failing to address social equality concerns. It is worth noting that scientists have issued a dire warning about the climate crisis, underlining the urgency of addressing environmental concerns[6].

On the other hand, if we prioritize the environment alone and cease the use of fossil fuels, vehicles, and other resources, innovation may stagnate, businesses may suffer, and we risk falling behind in a rapidly evolving world. Such a singular focus could jeopardize livelihoods and economic sustainability, and eventually social sustainability too.

The metaverse presents a trade-off scenario, where emphasizing one aspect may weaken the others. This is precisely why these three pillars are considered crucial. Achieving a sustainable metaverse necessitates a delicate balancing act.

Sustainability considerations for the metaverse

In this section, our focus shifts towards crafting a sustainable metaverse. Key considerations include defining what to measure and the crucial step of measuring it. We will also touch upon the creation of eco-friendly product experiences and dive deep into the business perspective of sustainability, encompassing risks, rewards, and reputation. These guiding principles will chart our course through the metaverse, anchoring us in a commitment to environmental stewardship, economic responsibility, and social well-being.

Defining and measuring sustainability index

In our quest to create a sustainable metaverse, one principle stands out: *You can't improve what you can't measure, and you can't measure without knowing exactly what to measure.* This philosophy underscores the critical importance of defining and measuring sustainability indexes within the metaverse.

To start, imagine these indexes as compasses guiding us in the vast digital landscape. We need these compasses for economic sustainability (making sure the metaverse can thrive financially), environmental sustainability (ensuring it does not harm the planet), and social sustainability (promoting fairness and inclusivity among users). Similarly, we also gauge these indexes for viability (how well it can continue to exist), bearability (its impact on our environment and resources), and equitability (how fair and accessible it is to all).

Every solution within the metaverse should take these metrics into account. It is like setting goals to make sure the metaverse is a good place for all. Think of it as setting speed limits on a highway – it keeps everyone safe and ensures we are all heading in the right direction.

However, it is not enough to define these metrics; we must continuously watch and improve them. Imagine steering a ship: you keep an eye on the compass and make adjustments to stay on course. This is vital because as the metaverse evolves, our goals may shift.

Consider the *Green Software Foundation*[7] as an example. They have defined ways to measure software's carbon intensity[8] (how much it pollutes). They define what is included in the "software boundary" (what counts as part of the software) and calculate how much energy each piece uses. They even create tools (like carbon-aware software development kits[9]) to help developers build eco-friendly software.

Similarly, the metaverse needs to define its sustainability indexes. However, the issue extends beyond carbon emissions. We need to consider how the metaverse affects society and the economy. Does it create jobs or take them away? How does it impact our economy, our way of life, our mental and physical health, and our environment? Does it produce a lot of electronic waste? And so on.

In essence, we have to make the metaverse *green* – not just in terms of the environment, but also in terms of making it economically strong, socially fair, and environmentally responsible. By defining and measuring sustainability indexes, we are essentially giving the metaverse a set of guidelines to follow, ensuring it grows in a way that benefits everyone.

Sustainable product and customer experience

Once we have established a robust system for measuring sustainability within the metaverse, the next crucial step is to ensure that these measurements are directly visible in the customer experience. Imagine it as making the sustainability information as visible and accessible as the price or features of a product you are about to buy.

For instance, think about booking a flight online. Google now displays not only the price and available services but also the carbon rating for each flight option. This allows travellers to make informed decisions, not only based on price and convenience but also on the environmental cost of their choice. In the metaverse, it is essential to incorporate similar **green nudges** that continuously prompt users to consider sustainability in their actions. *Figure 13.6* is a depiction of green nudges in the metaverse, that may guide the user to use the sustainable options:

Figure 13.6: *Depicting sustainability visual cues – green nudges*

These nudges should be like friendly reminders, keeping users aware of the choices they make and what those choices mean for the environment, the economy, and society at large. Just as we are aware of how many calories or fats we consume, we should also be conscious of how our actions in the metaverse impact resources and sustainability. It is the classic principle: *What you see determines how you act.*

Imagine if the metaverse constantly informs you about the impacts of your actions. For example, how much water you are virtually using every time you ask a question in ChatGPT[10]. The idea is to link the metaverse experience with the real world. Every action, every minute spent in the metaverse, comes with a cost. If one part of society overuses resources, it can lead to scarcity for others, and show it with green nudges.

However, not using the metaverse services would not be an option, instead, we can find ways to offset the associated costs. For instance, the metaverse products could promote users to contribute to environmental causes, like planting trees or supporting charitable organizations, to negate the impact of their actions.

Beyond environmental concerns, the metaverse should also actively create awareness about sustainability's broader implications. It should alert users when their usage may impact personal health, mental well-being, or societal harmony. It can help address issues like addiction or emotional impacts that prolonged immersion in the metaverse might bring about.

In essence, sustainable product and customer experiences in the metaverse go hand in hand. They not only empower users to make environmentally conscious choices but also promote an overall awareness of sustainability's multifaceted role in our lives.

Holistic product development process

Creating solutions for the metaverse is a complex undertaking. It involves a multitude of technologies and requires a holistic product development approach that extends far beyond the confines of mere software or hardware. To ensure sustainability within the metaverse, we must weave it into every phase of the product's life cycle, from inception and design to development, testing, rollout, pre-sales, sales, and after-sales services.

The cornerstone of this approach is optimizing resource utilization and selecting technologies/tools that maintain a net-neutral sustainability impact. The key is to consider sustainability at every step, acknowledging that products and processes will evolve, and each phase may require different measures. We must adapt each phase of the product's life cycle to its unique needs. While agility and adaptability are essential business considerations, we cannot simply discard products and replace them with newer ones without taking sustainability into account.

For example, changes in chip design or car engines cannot occur as frequently as software updates. Therefore, each component of the metaverse ecosystem must be managed differently. Consider reusability as a parallel to waste management, where we follow best practices to optimize resource utilization in a safer work environment, ultimately boosting sustainability. Communication and collaboration in the metaverse transcend traditional boundaries, involving a diverse array of devices, tools, and techniques.

The metaverse products should function as data products, continually measuring, suggesting improvements, and self-adjusting based on social usage, ratings, and usage patterns. This data-driven approach is vital at every phase of the product life cycle, involving data gathering and iterative enhancement. A central focus should be on making user onboarding smoother, accelerating skill acquisition and re-skilling, and facilitating ease of use throughout the product's lifecycle.

In essence, crafting sustainable metaverse solutions requires a holistic approach that integrates sustainability into every facet of product development. It is about creating a dynamic ecosystem that adapts, evolves, and ultimately thrives in harmony with both the digital realm and the real world.

Sustainability as a business

In the metaverse, ensuring sustainability is not a task solely for governments or corporations; it is a shared responsibility. This collective partnership is crucial to crafting a sustainable metaverse that benefits all, depicted in *Figure 13.7:*

Figure 13.7: Consider sustainability as a business for everyone

Imagine sustainability as a business within the metaverse itself. It is not just about staying competitive; it is also about survival. In the metaverse, sustainability is not just a buzzword; it is a statement of values and a pathway to long-term success. It is about linking sustainability with reputation, making it an integral part of a brand's identity. When sustainability becomes part of a brand's DNA, it sends a powerful message to users and competitors alike.

Think of it as a continuously evolving interconnected network of businesses. Each business within the metaverse has a role to play in this sustainability ecosystem. **Corporate Sustainability Responsibilities** (**CSR**) must be well-defined, with clear goals for achieving net-neutral or even positive impact.

This approach is not just about avoiding harm; it is also about actively contributing to the betterment of the metaverse and its users. It is about creating a culture where sustainability is not just an option but a necessity. When every player in the metaverse ecosystem aligns their interests with sustainability, it leads to a more harmonious and prosperous metaverse.

In this section, we have explored some of the crucial sustainability considerations for the metaverse, recognizing that these considerations are just the beginning, and more innovative approaches for sustainability will continue to evolve as this digital frontier expands.

Conclusion

Throughout this chapter, we have traversed three critical phases, each contributing to our understanding of how the metaverse can align with sustainable principles.

First, we established the foundation by comprehending the essence of sustainable development from economic, environmental and social perspective. This explained the importance of meeting current needs while safeguarding the capacity of future generations to do the same.

Next, we delved into the challenges posed by the metaverse. We recognized that the metaverse would bring economic, environmental, and social complexities that demand our attention. Our exploration illuminated the need for equilibrium among economic viability, environmental sustainability, and social equity as we navigate this complex terrain.

Further, we examined the vital considerations essential for shaping a sustainable metaverse. From defining sustainability indexes to promoting eco-conscious product experiences. Furthermore, we underscored that achieving sustainability in the metaverse is a collective endeavor, necessitating the collaboration of users, authorities, governments, academia, and industry stakeholders.

As we conclude, we recognize that the journey to a sustainable metaverse is ongoing, guided by innovation, responsibility, and collaboration, aiming for a future where the metaverse aligns harmoniously with economic, environmental, and social well-being.

Points to remember

Here are some points to remember from this chapter:

- Sustainability is backed by the three pillars ; environmental, economic, and social.
- The metaverse presents challenges in terms of economic viability, environmental impact, and societal equity.
- Sustainability must be integrated into all aspects of the metaverse.
- Achieving sustainability in the metaverse requires collective responsibility involving users, authorities, and industry stakeholders.
- The metaverse is a dynamic environment that continually evolves, offering both challenges and opportunities for sustainability.
- Sustainability in the metaverse involves balancing economic viability, environmental bearability, and social equity.
- A cultural shift towards sustainability is necessary within the metaverse ecosystem.
- The journey toward a sustainable metaverse is ongoing, requiring adaptation as the digital landscape evolves.

In this *Part 4 - Metaverse: The Concerning Part,* we delved into critical aspects of the metaverse, focusing on identity preservation, privacy protection, and sustainability.

- **Identity preservation and privacy protection:** We explored the metaverse's complexities, including the challenge of safeguarding digital identities as physical and virtual realms merge. Privacy, a fundamental human right, faces new dimensions in the metaverse due to interconnected data networks and AI, demanding innovative solutions.

- **Sustainability in the metaverse:** Our journey through sustainability in the metaverse revealed a digital realm brimming with potential and challenges. We emphasized the importance of sustainable development, balancing economic viability, environmental impact, and societal equity. Collaboration among users, authorities, and stakeholders is vital for metaverse sustainability, as it evolves as a responsible and inclusive digital frontier.

As we conclude *Part 4,* we look ahead to *Part 5 - Shaping the Metaverse: Standards and Practices.* We will explore the practical aspects of building metaverse applications, examining the emerging standards and best practices that are shaping the metaverse development.

References

1. **https://www.britannica.com/topic/Brundtland-Report**
2. **https://sustainabilityscout.com/the-three-pillars-of-sustainability-explained/**
3. **https://www.researchgate.net/publication/277729682_The_Potentials_threats_and_challenges_in_sustainable_development_of_Penang_National_Park**
4. **https://uwaterloo.ca/earth-sciences-museum/resources/detailed-rocks-and-minerals-articles/coltan**
5. **https://www.linkedin.com/in/knagarjun/**
6. **https://www.theguardian.com/environment/2023/mar/20/ipcc-climate-crisis-report-delivers-final-warning-on-15c**
7. **https://greensoftware.foundation/articles/software-carbon-intensity-sci-specification-project**
8. **https://www.thoughtworks.com/en-in/insights/blog/ethical-tech/calculating-software-carbon-intensity**
9. **https://github.com/Green-Software-Foundation/carbon-aware-sdk**
10. **https://www.businesstoday.in/technology/news/story/may-drink-a-500-ml-bottle-of-water-for-20-50-questions-chatgpt-data-centres-consumes-a-lot-of-water-warns-study-377473-2023-04-14**

Part - 5
Shaping the Metaverse: Standards and Practices

In the ever-evolving landscape of the metaverse, the path to its realization is filled with complexity and nuance. In this part, we will cover approaches, standards, and practices in shaping the metaverse, serving as a guiding beacon for all who wish to understand and participate in this transformative paradigm shift. We unfurl the roles and responsibilities of the diverse stakeholders who play pivotal roles at various stages of metaverse development, from visionaries and creators to policymakers and consumers.

We will explore the practices and tools that underpin metaverse development and understand the essential building blocks that lay the foundation for this digital universe, revealing the very tools and technologies that power its existence. In *Chapter 14, Getting started with metaverse development*, we offer an essential roadmap for those seeking to embark on their metaverse journey. This chapter meticulously unpacks the metaverse solution ecosystem, offering invaluable insights into leveraging existing digital transformations and navigating the path towards the metaverse. We will learn more about integrated development, where hardware and software converge seamlessly, and customizable operating systems and firmware usher in a new era of configurability and modularity in design.

As we go further, we will discuss the best practices and guidelines essential for metaverse product design, development, testing, and deployment. In *Chapter 15, Metaverse standards, practices, and initiatives*, we shine a spotlight on the emerging standards and initiatives shaping the metaverse's sustainable future. This chapter serves as a compass for ensuring that the metaverse meets the evolving needs of its inhabitants while adhering to ethical, responsible, and environmentally conscious principles.

In essence, this part offers a panoramic exploration of metaverse development, inviting readers to navigate the uncharted waters of this digital frontier. Whether you are a developer, entrepreneur, policymaker, or simply an enthusiast eager to understand the metaverse's inner workings, this section of our book promises to be your trusted guide, illuminating the path forward as we collectively shape the metaverse of tomorrow.

CHAPTER 14

Getting Started with Metaverse Development

Introduction

Welcome to the gateway of metaverse development. In this chapter, we will explore the essential steps and tools for embarking on your journey into this transformative world. From **Extended Reality** (**XR**) app development to understanding the metaverse ecosystem, we will equip you with the knowledge to begin crafting your virtual experiences. Whether you are a developer, a content creator, or simply curious, this chapter will lay the foundation for metaverse development.

At the heart of the metaverse development lies XR app development, a cornerstone of creating immersive experiences within this digitally enhanced world. We will also look into enterprise metaverse, explore WebXR development, introduce you to a range of **software development kits** (**SDKs**) and learn to customize the operating system. So, let us dive in and discover the keys to unlocking the metaverse's infinite possibilities.

Structure

In this chapter, we will discuss the following topics:

- Understanding the metaverse solution ecosystem
- Basics of the metaverse application development
- Metaverse Development Kits

- Operating system to support the metaverse
- Modular and configurable metaverse devices
- Meeting the enterprise metaverse

Objectives

This chapter's objective is to provide readers with a comprehensive understanding of the fundamental aspects, skills, and tools necessary to embark on a journey into metaverse development. The readers will gain insights into configurability and modularity in hardware, firmware, and operating systems to meet the dynamics of the metaverse and enterprise needs. By the end of this chapter, you will have a comprehensive understanding of the metaverse's foundational elements and the tools at your disposal.

Understanding the metaverse solution ecosystem

In our journey through the metaverse, we have seen how technology is evolving to create this incredible digital world. The metaverse is the next evolutionary stage of the internet where different technologies come together to make our everyday online experiences seamless and exciting.

Imagine the metaverse as a giant puzzle made up of three main pieces:

- Tools to build metaverse apps,
- Devices to use these apps,
- The operating system to run everything smoothly.

These pieces fit together to make the metaverse work like magic in the interconnected environment.

Figure 14.1 serves as a visual guide, illustrating the intricate interplay of components within the metaverse solution ecosystem. The subsequent sections will dive deeper into the specifics of this ecosystem, shedding light on the technology and infrastructure, and people that make the metaverse a reality.

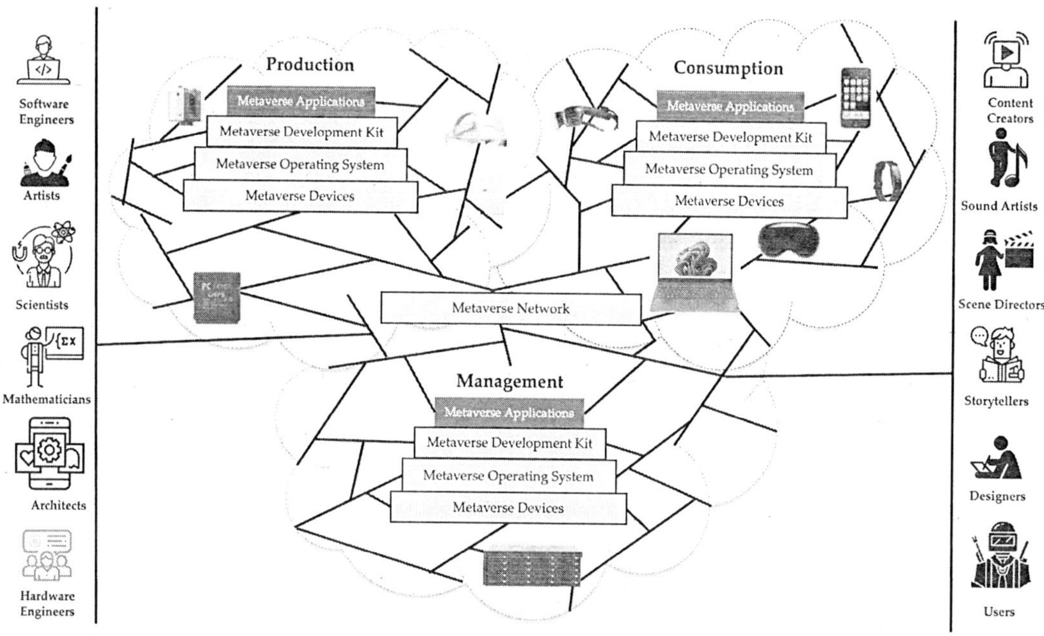

Figure 14.1: *Depiction of the metaverse solution ecosystem*

The metaverse solution stack

The metaverse solution stack is like a recipe made from lots of different ingredients. Each ingredient is a special tool or technology that when combined, creates the magic of the metaverse. In this section, we will understand these essential components that would make the metaverse work smoothly. Here are the key parts of the metaverse solution stack:

- **Metaverse applications:** These are like the apps you use on your phone or computer, but are supercharged for the metaverse. The metaverse apps connect people, businesses, technology, and others over the internet. They can do many things and follow the characteristics we talked about in *Chapter 2, Metaverse various forms and interpretations* when we defined the metaverse. These apps come in different forms –mobile apps, web apps, native system apps that use cloud, edge or IoT technologies. They work on various devices and networks, following certain rules and standards.

- **Metaverse Development Kit (MDK)**: Imagine you want to build a metaverse app for your smart glasses, watch or other devices. MDKs are like toolkits for developers. They help create and integrate apps for different metaverse devices. These toolkits let apps use the special features of the devices and interact with them. For example, they can access location data or make your device do something when the app says so. MDKs wrap around the device's operating system and connect apps to devices securely. They make it easier for developers to create apps and customize them.

- **Metaverse Operating System (mOS):** In the metaverse, safety, security, privacy, and identity protection are extremely important. The regular operating systems on devices are not always enough for the metaverse. Some devices have their own custom operating systems, while others use traditional ones like Android or Linux. We will learn in depth what the mOS should be like in this chapter to meet the unique needs of the metaverse.
- **Metaverse devices:** In the metaverse, devices would come in various shapes and sizes, each with varied capabilities. What would set them apart from traditional devices would be their configurability. These devices need to be designed to be flexible and adaptable through **over-the-air (OTA)** updates. They can be optimized for specific tasks or business needs, making them as modular as possible. This adaptability is a key feature of metaverse devices, allowing them to transform for different purposes.
- **Metaverse network:** This is like the internet of the metaverse. It connects all the devices following the mOS specs, creating one big metaverse internet. Any app on this network can communicate, share, and perform tasks safely. The network has rules to keep things secure and monitor for any unsafe actions. If something seems harmful, it can block access or remove the bad actors automatically. This network will make the location of people and data less important, as data may be stored in a decentralized or isolated way, giving users more control.

In the following sections of this chapter, we will dig deeper into these building blocks. We will explore their details, additional considerations, and specifications. By the end of this section, you will have a clear picture of how these parts come together to create metaverse's incredible world.

Categories of metaverse applications

The metaverse, like our real universe, is a dynamic and evolving space. Just as in our physical world, some parts of the internet will contribute to building the metaverse, while others will consume its services. Some applications are responsible for managing and governing the production and consumption of this digital universe. *Figure 14.1* covered these categories, let us explore them in more detail.

Building the metaverse using production applications

In the metaverse, production applications stand as the architects and builders, crafting the digital landscape that surrounds us. They are the creative powerhouses responsible for shaping this interconnected world. Some of the responsibilities and roles that define this category are:

- **Content creation tools:** The production applications are at the forefront of content creation. They are responsible for generating diverse and captivating digital experiences that captivate the audience. These experiences could range from immersive games and interactive storytelling to 3D modeling and virtual simulations.
- **Environmental scanning:** To bring metaverse to life, it is crucial to scan and capture the environment accurately. Production applications use technologies like **augmented reality** (**AR**) and **virtual reality** (**VR**) to create digital representations of the real world or construct entirely new environments.
- **Experience designing:** Collaboration is at the heart of the metaverse development. Production applications enable multiple users to collaborate on content and designs simultaneously. They facilitate real-time teamwork, whether it is in virtual design studios or during multiplayer gaming sessions. The metaverse's user interface is a critical component of user experiences. Production applications are the tools and techniques used to design intuitive and user-friendly interfaces that make navigating this complex digital world a breeze.
- **Setting standards:** Production applications establish the standards for how the metaverse devices should operate. This includes defining protocols for communication, interaction, and security. By doing so, they ensure that all metaverse experiences are coherent and seamless.
- **Development kits and tools:** To empower other developers and creators, production applications build development kits and tools. These kits provide access to sensors, interface with hardware, and offer the essential building blocks for crafting metaverse experiences.
- **Device and service creation:** In the metaverse, a diverse array of devices is required, each serving a different purpose. Production applications help create these devices and services, ensuring that they align with the vision of a connected and immersive digital universe.
- **Frameworks and platforms:** Many production applications take the form of frameworks and platforms. These serve as the foundation for the metaverse, allowing other developers to submit their applications and content while adhering to specific standards and best practices.

Production applications are the driving force behind the Metaverse's growth and innovation, shaping a digital world that thrives on creativity, collaboration, and immersive experiences. They are the architects of our virtual future.

Governing the metaverse using management applications

In the Metaverse's intricate web of creation and consumption, management applications serve as the guardians and overseers, ensuring order and security within this sprawling digital realm. Let us understand some of responsibilities and functions that define this category:

- **Content storage:** Managing the vast amount of data generated within the metaverse is a monumental task. Management applications take on the crucial role of content storage management. They securely store and organize the vast troves of digital content created in the metaverse. This includes everything from images and videos to 3D models and virtual environments.
- **Versioning:** To manage the constant evolution of content, versioning is essential. Management applications track changes, revisions, and updates to ensure that users have access to the most current and relevant content.
- **Device provisioning:** Metaverse devices must be provisioned and managed efficiently. Management applications handle the process of setting up, configuring, and maintaining devices, ensuring they are ready for use.
- **Remote access management:** In the metaverse, remote access to various resources and services is common. Management applications govern and oversee who can access what, implementing access controls and authentication mechanisms. They manage permissions, authentication, and access controls to maintain the integrity and security of the metaverse.
- **Privacy and policies:** Upholding privacy and adhering to established policies is of utmost importance in the metaverse. Management applications define and enforce privacy rules, ensuring that user data is safeguarded and that policies are adhered to.
- **Ensuring compliance:** Compliance with legal and ethical standards is a critical aspect of metaverse operation. Management applications ensure that all activities within the metaverse align with these standards, mitigating risks and legal concerns.
- **Content publishing:** Management applications facilitate the publication of content, ensuring it is accessible to the intended audience. They enable various methods and channels for content dissemination, including integrations with hardware, software, and businesses.
- **Strengthening the metaverse network:** Management applications play a pivotal role in fortifying the metaverse network. Their actions, such as access control and data management, contribute to creating a safe and secure environment for both, production, and consumption applications.

These applications are the custodians of the metaverse's stability and governance. They work tirelessly behind the scenes to ensure that the digital universe operates smoothly and securely, fostering an environment where creators and consumers can explore, collaborate, and interact with confidence. Their presence is integral to the metaverse's continued growth and success.

Experiencing the metaverse using consumption applications

In the ever-expanding metaverse, consumption applications take center stage, catering to the diverse needs and desires of users. These applications focus on the experiences within the metaverse, ensuring that users can seamlessly engage with this digital realm.

In *Part 3, Metaverse: an opportunity to extend the beliefs,* we unveil the extraordinary potential of the metaverse, diving deep into its applications across various domains. We discussed the profound impact it has on gaming, entertainment, social connection and engagement, healthcare and fitness, training, onboarding and formal education, various industry use cases, and the ever-evolving digital economy. We have also discussed reimagining commerce and retail to transform social engagement, the metaverse reshapes how we interact with the digital world. In *Part 4, Metaverse: the concerning part,* we have also covered the side effect of this adoption.

Figure 14.2 illustrates a user consuming the metaverse content and applications in this category, a boundless realm of possibilities:

Figure 14.2: *Depiction of consumption application of the metaverse*

A brief of the roles and responsibilities that define this category are :

- **Visualizing content:** Consumption applications excel at bringing content to life. They enable users to visualize and experience digital creations, whether it is exploring a virtual art gallery, trying out a new piece of clothing in an AR dressing room, or wandering through a digital city.
- **'Try Before Buying' experiences:** One of the unique aspects of the metaverse is the ability to try products and services before making a purchase. Consumption applications offer *try before buying* experiences, allowing users to virtually test products, from furniture to vehicles, ensuring they make informed decisions.
- **Facilitating collaboration on services:** Collaboration is a core feature of consumption applications. Users can collaborate on services, work together on projects, or share experiences. Whether it is collaborating on a virtual workspace or engaging in real-time multiplayer games, these applications make it possible. They provide spaces for users to socialize, connect, and collaborate, bridging the gap between the physical and digital worlds.
- **Remote assistance:** Consumption applications often provide remote assistance, connecting users who need help from experts or peers who can offer guidance. This feature is particularly valuable for troubleshooting, learning new skills, or receiving support in various contexts.
- **Managing communities:** Community management is a significant role within this category. Consumption applications create and manage communities where users with shared interests or goals can interact, share insights, and participate in events.
- **World anchors:** World anchors are vital for pinning digital content in physical locations within the metaverse. Consumption applications enable users to create and manage these anchors, ensuring that digital objects and experiences are tethered to specific real-world locations.
- **Hosting events:** Events are a cornerstone of the metaverse. Consumption applications provide the tools and infrastructure for hosting a wide range of events, from virtual conferences and concerts to gatherings in unique virtual spaces.
- **Buying, selling, and renting products:** Economic activities within the metaverse are supported by consumption applications. Users can buy, sell, or rent products and services, just like in the physical world. These applications create virtual marketplaces that facilitate transactions and commerce.

These consumption applications leverage the services provided by production and management applications, offering users a broad spectrum of engaging, interactive, and immersive experiences within the metaverse. They enable users to explore, create, connect, and participate in a dynamic digital universe that continues to evolve and expand.

These three categories; production, management, and consumption application work together to shape the metaverse, creating a dynamic digital ecosystem that caters to the diverse needs and desires of its inhabitants.

The changing role of people in the metaverse

The advent of the metaverse is not merely a technological shift; it is a profound transformation that redefines the roles and skills of individuals across various domains. Whether you are a creator, developer, or consumer, your role in this digital universe will undergo significant changes.

Let us explore some the change that impacts different facets of human involvement, however, this list is ever evolving:

- **Software engineering converging with science and arts:** In the metaverse, technology is no longer just about code and algorithms or AI; it must seamlessly blend with principles from the fields of science and arts. Traditional development roles like programmers, testers, and business analysts now require proficiency in mathematics, physics, and artistic sensibilities. This fusion of disciplines is essential to create and test immersive and user-centric experiences within the metaverse.
- **Digital business transitioning into movie making:** The traditional landscape of digital business is shifting towards a more cinematic approach as depicted in *Figure 14.3*. Business analysts and product managers, who once focused on 2D screens, pages, and functional steps, must now think in terms of scenes, lighting, action, and sound. They are, in essence, becoming movie directors of digital narratives. In addition, new roles like storytellers are emerging as critical contributors to metaverse development, shaping captivating and engaging digital experiences.

Figure 14.3: *Metaverse development is like making a movie*

- **User experience designers as multimedia artists:** User experience designers in the metaverse take on the role of multimedia artists. Their canvas extends beyond traditional screens, encompassing virtual worlds, interactive elements, and immersive environments. Their work involves crafting holistic user experiences that merge visual, auditory, and interactive elements seamlessly.
- **Rise of freelancers and community content creators:** The metaverse welcomes a new era where freelancers and community content creators take center stage. Their contributions become mainstream, and they play a pivotal role in content creation and curation, often surpassing traditional office job roles.
- **Transformation from testers to players:** The role of testers and quality assurance professionals evolves into something akin to *players*. Testing methodologies will also undergo significant change. Instead of simply detecting bugs and issues, they actively engage with and experience the metaverse to ensure its functionality, immersion, and user-friendliness.
- **Metaverse strategists to replace social media strategists:** As the metaverse would become a primary stage for human interaction, professionals engaged in social media strategies must pivot towards becoming metaverse strategists. Marketers and analysts will be challenged to re-evaluate their roles and strategies, adapting them to the dynamic and interconnected nature of the metaverse.
- **Artificial people as the creative assistant:** AI is on the rise, and would be fuelling the metaverse as explained in *Chapter 4, AI Empowering the Metaverse*, this would become more experienced and integral to the creative process. Traditional creative tasks shift towards artificial people of the metaverse, co-working as creative assistants with the real ones. They not only complement human creativity but also autonomously complete creative tasks, ushering in a new era of innovation and collaboration.

The metaverse is not only revolutionizing technology; it is also reshaping the very roles and skills that drive its development and use. Those who embrace this transformation will find themselves at the forefront of a new digital era, where the boundaries between science, art, business, and technology blur, fostering innovation and creativity on an unprecedented scale.

Basics of metaverse application development

The metaverse is an expansive world, brimming with diverse technologies, applications, devices, use cases, and complexities. While we may not cover every facet in this journey, we will begin with the fundamental building blocks of application development and gradually explore more intricate aspects in the subsequent sections.

At the heart of metaverse creation lies XR, a dynamic fusion of game development and software engineering. Transitioning from the 2D world to the 3D landscape of XR entails significant changes in software development practices, a transformation we will explore in detail, along with other backing blocks of the metaverse.

In this section, we embark on a gradual journey, extending the principles of game development to the metaverse application development that sets the stage for a deeper exploration of metaverse application development, paving the way for an exciting and innovative journey into the heart of the digital universe.

Scene and environment

Metaverse development draws inspiration from the world of gaming, fundamentally transforming the machine and computer experience. If you have ever played a video game, you are already familiar with one of the building blocks of the metaverse: the *Scene*. Unlike traditional apps that revolve around screens, the metaverse applications aim to create a digital world, mirroring the physical environment around us. In this digital world, just as in the real world, everything is an object. These objects, often referred as *Game Objects*, have shapes, appearances, and behaviors based on the materials they are made of, similar to objects in our physical environment.

Consider a simple example: a physical ball, that is defined by its spherical shape, color, plastic material, hard texture, and a certain weight. When you throw the ball or apply force to it in a specific direction, it obeys gravity and follows the rules of physics. It might even produce sounds upon impact. This behaviour is added to the digital ball through a component called a *Game Engine* or *Physics Engine*.

Various platforms and tools are available as a game development environment. Popular choices include Unity3D[1], Unreal Engine[2], Godot Engine[3], and more. While these platforms may use different terms for game objects (for example, Unreal calls them Actors; Godot calls them Nodes), they all come equipped with game and physics engine capabilities by default. *Figure 14.4* depicts making of a game roll a ball in Unity 3D[4]:

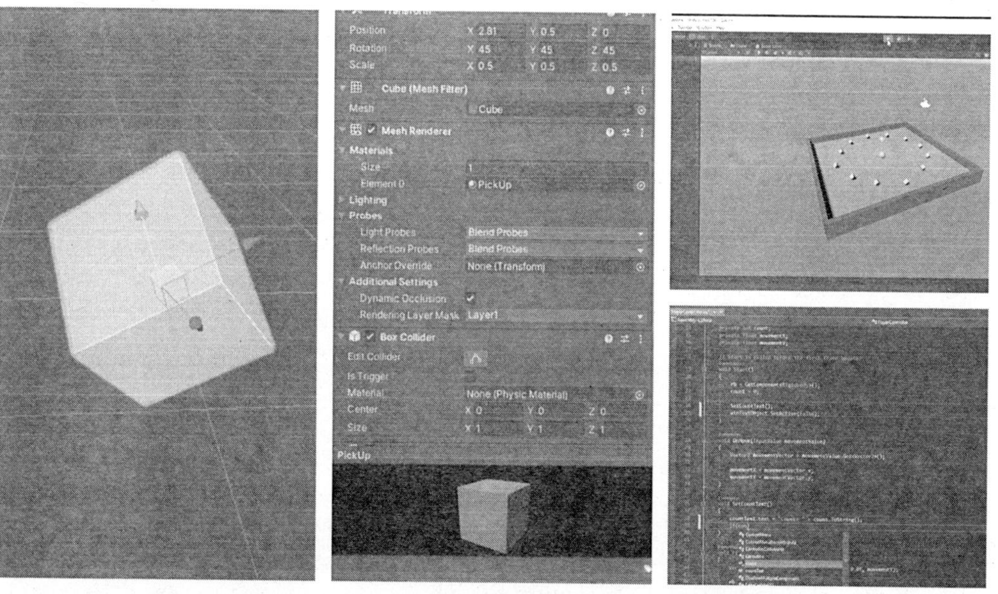

Figure 14.4: *Game scene and environment in game engine*

Game objects possess a transformation that includes their position, rotation, and scale in three dimensions: x, y, and z. By altering this transformation, you can change the position and orientation of game objects, and simulates applying forces in specific directions over time. This movement continues until the force acting on the object ceases, and friction gradually brings it to a stop.

Since objects in this game environment can move around and interact, they might collide with one another if they have a rigid body type. Objects with different body types may simply pass through each other, much like in movies when spirits pass through living beings. Game engines provide capacities for **collision detection**, and handle them. The **elasticity** of the materials determine how the shape of objects change upon collision. Each game object is associated with a shape based on the **mesh** attached to it, and the rendering of the object in that specific shape is accomplished using static or dynamic **mesh renderers**.

The metaverse applications are designed in layers where objects in the foreground can hide those in the background, a phenomenon known as **occlusion**. Game engines offer occlusion techniques to make the digital world more realistic.

Game objects can form hierarchies, following rules based on their position in the hierarchy and grouping behaviors. This hierarchical structure can represent complex game scenarios, including 3D models, vehicles, entire buildings, and more, with behaviors attached to individual game objects.

These development environments provide a way for developers to test their games by playing within the simulated environment. The game objects can also be linked to custom **scripts** written in various programming languages like C#, C++, and JavaScript, to customise the behaviours and implement business logics for the metaverse applications. In the following section, we will explore how these scripts can be linked to various input methods, making metaverse applications as interactive as real life.

Interactions and navigation

In the previous section, we explored how to control game objects, which we can also call actors or game characters, by handling their transformation programmatically. However, for a game to be realistic, we need to connect it with various input methods that allow people to interact with it, using the interfaces that allow humans to interact with machines.

In the world of video games, you might be familiar with using keys or buttons to move characters left, right, up, down, make them jump, roll, or perform other actions. You might have used game controllers, joysticks, game consoles, or even a mouse for navigation. With the introduction of mobile phones, touch screen-based controls have become popular for allowing game characters move around in the game world.

Game development environments provide all the tools and integrations needed for these **input methods**, making it easier to develop and test game apps. They offer configurations for the game and player inputs, allowing different types of input methods to be mapped.

Depending on the target platform, these inputs are automatically converted to match the platform.

Another essential aspect of a game is the camera. The camera serves as the eyes of the game, determining the player's point of view. Similar to the real world, what we see from our eyes is call first person view. This is where we see our hands and legs along with the world and people around us from a first-person perspective. However, what others see from their eyes is called third-person view, they see our whole body along with the environment. Similarly, in a game, you can experience it from either a first-person or third-person perspective. When you control a character in a game, it can simulate a real-life character's movements based on the inputs you provide. The *perspective* you choose, first or third person, impacts how you experience the game. See the position of camera in *Figure 14.5* that makes this perspective:

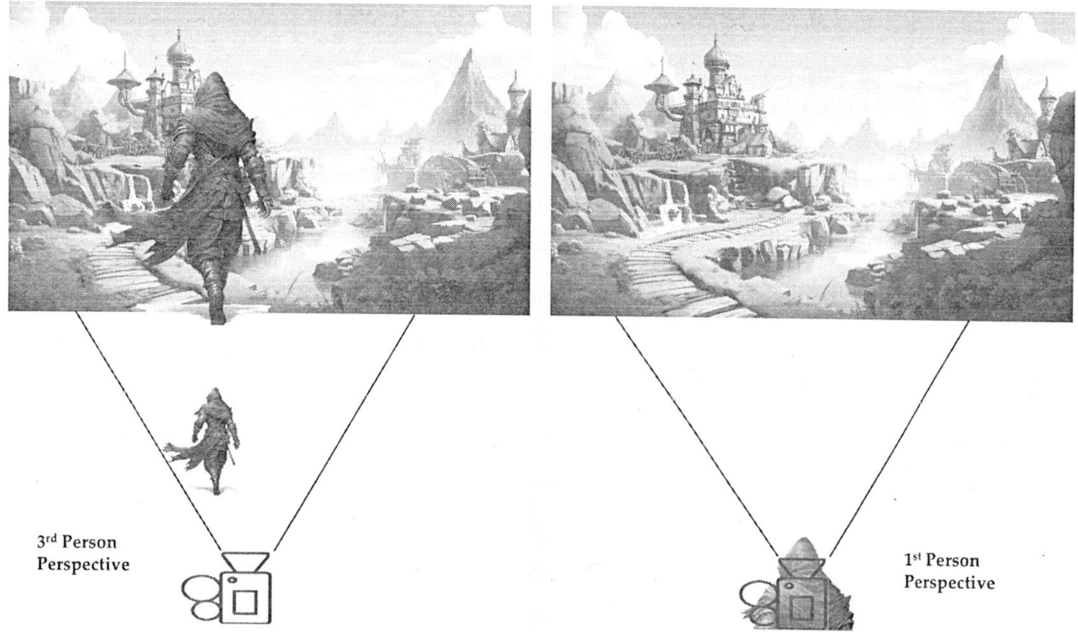

Figure 14.5: *Perspective in the game*

Behaviors in game characters can also be automated using AI. This includes simulating things like airflow, water waves, heat, gravity, fire, collisions, fluid mechanics, and the movement of humans, animals, or objects. AI can even automate walking patterns. Unity[5], Unreal[6] and others[7] provide **navigation systems** that allow you to create characters that can navigate the world environment just like physical characters. These systems also enable AI-based pathfinding, making it possible for characters to move through the environment intelligently.

These techniques are the building blocks of the metaverse applications. They let you create human-like characters and real looking objects in the digital world, allowing them to navigate the environment just like they would in the real world. This is where the journey into the metaverse applications begin. However, when we introduce shared experiences with people's collaboration and social engagement into these applications, we take a step closer to the full-fledged metaverse experience. We will dive deeper into that aspect in the next section.

Collaboration and social engagement

We have explored the fundamental components that can create an interactive gaming experience, perfect for single users within confined environments. However, the metaverse goes beyond these confinements; it is a concept rooted in the internet, so online collaboration is the key to metaverse applications. Fortunately, there are already well-established web-based development practices that we can leverage. The web has evolved significantly, moving from Web 1.0 to the faster-paced Web 3.0, a journey we cover in *Chapter 1, Exploring the metaverse origin*.

A typical web-based solution offers a graphical user interface served from the cloud servers over the internet, with the cloud servers backed by database servers. This infrastructure is designed to scale dynamically, handling user requests as needed. Web interfaces are accessed through a browser on standard PCs or mobile devices. Even typical mobile apps rely on web services hosted over these servers, using standard web protocols like HTTPS. Over the years, social collaboration has seen a tremendous increase, with real-time collaboration and shared experiences being made possible through technologies like **Asynchronous JavaScript and XML** (**AJAX**), web sockets, and WebRTC[8].

Using these technologies, the gaming applications can also be connected to the internet, and be played by multiple users at once. Everyone can log in and play together, competing against each other. They can see the shared game environment, and their actions are replicated in real-time across all the devices involved. Multiplayer online games are extremely popular, with titles like *Fortnite*[9], *Roblox*[10] and *Minecraft*[11] bringing millions of people together on these platforms. These platforms are typically supported by strong backend systems. Similarly, various collaboration applications, such as *Zoom*, *Microsoft Teams* and *Google Workspace*[12], have allowed us to work together, irrespective of our physical locations. These tools proved invaluable during the COVID-19 pandemic, ensuring business continuity. Social media platforms have also fostered extensive collaboration, with individuals using them as tools for business and income generation.

These platforms can be backed by centralized but distributed systems to meet scaling requirements, or they can use decentralized backends to provide trust and local relevance with near real-time capabilities. Some metaverse applications are built on blockchain or **Distributed Ledger Technology** (**DLT**) based backends. These backend can also be derived from standard web-development stack[13]. Ethereum[14] enables the development of **decentralized apps** (**DApps**) that communicate with smart contracts written in Solidity[15]. Truffle[16] offers comprehensive tools for smart contract development. This architecture creates a decentralized and immutable data structure that maintains a connected block of information. Each block is linked to the previous one using a hash, and every new block is validated (mined) before being added and replicated. *Figure 14.6* depicts a typical decentralized architecture where each node serves the client interface locally, and while data get synchronized across the participating nodes wherever required, all the nodes forms an interconnected network of blockchain:

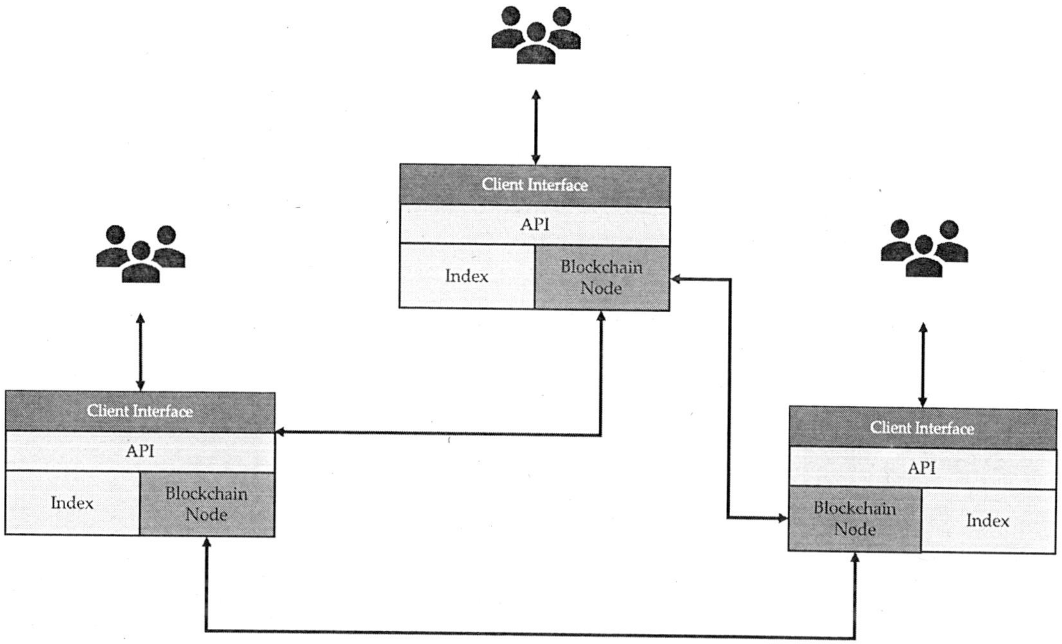

***Figure 14.6:** Typical decentralized backend*

Protocols like beckn[17] are evolving to enable sellers, buyers, and other stakeholders communicate and transact within platforms like[18] **Open Network for Digital Commerce (ONDC)**. Decentralized development is still evolving, and it may add complexity to the architecture, which comes with its costs, if not managed well. It is essential to carefully consider these factors before choosing a backend. More protocols for Web3.0 or future internet iterations need to evolve to provide a strong foundation for the metaverse, especially in the context of 5G, 6G, and beyond.

Now, we will shift our focus back to the user experience in the metaverse applications. We have discussed the developing gamified experiences mostly within the virtual world, often associated with screen based games. However, there is a significant aspect left to explore, one that bridges the gap between virtual and real-world metaverse applications. We will discuss this further in the next section.

Real-world integration

In virtual world games or applications, we typically aim to recreate everything from the real world within the virtual space. But modern devices come with more than just screens and speakers; they have eyes, ears, and sensors that allow them to perceive and interact with the real world. Let us take a basic example, *Thoughtarena* by Thoughtworks[19], that integrates a virtual whiteboard in the real-world, as shown in *Figure 14.7*, brings a virtual whiteboard into the physical environment, where it can be placed on a wall, or a floor, or anywhere we prefer. Multiple users can join the space with a copy of whiteboards in their environment and interact with them in real-time. All the actions on these whiteboards are instantly synchronized with others, creating a seamless collaborative experience. The whiteboard effectively becomes a part of the physical surroundings, just like a real whiteboard.

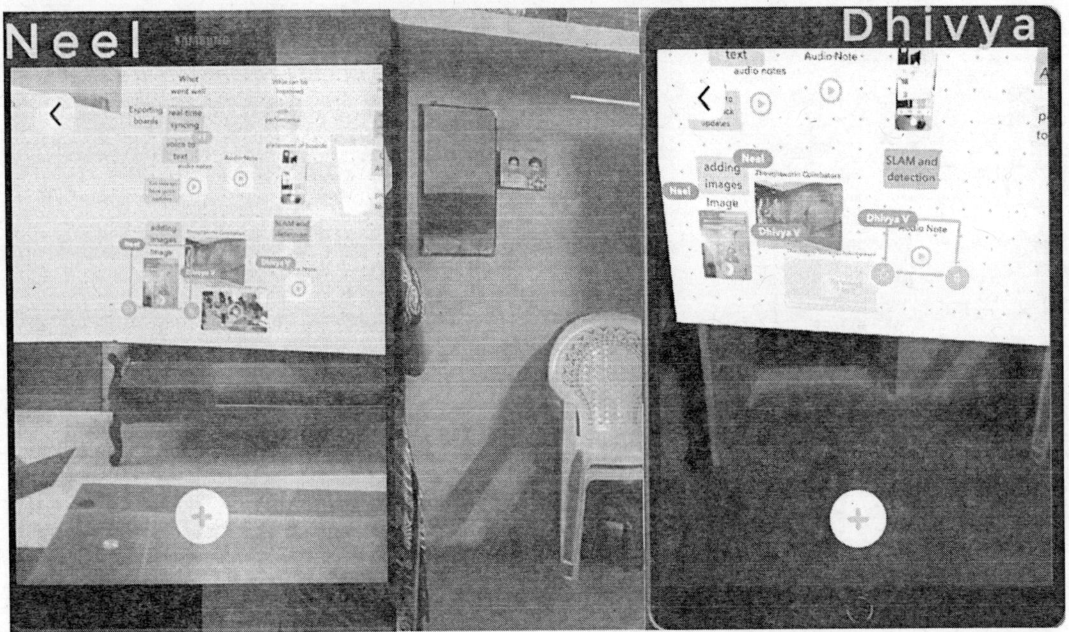

Figure 14.7: *Real-time collaboration on a virtual whiteboard at different user locations*

This experience of anchoring the whiteboard in a physical environment is made possible through a combination of sensors, such as **Inertial Measurement Unit** (**IMU**) and the device's camera, that track the environment and the device's position within it. This integration with the real world is known as AR or **Mixed Reality** (**MR**) applications.

Camera-based scanning of objects, like QR codes and barcodes, is already common. **Bluetooth Low Energy** (**BLE**) or infrared sensors can enhance this capability for specific use cases. However, devices equipped with IMU and depth sensing capabilities become powerful tools in the metaverse. Whether you are developing a mobile app or a web-based application, we can add these capabilities to the project using editors provided by game development platforms like Unity, Unreal and others. But to access these advanced features, we need to integrate **Software Development Kits** (**SDKs**), which we will explore in the next section. Additionally, we will cover head-mounted devices or smart glasses, which come with more sophisticated sensors and interaction methods, providing a truly immersive experience in the metaverse.

In summary, we can leverage traditional software development practices and extend them with new ways of interaction to build metaverse applications. To fully harness the capabilities of the metaverse devices and environments, it is crucial to integrate software development kits into your applications.

Metaverse Development Kits

In the metaverse, applications are set to thrive in a realm where internet speed is significantly faster than what we are used to, and devices are turbocharged with AI, creating immersive experiences that blur the line between the physical and virtual worlds. These sophisticated devices come with advanced capabilities, and to harness these capabilities, application developers need a set of tools and resources that can be called **Metaverse Development Kits (MDK)**. MDKs encompass various elements like tools, libraries, APIs, frameworks, and platforms. These kits unlock and securely encapsulate the underlying device capabilities, enabling developers to create immersive applications without compromising the standards.

Now, let us explore MDKs for different types of metaverse applications:

Development kits for mobile apps

For standard devices like Android/iOS phones and Mac/Windows PCs, application development kits are included in source code editors, also known as **Integrated Development Environments (IDEs)**. However, for the metaverse applications, including AR and VR experiences requires additional development kits. Here are some essential tools that combine to form a metaverse development kit for mobile-based XR applications:

- **ARCore**: Developed by Google, ARCore[20] is an SDK for creating AR applications. It tracks device motion, understands the environment, and lighting conditions, and allows developers to integrate virtual content with the real world. ARCore also supports features like world anchoring and depth understanding on some of the supported devices[21].
- **Cloud APIs:** Geospatial APIs[22] enable the remote attachment of content to locations that can be visualized in Google Street View[23], allowing developers to create AR experiences on a global scale. Cloud anchors[24] provide a way to store anchors in world coordinates. Most cloud providers come with services that can be integrated in the metaverse applications.
- **ARKit:** Apple's ARKit[25] is the AR platform for iOS devices. It enables developers to create apps that interact with the real world using the device's cameras and sensors. ARKit combines device motion tracking, world tracking, scene understanding, and display features to simplify AR development.

- **RealityKit:** *RealityKit*[26] is a high-quality rendering technology that delivers hyper-realistic experience. It includes features such as skeletal animations, realistic shadows, lights, reflections, and post-processing effects. It also supports photogrammetry from Object Capture[27] to transform 2D images into 3D models.
- **RoomPlan:** Powered by ARKit, *RoomPlan*[28] scans the surrounding environment using the camera and Lidar scanner on iPhone and iPad, creating a 3D plan, and providing a convenient way to incorporate the real world into applications.
- **Cardboard SDK:** The open-source *Cardboard SDK*[29] allows developers to build immersive cross-platform VR experiences for Android and iOS. These experiences are designed for mobile phones, but are viewed through head-mounted cardboard devices.

These SDKs empower the creation of reality-aware XR applications for mobile or PC-based platforms. In the next section, we will discuss development kits tailored for smart glasses and head-mounted devices.

Development kits for HMD and smart glasses apps

When developing for head-mounted devices and smart glasses, a different set of interactions are required. Users wear the device on their heads, leaving their hands free for other tasks. Some devices come with dedicated controllers for precise interactions, while others provide gaze tracking and gestures like hand and eye tracking for interactions. Here are some types of SDKs for devices that make this possible:

- **Proprietary XR development kits:** These development kits need to build applications for the proprietary devices and access the capabilities of these devices. Some of the examples include the **Mixed Reality Toolkit** (**MRTK**)[30] for Microsoft's XR devices[31], Oculus' own development kit, MagicLeap's LuminSDK[32], and the ThinkReality SDK for Lenovo's XR devices[33]. The metaverse development favors the open eco-system, and most of the proprietary development also adopted OpenXR standards. However, some proprietary systems like Apple's Vision Pro developer kit[34], continues to expand their own standards.
- **OpenXR development kits:** OpenXR[35] is an open-source standard for accessing VR and AR platforms and devices. It was developed by a working group managed by the Khronos Group consortium. Most XR device makers consider complying with OpenXR. For instance, MRTK[36] has become open-source and conforms to OpenXR standards. Similarly, Meta Quest devices support OpenXR[37], and Lenovo's ThinkReality devices have adopted OpenXR via the Qualcomm Spaces SDK[38]. Qualcomm has made significant strides[39] in developing chipsets for metaverse devices and fostering a developer community around them. Unity has also taken a proactive approach by offering a simplified development experience through AR Foundation[40], which abstracts the underlying SDKs and provides developer-

friendly interfaces. *StereoKit*[41] also became a lightweight alternative for OpenXR based app development. This approach allows developers to create applications that can run seamlessly on multiple devices. For instance, an application built using MRTK can be easily adapted to run on Lenovo's *ThinkReality device*[42]. This compatibility streamlines the development process and enhances cross-device functionality.

These SDKs provide access to features like raycasting, gaze pointers, gesture-based interactions, and controllers, enhancing the overall user and developer experience. The development will continue in both directions, with open ecosystems bringing wider adoption of the metaverse, and proprietary development kits catering to specific enterprise needs and objectives. The list is ever growing with *SparkXR*[43] emerging as the metaverse builder, and *SteamVR*[44] powering the PC and VR based integrated gaming. In summary, these development kits provide developers with the tools needed to create immersive metaverse applications that can run on various devices.

Development kits for web apps

As the world of metaverse development continues to evolve, we are not just seeing growth in the number of devices and development kits for native applications but also in web-based XR development. Web-based development has been around for decades and has transformed the landscape of internet-based applications. It is natural that the metaverse features are being integrated into web-based applications, and WebXR is making it possible with popular JavaScript SDKs and tools. The significant advantage here is that users do not need to download a separate app to their devices.

Here are some noteworthy developments:

- **Google Scene Viewer:** This immersive viewer empowers android users to easily preview, place, view, and interact with web-hosted 3D models in their environment[45]. It is well-integrated into Google Search, allowing users to view a wide range of objects in AR.
- **Three.js**: It is a cross-browser JavaScript library to create and render animated 3D graphics in web browsers. It supports WebXR device APIs, making it a solid choice for rendering XR content and accessing camera and controllers of XR devices while running web applications in web-browsers[46].
- **A-Frame:** A-Frame[47] offers a powerful and extensible structure built on top of Three.js, simplifying the development of VR content. A-Frame's goal is to create fully immersive XR experiences that go beyond basic 360° content, utilizing positional tracking and controllers to build 3D, AR, and VR experiences for various devices.
- **Babylon.js:** Babylon.js is a real-time 3D game engine that renders 3D graphics in web browsers. It is already being used in various world-building games such as Minecraft, Space Invaders, Temple Run, and more. The engine has a robust community with many available demos[48].

- **8th Wall:** As a leading development platform for web-based reality content, 8th Wall offers a comprehensive solution for creating, publishing, and distributing WebAR and WebVR content. This includes the Cloud Editor, AR Engine, and Built-in Hosting. It is worth noting that 8th wall is now part of *Niantic*[49], known for their real-world metaverse.

While these are some of the popular options, the list continues to expand. No-code platforms like *Hololink*[50] and *Onirix*[51] are entering the scene, which can significantly speed up development. Additionally, expect more tools and platforms driven by Generative AI to emerge that will further accelerate the pace of metaverse development.

Development kits for peripheral devices

The metaverse is an ever-expanding realm of development, where the goal is to create increasingly realistic as well as imaginative experiences. Some of these experiences may seem purely imaginary, such as feeling and sensing the virtual content or interacting with devices using only your thoughts. However, these imaginative experiences are becoming possible through the use of peripheral devices that can be attached to XR devices, and require specific development kits to enable these new capabilities.

Some noteworthy development includes TeslaSuit SDK[52], that allows developers to create applications that can interact with the user's entire body by providing full-body sensing capabilities. It is a significant step toward bringing immersive touch and feel to virtual content. Similarly, HaptX SDK[53] give tools to developers to build haptically enabled applications. However, it does not stop here; technology is emerging to use ultrasonic ware to get haptic sense of metaverse with bare hands[54]. On similar lines, development kits for **Brain Computer Interfaces (BCI)** are also evolving, and OpenBCI[55] is bringing biosensing and spatial computing together to build future metaverse solutions, where imagination is the reality. Galea SDK[56] for Varjo headset is a showcase for the growth in this direction.

While these peripheral devices and development kits are paving the way for remarkable possibilities, and becoming a part of the main device, it is important to note that these are still in their early stages and need further evolution to gain consumer trust and widespread adoption. Imagining these futuristic experiences is one thing; turning them into a reality that works seamlessly and safely for users is another, and it may take some time to bridge that gap.

In summary, metaverse development kits consist of essential tools designed to expose the core capabilities of these devices to developers. They offer user-friendly interfaces that empower developers to create applications without having to navigate the intricacies of lower-level components, including firmware, operating systems, and hardware. These development kits serve as a protective layer, encapsulating the underlying ecosystem while concealing any potentially insecure or sensitive elements within those lower layers.

Nevertheless, the metaverse landscape is not just about an application on the device. It also demands a higher degree of flexibility and customization at the operating system and device level, which we will explore in the next section.

Operating system to support the metaverse

Operating System (**OS**) play a crucial role in managing the operations and interactions of the devices, often providing seamless interfaces that we interact with daily. These systems handle core functions like connecting to the internet, managing storage and content, and navigating through files and folders. They are responsible for handling extensive operating settings and personalization, supporting enterprise integration with single sign-on capabilities, device provisioning, and enrolment. Operating systems also oversee web browsers, allowing users to access the vast world of the internet. Furthermore, they execute applications and provide access to attached hardware capabilities through SDKs, as discussed in the previous section.

Many XR devices are based on the android operating system, which was originally designed for flat-screen devices but gets customized to function with smart glasses or **Head-Mounted Display** (**HMD**) devices. However, this level of customization is not sufficient to meet the evolving needs of the metaverse. Supporting metaverse at OS level means, the underlying OS should support 3D spaces from ground up and not as an extension, for example, the spatial tracking of environment need to an integral part of OS. Apple's VisionOS[57] and Nimo OS[58] have taken steps towards creating an operating system designed for spatial computing, which aligns towards the metaverse. As metaverse devices become more complex with additional sensors, increased computing power, and enhanced networking capabilities, there is a growing need for the operating system to address specific challenges as outlined in *Part 4, Metaverse: the Concerning Part* of the book, while maintaining standard operating functionalities.

***Figure 14.8:** Depiction of connected metaverse operating system*

The **metaverse operating system** (**mOS**) should offer greater flexibility without compromising safety and security. *Figure 14.8* depicts the connected eco-system of the metaverse. Here are the several key aspects that must be considered in the development of the mOS to support this ecosystem:

- **Identity and privacy:** The mOS should have the capability to recognize the user's identity, even by simply wearing smart glasses. It should automatically load user preferences based on identity recognition. The operating system should allow users to join various metaverse applications but only with verified identities. It should also have mechanisms to detect unauthorized access and take appropriate action.

- **Data safety:** The mOS must ensure data isolation at the operating system level, even when multiple users share a single device. This means data should remain isolated and only accessible by the data owners.

- **Monitoring and telemetry:** The operating system should be equipped to monitor device usage telemetry, analyze it for safety, and report any unsafe usage. This can encompass health, economic, and sustainability concerns, and the OS must take measures to address such issues.

- **Internet network:** The mOS should be responsible for not only safeguarding data on the device but also protecting data in transit over the internet network. A novel concept for connecting to a metaverse identity may need to be developed, similar to the way we connect to the internet via IP addresses.

- **World explorer:** The web browsers integrated into the mOS will act as *world explorers*. They will be capable of running spatial computing-aware applications and managing assets related to these applications. The applications will always be available on the internet and the explorer would make these applications accessible for common use.

- **Open ecosystem:** The mOS should be supportive of an open ecosystem and customizable to meet different business and privacy needs. While flexibility is key, the operating system should also maintain a strict certification process for any customizations. Compliance suites for the metaverse should be established to ensure uniform standards, similar to *Compatibility Test Suite*[59] for **Android Open Source Project** (**AOSP**). BharatOS (BharOS)[60] is another example of open OS.

- **Decentralized operating systems:** Decentralized operating systems, such as EthereumOS[61] and other blockchain-based alternatives, are emerging to support the decentralized metaverse. They offer environments where users have more control over data, identity, and interactions. These operating systems aim to enhance security, privacy, and user ownership in the metaverse, shaping a decentralized, user-centric future.

- **Over-the-Air updates:** Managing the mOS remotely and keeping it up-to-date is crucial. Upgrading the OS can provide users with the feeling of a new device, extending the life of their hardware and contributing to sustainability. This practice will apply not only to digital devices but also to physical objects like cars and televisions in the metaverse.

While the aspects discussed here are just a few of the considerations for the metaverse operating system, the overall goal is to encapsulate tools that allow users to operate safely within the metaverse. At the same time, the mOS should offer flexibility for building applications through SDKs and the ability to customize the operating system, all while adhering to standards and best practices. The dynamic nature of the metaverse may necessitate ongoing developments in this domain, and the discussion continues in the next section, where we will explore the modularity and customization of devices.

Modular and configurable metaverse devices

Metaverse devices would come in a variety of forms, from fixed installations to standalone mobile units and wearables. These devices will be used in various environments, both indoors and outdoors, and tailored to specific use cases, each with unique requirements. One-size-fits-all solutions would not suffice, and wearables, in particular, present complex challenges due to the need for personalization.

Here are some key considerations for designing metaverse devices:

- **Modular and extendable architecture:** One of the key considerations for designing metaverse devices is the notion of a modular and extendable architecture. This approach allows users to customize their devices based on specific use cases and needs. Components such as cameras, depth sensors, gesture trackers, and eye-tracking modules can be chosen and attached as required. Additionally, these devices should be extendable, enabling users to attach additional components for purposes like extended battery life, enhanced computing power, display options, improved rendering capabilities, and additional memory. Importantly, these extensions should be hot-swappable, providing flexibility. The devices may also be powered by additional capability by edge or cloud resources, which can well meet the scaling and metaverse dynamics.

- **Immersive configurability:** Another critical aspect of metaverse devices is the ability to configure their immersiveness. Users should have the option to determine the level of immersiveness they desire when using the device. They can choose to be fully immersed in virtual content, experience a blend of the virtual and real worlds, or focus on extending the experience of the real world. Future metaverse devices aim to serve both, AR and VR use cases, and configurability will be a defining feature. Some XR devices are already evolving to provide realistic passthrough capabilities, enhancing the user experience.

- **Sensing with consent:** In the context of privacy and user consent, metaverse devices need to address concerns related to environment scanning. Many immersive devices scan the user's surroundings, raising privacy questions. To address this, these devices should provide visible indications when scanning the environment. This will create awareness among both users and non-users about the device's impact, data storage, access, and any recording activities, fostering a sense of safety and informed usage. When individuals observe VR users, they may feel vulnerable, as they are uncertain on where the user is looking or if they are recording their surroundings. This perception can lead to a sense of isolation or discomfort. However, features like VisionPro's eyesight[62] feature aims to address these concerns by ensuring that users remain connected to the real world while using immersive devices. This technology represents a positive step towards creating a more inclusive and secure metaverse experience.
- **Personalization and comfort:** Personalization and comfort are vital considerations for metaverse devices, which are intended for everyday use. Personalization can encompass fit, comfort, style, and functionality. Smart glasses, for example, should offer configurations that automatically adjust to users' **interpupillary distance (IPD)** and allow for diopter adjustments to accommodate varying eyesight, similar to the capability of Ajnalens[63]. Additional aspects of personalization include ensuring comfort during prolonged wear, effective heat management, and a secure fit while users engage in various activities like walking and jumping.

These considerations are key parameters in designing metaverse devices, but the list of considerations can be extensive. Devices will continue to evolve, some designed for specific use cases, such as blockchain phones[64] emphasizing security. Furthermore, increased configurability comes into play when discussing peripherals and implants that connect with BCIs. Metaverse devices will advance towards being more natural in appearance and function, extending users' vision, hearing, senses, emotions, and overall life experiences.

Meeting the enterprise metaverse

Enterprise metaverse development needs address several crucial considerations at all levels, spanning applications, operating systems, network infrastructure, and devices. These considerations are vital as the enterprise and consumer aspects of the metaverse are closely intertwined. If there are no consumers, there is little incentive for metaverse businesses, and if there are no enterprise use cases, the adoption by consumers may also be limited. Here are some specific considerations for enterprise metaverse development across various layers:

- **Enterprise integration:** Enterprise solutions must seamlessly integrate with various systems, such as **Identity and Access Management** (IAM), **Enterprise Resource Planning** (ERP), **Customer Relationship Management** (CRM), and Learning Management Systems. Compliance with organizational standards, processes, and policies is essential, hence integration with **Mobile Device Management** (MDM) solutions is critical for enforcing security and device management policies in the metaverse. A consistent user experience across web, mobile, and metaverse applications, possibly with single sign-on, is crucial and needs support at both the native OS and device levels.

- **Metaverse content management:** While discussions about metaverse content often revolve around visual quality and immersive experiences in the consumption side, actually the content management begins well before with content generation. Tools like Blender[65], 3ds Max, Maya, and creative design skills are essential for creating content. Traditional CAD[66] designs may also be used but they need to be transformed into metaverse-compatible formats, followed by optimization with tools like Convrse.ai[67] or other dissemination tools. The content then undergoes further refinement in terms of texturing, lighting, and animation, called skinning phase. It is essential to have tools that facilitate publishing content in various formats for seamless integration across different media platforms and channels. AI-assisted content generation[68] is evolving and will play a significant role in enterprise content production.

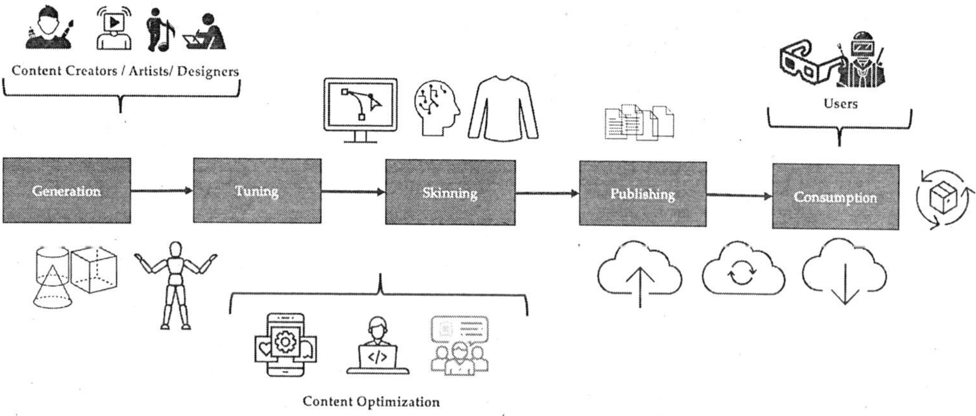

Figure 14.9: A typical content management flow for XR content

- **Customizations:** Enterprise solutions demand a high degree of customization and interoperability across devices, software, and hardware. These solutions must be compatible with different environments, including on-premises, cloud, and hybrid setups. Integration with evolving infrastructure is equally important. Enterprise metaverse adoption benefits from a vibrant partner ecosystem that ensures compatibility with a range of devices and development frameworks discussed in last section. Leveraging existing investments is also a key consideration to avoid the unnecessary replacement of current solutions.
- **Monetizing solutions:** Metaverse solutions can offer measurable **return on investment** (**ROI**) for organizations. Implementing turnkey solutions for remote assistance, guided workflow and training, remote data visualization, design

collaboration, and compliance can be monetized by offering them to a broader industrial audience. Some organizations may explore the creation of a marketplace for metaverse solutions or develop super apps and comprehensive platforms to aggregate the necessary components for various use cases.

- **Standardization:** In the enterprise space, it is vital to establish and adhere to the best practices for metaverse development. Drawing from existing principles such as Agile methodologies, open-source practices, extreme programming, and test-driven development can significantly benefit the development of metaverse solutions. Standardization is critical due to the diversity of tools and technology stacks used in metaverse solutions. Detailed discussions on standardization will be covered in the next chapter.

In essence, the development of enterprise metaverse solutions is closely linked to consumer metaverse development. Metaverse creators must also be considered as consumers, and enterprises should prioritize creating user-friendly interfaces , training and onboarding for the creators. This approach empowers creators to focus on building a consumer-friendly ecosystem within the metaverse.

Conclusion

In this chapter, we embarked on a journey to get started with metaverse development. We explored various facets of the metaverse solution ecosystem, exploring the essential components that make up the metaverse, from both consumer and enterprise perspective. We discussed Metaverse Development Kits, uncovering the tools and platforms that bridge the virtual and real, ensuring the metaverse thrives. We highlighted the role of the operating system for the evolving complexity of metaverse devices and emphasized the need for modular and configurable devices to create personalized metaverse experiences. The intersection of enterprise solutions and the metaverse was discussed, focusing on integration, standards, user experiences, and value-driven considerations.

Conclusively, the metaverse emerges as a dynamic realm with limitless opportunities, promising transformation through a vibrant and interconnected ecosystem, guided by the right tools and foundational knowledge.

In the next chapter, we will explore the standards and practices evolving around the metaverse, and initiatives aimed at making the metaverse a safe and secure place. This is a crucial aspect of ensuring that the metaverse can grow and flourish while protecting the interests and well-being of its users.

Points to remember

Here are some points to remember from this chapter:

- The metaverse is a vast ecosystem, involving interconnected applications, devices, operating systems, and development kits that enable immersive digital experiences.

- Metaverse applications are categorized as production, management, and consumption applications.
- Software engineering is converging with science and the arts, with digital business becoming analogous to movie making, incorporating new roles like storytellers and sound artists.
- Metaverse development kits, whether proprietary or open-ecosystem-based, are essential tools for building metaverse applications.
- Metaverse operating systems require robust features for identity and privacy, data safety, monitoring, network integration, and more.
- Metaverse devices needs to be modular and configurable to meet diverse needs.
- Enterprise metaverse development must consider integration with enterprise systems, content management, customization, monetization, and standardization of best practices.

References

1. **https://unity.com/**
2. **https://www.unrealengine.com/en-US**
3. **https://godotengine.org/**
4. **https://learn.unity.com/project/roll-a-ball**
5. **https://docs.unity3d.com/Manual/nav-NavigationSystem.html**
6. **https://docs.unrealengine.com/4.27/en-US/InteractiveExperiences/ArtificialIntelligence/NavigationSystem/**
7. **https://docs.godotengine.org/en/stable/tutorials/navigation/navigation_introduction_3d.html**
8. **https://webrtc.org/**
9. **https://www.fortnite.com/**
10. **https://www.roblox.com/**
11. **https://www.minecraft.net/en-us**
12. **https://workspace.google.com/intl/en_in/products/chat/**
13. **https://dzone.com/articles/intro-to-blockchain-with-ethereum-web3j-and-spring**
14. **https://ethereum.org/en/**
15. **https://soliditylang.org/**

16. https://trufflesuite.com/
17. https://becknprotocol.io/
18. https://ondc.org/
19. https://www.thoughtworks.com/en-in/insights/articles/navigating-new-normal-ar
20. https://developers.google.com/ar
21. https://developers.google.com/ar/devices
22. https://developers.google.com/ar/develop/geospatial
23. https://www.google.com/streetview/
24. https://developers.google.com/ar/develop/cloud-anchors
25. https://developer.apple.com/augmented-reality/arkit/
26. https://developer.apple.com/augmented-reality/realitykit/
27. https://developer.apple.com/augmented-reality/object-capture/
28. https://developer.apple.com/augmented-reality/roomplan/
29. https://developers.google.com/cardboard/
30. https://learn.microsoft.com/en-us/windows/mixed-reality/develop/unity/unity-development-overview
31. https://www.microsoft.com/en-us/hololens
32. https://ml1-developer.magicleap.com/en-us/learn/guides/develop-choose-platform
33. https://techtoday.lenovo.com/us/en/solutions/thinkreality
34. https://developer.apple.com/visionos/developer-kit/
35. https://www.khronos.org/openxr/
36. https://learn.microsoft.com/en-us/windows/mixed-reality/develop/unity/new-openxr-project-with-mrtk
37. https://developer.oculus.com/documentation/native/android/mobile-openxr/
38. https://spaces.qualcomm.com/sdk/
39. https://www.qualcomm.com/products/technology/metaverse
40. https://unity.com/unity/features/arfoundation
41. https://stereokit.net/
42. https://www.youtube.com/watch?v=6hzaVZrarDA

43. https://www.sparkxr.com/
44. https://store.steampowered.com/steamvr
45. https://thinkuldeep.com/post/try-everything-in-your-space-webxr/
46. https://threejs.org/examples/?q=xr
47. https://aframe.io/
48. https://www.babylonjs.com/community/
49. https://nianticlabs.com/news/welcome-8thwall?hl=en
50. https://www.hololink.io/
51. https://www.onirix.com/
52. https://teslasuit.io/software/sdk/
53. http://support.haptx.com/docs/sdk/index.html
54. https://www.weforum.org/agenda/2022/05/metaverse-vr-ultrasonic-tech-emerge/
55. https://openbci.com/
56. https://galea.co/# home
57. https://developer.apple.com/visionos/
58. https://www.nimoplanet.com/
59. https://source.android.com/docs/compatibility/cts
60. https://bharos.net/bharos
61. https://www.ethosmobile.org/
62. https://www.makeuseof.com/vision-pro-eyesight-feature-explained/
63. https://www.ajnalens.com/ajnaxr-PRO
64. https://learn.bybit.com/web3/crypto-phones-web-3-blockchain/
65. https://www.blender.org/
66. https://www.autodesk.in/solutions/cad-software
67. https://www.convrse.ai/
68. https://www.thoughtworks.com/en-ca/insights/blog/machine-learning-and-ai/ai-content-xr

Join our book's Discord space

Join the book's Discord Workspace for Latest updates, Offers, Tech happenings around the world, New Release and Sessions with the Authors:

https://discord.bpbonline.com

CHAPTER 15
Metaverse Practices, Standards, and Initiatives

Introduction

This chapter is a journey into the ever-expanding horizons of the metaverse, that goes beyond traditional software boundaries. We will explore the best practices necessary for crafting immersive and captivating metaverse experiences. The topics include user experience design principles, content creation strategies, testing methodologies, and iterative product development. We emphasize the importance of understanding user behaviour and harnessing emerging technologies to elevate user experiences. Additionally, you will be introduced to development best practices, coding, optimization, and collaboration within the metaverse context. As we progress, we uncover emerging standards and collective initiatives that are shaping the metaverse, forging a path toward a safer and more cohesive digital realm. We unveil the secrets to creating a metaverse that transcends software, opening doors to a transformative world filled with boundless possibilities.

Structure

In this chapter, we will discuss the following topics:

- Metaverse beyond software horizon
- Best practices for metaverse development
- Emerging standards and protocols

- Collective initiatives shaping the metaverse

Objectives

The objective of this chapter is to provide readers with comprehensive insights into the expanding horizons of the metaverse. They will learn some best practices for metaverse development, explore emerging standards, and understand the significance of collective initiatives in shaping this transformative digital realm.

Metaverse beyond software horizon

So far in this book, our exploration of the metaverse has been comprehensive, covering its fundamental definition, the building blocks that compose it, a wide range of practical use cases, and the potential concerns it may raise. However, we must embark on a journey that takes us beyond the conventional boundaries of software development.

Our voyage into the metaverse has revealed its profound impact, a transformative force that extends well beyond the confines of software. Much like the industrial revolution revolutionized machines and processes, the digital era has pervaded every facet of our lives, branding nearly every modern product with the *digital* label. This digital landscape, though, is often synonymous with software, and now getting rebranded with **Artificial Intelligence** (**AI**). But, does modern equate to digital, and does digital exclusively mean software or AI?

$$\text{Modern} \approx \text{Digital} \approx \text{Software} \approx \text{AI?}$$

It is important to note that while a modern product may or may not encompass digital, software, or AI components, the impact of software development practices on modern product development or evolution of these practices cannot be underestimated. These practices and processes have undergone significant evolution over the years.

In the realm of software development, we have established well-defined phases that guide the journey from requirements gathering to design, development, testing, and eventual rollout. The traditional, linear model of this process was famously known as **waterfall development**[1],which was less adaptable to change. However, the inherent flexibility of software allowed for a shift towards more agile methodologies. Agile development ushered in a new era by introducing iterative approaches. This transformation enabled developers to incorporate changes and refinements throughout the development lifecycle. The Agile Manifesto[2], a pivotal document, outlined key principles that have become the bedrock of modern software development practices. These principles, in conjunction with evolving standards and methodologies from CMMI[3] and ISO[4] have played a vital role in shaping the software development landscape.

These practices and standards have been followed, adapted, and questioned over the years. While agile methodologies were a significant improvement, they had their limitations, especially in need of location independent development. With the advent of asynchronous-first ways of working[5] and remote collaboration, it became clear that traditional agile practices were not entirely suited for the modern technology world. What we traditionally measure and plan to improve are also being challenged by initiatives like EEBO metrics[6] to focus on engineering excellence and business outcome. The metaverse encompasses a vast spectrum, extending beyond traditional software. It involves hardware, firmware, operating systems, software, as well as business, people, and environment. *Figure 15.1* depicts the metaverse elements that all need to bring together while shaping its practices and standards. Just bringing technology at the core of business is not enough, we need to bring people, process and the working environment also at the core.

Business + Technology + People + Process + Environment

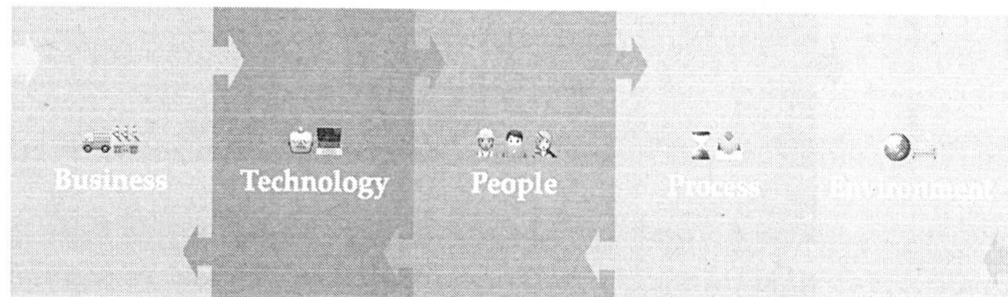

***Figure 15.1**: Element of the metaverse*

The metaverse must evolve beyond the traditional software-centric approach, and shape up practices and standards that is agnostic to specific hardware, software, technology, location, and environment. These practices and standards need to provide flexibility and agility to build future metaverse products. The book *Agile IT Organization Design*[7] explains how structural, political, operational, and cultural facets of organization design influence overall IT agility. The organizational design of metaverse companies will also need to evolve to create metaverse products that can adapt and thrive. Long-lived metaverse products must embody the agility that the metaverse demands. Organizations that prioritize independence and openness for technology, people, and environment at the core of their business will succeed in the metaverse.

It is essential to recognize the need for change to prepare for the future, collaboratively define standards and practices, and stay at the forefront of metaverse development. In the next section, we will discuss some of Metaverse's best practices that have evolved over time, leveraging existing practices and standards while exploring emerging standards and initiatives.

Best practices for metaverse development

The metaverse is a vast and multifaceted concept, making it challenging to establish one-size-fits-all best practices. Metaverse needs to go beyond software horizon, but software would remain a cornerstone of the metaverse, its diverse components require a tailored approach. Best practices cannot be uniformly applied across the metaverse; they must be fine-tuned based on specific use cases. For instance, hardware development might still lean on a more structured, less flexible approach compared to software. We have explored the need for modularity and flexibility in this context, although its full realization is an ongoing journey.

In this section, we delve into practical insights for metaverse application development, with a primary focus on XR and decentralized development. Please note that this section does not encompass well-established web development practices, readily available in various forms across the internet. It also refrains from delving deeply into rapidly evolving domains like AI, IoT, advanced computing, and network technologies.

Product definition practices

The metaverse characterized by rapid technological evolution and the emergence of various products catering to diverse business needs, building and defining mature products can be a complex task. Metaverse-based products are still in their infancy, and there exists a lack of established standards and practices for assessing their maturity. This section provides some insights about product definition practices within the dynamic and ever-evolving metaverse:

- **Embrace lean inception:** In traditional product development, inception marks the phase for defining a product and charting its roadmap. However, due to the metaverse's inherent evolutionary nature, products may not be well-defined from the outset, regardless of the amount of initial planning invested. To address this, a lean inception approach[8] is recommended. It involves quick-start initiatives with iterative processes to discover the **Minimum Viable Product** (**MVP**). This typically commences with brief meetings involving stakeholders from diverse domains such as business, marketing, technology, and end-users. The aim is to gather a bare minimum aspiration and agree on an initial feature list, eventually culminating in the **Bare Minimum Viable Product** (**BMVP**). The entire process should be swift, typically not exceeding a couple of days.
- **Expect evolution:** The metaverse is a dynamic and evolving space, and metaverse products should mirror this dynamism. By making stakeholders aware of the product's evolving nature, sharing a clear plan for that evolution, and being flexible in feature sets, the product developers can create metaverse products that remain relevant, user-centric, and competitive in the ever-changing metaverse landscape. This approach ensures that metaverse products continue to meet user needs and expectations as the metaverse itself continues to grow and evolve.
- **Diverse user group recruitment:** A diverse user group holds the key to guiding metaverse product development in the right direction. This group should ideally mirror the real-world user base. Their skill sets, backgrounds, and experiences should encompass a wide spectrum to ensure unbiased feedback and inputs.

Diversity, in this context refers to not only ethical backgrounds but also professional backgrounds, including IT, operations, delivery, experience design, marketing, and support.

- **Identify risky assumptions:** One of the critical steps in product definition is identifying and stating risky assumptions. This practice aids in understanding the potential challenges and unknowns associated with a metaverse product. For instance, when developing an XR product, risky assumptions may revolve around beliefs such as 3D experiences being superior to 2D experiences, the readiness of the chosen technology, or the potentially long-lasting impact of metaverse products on users.

- **Plan assumption validation:** After outlining the risky assumptions, the next step is to plan their validation, both quantitatively and qualitatively. Address the assumptions with concrete facts and figures. We may not have these facts and figures at the start, but plan the collection of these overtime that should have the feedback of the products' evolution. For instance, for an XR product, validation might involve assessing whether the product genuinely needs 3D or spatial computing and whether spatial experiences are indeed enjoyable. Develop prototypes, which can be in a crude, rough, or unfinished form, to provide an early visualization of the idea and validate feasibility. Prototypes don't necessarily have to be in software form; they can be conveyed using cut papers, drawings, or comical storyboards. The goal is to convey how the idea might look and function at the earliest stage of development.

- **Prioritize problem solving:** The user experience should resonate with the flexibility and intuitiveness of a physical space. If the product introduces elements that are significantly different from physical reality, it must provide an exceptional onboarding experience. Without this, users may struggle to understand and use the product effectively. Moreover, a metaverse product must be built with a strong focus on solving real-world business problems. An impressive initial experience alone is not sufficient to ensure the product's success.

- **Content lifecycle and diversity:** Metaverse products, especially those designed for social collaboration, should support users at every stage of the content lifecycle. This includes content creation, reorganization, and consumption. The product should offer a diverse range of content types, including freehand drawings, shapes, flowcharts, images, audio, videos, and 3D models.

- **Adapt to user context:** Metaverse products should be adaptable to users' contexts. This means users should be able to engage using the devices they have, in different environments, and according to their physical abilities, all without compromising the user experience.

- **Market analysis and coverage:** In-depth analysis of similar products in the market is essential. It helps understand the competitive landscape, prioritize product features, and ensure feature parity. Even if similar products are not as immersive as the one under development, examining their journey, feature evolution, user demographics, and market adoption can provide valuable insights. This analysis, in turn, guides the development of the metaverse product, ensuring it aligns with the target audience and addresses the market's specific needs.

- **Familiarize with technological constraints:** Before defining a product, it is crucial to conduct a feasibility check and understand the technological limitations. In cases like developing decentralized metaverse products, it is essential to acknowledge that technology like blockchain might not support real-time, highly transactional systems at this stage. Additionally, challenges related to backward compatibility and cost optimization should be considered while planning the product's evolution.
- **Legal and compliance:** At the outset, prioritize data privacy and adherence to legal regulations. Incorporating these considerations early in the product development process can prevent costly revisions later. Ensure transparency with stakeholders and remain agile in addressing evolving legal requirements and expectations, a critical focus area for the metaverse.

In the rapidly evolving metaverse environment, these are just a few essential practices that can form a strong foundation for effective product development. While many more practices will emerge over time, adhering to these guidelines empowers product developers to create solutions that address real-world needs and thrive within the dynamic metaverse ecosystem.

User experience design practices

In metaverse, where the lines between reality and virtuality blur, the design of user experiences takes center stage. The metaverse aims to seamlessly blend the digital world with the physical one, creating an environment where users interact with digital elements just as naturally as they would with real objects. To achieve this goal, following user experience design practices are crucial:

- **Continuous experience:** In the metaverse, minor glitches in immersive applications can disrupt the user's sense of reality. Just as in the real world, it is crucial to offer a continuous experience with dynamic, ever-changing content. Repetition can lead to disengagement, emphasizing the need for variety and novelty. Developers must ensure reliability, agile responses to issues, and user-centered design to keep users immersed without interruptions. A seamless, dynamic experience is essential for the metaverse to fulfil its promise of blending real and virtual worlds.
- **Adequate onboarding:** The ever-evolving landscape of the metaverse and its immersive technologies can be overwhelming for first-time users. These individuals are accustomed to conventional 2D interactions on flat screens and may initially struggle to grasp the transition to a 3D digital environment. Concepts

like spatial computing, where users' gestures and gaze dictate interactions, may not come naturally. It is akin to a newcomer attempting to control a cursor with a mouse or trackpad – unfamiliar at first but intuitive with practice. Without a well-crafted onboarding process, even exceptional products can leave users feeling disoriented and hinder their ability to adapt to this new digital realm. Adequate onboarding becomes the bridge that guides users from their familiar 2D world to the promising but initially unfamiliar 3D metaverse, enhancing their overall experience and interaction.

- **Alternative interactions:** In the metaverse, flexibility in interaction modes is key to accommodating various user preferences. Users differ in their preferred methods of engagement, and as such, the metaverse solutions should offer a variety of interaction options. For example, it should seamlessly support gaze-based interactions, hand gestures, voice commands, and more, allowing users to effortlessly switch between modes as needed. Take the concept of zooming in and out as an example: in a 2D environment, this often involves specific buttons or trackpad gestures. In the 3D, zooming can be as simple as moving closer to an object to magnify it. However, some users may prefer the familiarity of traditional zoom controls, while others may opt for physically manipulating objects. Thus, the metaverse immersive solutions must embrace hybrid interactions, combining elements from both the physical and digital worlds, ensuring users can engage in a manner that best suits their individual preferences and needs. *Figure 15.2* depicts experience designing for metaverse applications:

***Figure 15.2:** Experience designing for metaverse immersive applications*

- **Understanding the real-world context:** In metaverse, a thorough understanding of users' real-world needs and environments is paramount. When designing metaverse solutions, it is crucial to take into account the diverse use cases along with the lighting conditions, temperature, airflow, noise level, and various real-world settings where the users will engage with the product. Whether it is a compact apartment, an expansive outdoor field, or bustling public spaces, the metaverse product must cater to these varying scenarios. Providing users with clear guidance on the spatial requirements and ideal usage conditions is essential. This ensures that users can seamlessly integrate the experience into their specific surroundings, making it practical and user-friendly across a range of environments.

- **Cautious introduction of new interaction language:** When navigating the uncharted territory of immersive technology, it is essential to exercise caution when introducing novel interaction methods. Immersive experiences themselves are new to many users, making it potentially overwhelming to introduce a completely unfamiliar interaction language. Following *Jakob's Law* of **User Experience** (**UX**)[9], which suggests that users prefer consistency across different websites or platforms, gradual implementation of new interaction paradigms is advisable. For example, when presenting a image, PDF, or canvas in 3D, it may be more user-friendly to incorporate familiar interactions from the existing 2D realm of scroll, next/last page, zoom in/out, rather than radically introducing entirely new methods. By doing so, users can adapt at their own pace, ensuring a smoother and more intuitive transition to immersive experiences.

- **Minimise cognitive load of spatial design:** Spatial design plays a crucial role in user experience, and it is imperative to consider how users perceive and interact with objects in both 2D and 3D environments[10]. In this context, the 3D arrangement of content is generally preferred as it reduces cognitive load, provided the objects are distinct in appearance and limited in number. However, a cluttered arrangement of numerous similar objects in a 3D space can overwhelm the user and hinder their ability to process information efficiently. To strike the right balance, it is essential to carefully assess the amount of information and level of detail presented to users, ensuring that the cognitive load remains manageable. In essence, the goal is to create a spatial environment that maximizes user comfort and comprehension.

- **Text input challenges :** In spatial environments, text input poses a unique challenge. Typically, a virtual on-screen keyboard is presented to users, but it can be challenging to use and may disrupt the immersive experience. Recent advancements, such as those seen in devices like VisionPro and Quest 3, have shown promising improvements in text input within spatial environments.

  To further enhance text input, additional methods can be considered. Bluetooth keyboards or voice input are viable alternatives. However, it is crucial that these alternative input methods are seamlessly integrated into the user experience without breaking immersion. The goal is to provide users with practical and user-friendly options for text input, ensuring that it complements the immersive nature of spatial environments rather than detracting from it.

- **Aesthetics and design system:** In the metaverse immersive applications, visual and auditory elements significantly impact user experience. Define a colour palette, lighting conditions, and soundscapes that align with your product's identity. Tailor the theme of your user interface to suit the product's purpose and its usage environments. You should also create an appealing application logo to enhance brand recognition. Consider user feedback through surveys to refine these design elements, ensuring an engaging and memorable metaverse experience.

In spatial design, understanding ergonomics and human anatomy[11] is crucial. Here are key considerations to follow:

- **Designing for movement in spatial apps:** Spatial immersive applications enable users to move freely, potentially promoting creativity and a healthier work style. However, it is essential to design interactions carefully, considering:
    - **Physical fatigue**: Excessive movement within the metaverse can lead to physical fatigue, so balance is key.
    - **Awareness of real environment**: In immersive environments, users must remain conscious of their physical surroundings to avoid accidents.
    - **Designing**: Design mobile-based spatial apps with ergonomics in mind to prevent strain during prolonged use.
- **Field-of-View**: Considering the **Field-of-View (FOV)**[12] is critical in designing for both physical reality and virtual content. A user's FOV is what they can see while looking straight ahead, and the average human FOV is around 200° with comfortable neck movement. XR devices with limited FOV provides a less natural experience. Prioritize devices and designs that offer a wider FOV to create a more immersive and realistic experience in the metaverse.
- **Field-of-Regard:** Considering **Field-of-Regard (FOR)**[13] encompasses the space a user can see from a given position, accounting for eye, head, and neck movements. Understanding and designing for a user's FOR is essential in creating metaverse experiences. Designs that adapt to a user's natural head and eye movements provide a more seamless and intuitive interaction, enhancing their overall experience.
- **Optimize content positioning:** Careful consideration of content positioning is vital for user comfort in the metaverse applications. Users' eyes are naturally comfortable focusing on objects ranging from half a meter to 20 meters in front of them. Content placed too close or too far can strain the eyes or blur their vision. The ideal viewing distance falls within the range of 0.5 meters to 10 meters. To provide a user-friendly experience, metaverse designs should allow users to adjust content depth to match their preferences within this range.
- **Neck/hand movement:** When designing the user interface in the metaverse, it is crucial to strategically position UI elements to ensure accessibility and comfort. The primary UI elements should be located within the user's direct FOV without requiring neck or hand movements. Secondary UI elements can be placed in areas where some neck or hand movement is necessary.

Furthermore, designers should be aware of the user's arm's length, as it plays a vital role in interaction. Placing fundamental interactions and essential UI elements within the user's arm's reach makes for a more user-friendly and comfortable experience. Designing with these considerations in mind ensures that users can seamlessly interact with the metaverse without physical strain.

These are just a few of the essential guidelines for designing within the metaverse. Device manufacturers also offer their own design guides tailored to their specific devices. For instance, *VisionPro*[14], *Spaces SDK*[15], and *ThinkReality*[16] provide valuable best practices to ensure the best user experience.

Development practices

Metaverse development encompasses a wide range of technologies and tools, leading to the need for specific development practices. While established practices like **Test Driven Development** (TDD)[17], **Domain Driven Design** (DDD)[18], **eXtreme Programming** (XP)[19], and Agile development remain relevant for software-centric metaverse development, some practices need adjustment or specialization for hardware, firmware, and other areas. In this section, we will focus on what distinguishes metaverse development and its unique requirements. Below are key practices drawn from immersive metaverse application development for various devices:

- **Plan for Proof of Concepts (PoC):** Metaverse applications are relatively new, so anticipate PoCs in development. These PoCs involve validating hypotheses, conducting feasibility studies, usability analyses, and exploring performance and security aspects to uncover unknowns and mitigate uncertainties.

- **Embrace refactoring:** Managing source code complexity is critical for metaverse development due to inherent complexity of the metaverse solutions. Encourage teams to continuously refactor the code, supported by a comprehensive test suite. Regular and incremental refactoring[20] avoids accumulating technical debt.

- **Decision analysis and resolution:** Maintain decision records[21] for each choice made throughout development. This includes selecting development platforms, backend servers, tools, architectural approaches (for example, distributed vs. decentralized), and deciding between low-code or custom development, among others.

- **Plan for continuous tech evaluation:** Develop a strategy for regularly evaluating the suitability of chosen technologies. This is especially relevant for emerging technologies and their readiness for mainstream use. Regular spikes and assessments ensure that technology choices remain valid and meet evolving requirements.

- **Evolutionary architecture:** Design your architecture with flexibility in mind[22]. Keep input systems loosely coupled from the business logic, allowing for potential replacement or upgrade of components. Plan for the evolution of technologies and systems, including hardware, software, firmware, and tools, from the outset. Continuous refactoring and adaptation are key to staying current.

- **Consider tech limitations:** For XR applications, initialization speed varies based on hardware and OS capabilities. Shaking the device disrupts environment tracking, making control challenging. Prolonged XR usage can heat up the hardware and drain the battery due to CPU-intensive algorithms. While XR technology is advancing, it still relies on high-quality hardware. XR Cloud anchors, though promising, require proper calibration and often more extensive scanning for reliable results. Consider these while developing metaverse immersive solution and offering excellent onboarding to address these challenges. Similarly, it is also important to be aware of capacity and capability of software and hardware we choose and design the solutions accordingly.
- **Real-time collaboration cost:** Define session duration and plan for graceful handling of disconnections. Address scaling sessions considering the introduction of distributed cache management for session control. Also, ensure that the hosting platform supports this scaling approach.
- **Consider multi-tenancy:** Multi-tenancy should be a fundamental consideration, spanning layers such as end-user clients, APIs, authentication, indexes, decentralized systems, and integrations. Incorporating multi-tenancy early streamlines project design and reduces complexity.
- **Prioritize security:** Given the distributed and decentralized nature of the metaverse projects, security becomes more complex. It is crucial to safeguard critical points across various network nodes owned by different participants. Security does not come as a default even for blockchain solutions, it needs to define and adhere to comprehensive security processes at all different layers and integrations points.
- **Hybrid data solution:** Achieving a robust and secure data solution is vital, but relying solely on such a sophisticated system to meet the performance demands of multiple metaverse users can be challenging. To address this, it is advisable to establish local or near-local secure data boundaries with data replication. Striking a balance between real-time and eventual-real-time data access is key. Consider leveraging data indexes or caches, whether based on SQL or NoSQL databases, to enhance system performance and synchronize this data across various devices. For instance, when dealing with blockchain-based interfaces, a recommended approach involves maintaining read caches that subscribe to blockchain smart contract transaction events[23], facilitating the creation of data indexes or caches for faster and more efficient data retrieval. It is also important to ensure synchronization of master data across decentralized participant nodes. Inconsistencies may lead to transaction failures.

- **Business validation:** Metaverse applications require a high degree of interactivity, and rigorous business validation during user interactions. This may come at a cost to user experience and frame rates, potentially resulting in a suboptimal experience. Similarly, implementing business validation in blockchain-based smart contract applications can significantly impact transaction performance, potentially leading to out-of-gas issues[24]. As such, business validations must be carefully considered. They are undoubtedly important but need to be optimally managed to avoid compromising application performance. For example, one effective approach is to validate requests before they reach critical blocks, striking a balance between user experience and performance.

- **Handling failures and exceptions:** In the metaverse, when user requests encounter errors or exceptions, it is crucial for the solution to handle them gracefully, akin to how we expect issues to be resolved in the physical world and provide proper acknowledgment. The user experience is typically a series of interactions, and determining whether to wait for issue resolutions or to log errors and proceed is a critical decision. This choice should be made while considering its potential impact on the business. In the context of decentralized systems, the sequence of actions becomes particularly important, and we must thoughtfully decide between waiting for actions to be resolved or proceeding with alternatives.

- **Observability and tracing:** Observability plays a crucial role in guiding business and product functions, helping to determine where to focus resources and investments, and providing insights into the level of engagement. For example, in modern web applications, every request's journey is traced, from the web or mobile interface to the API services and backend servers. It is highly advisable to incorporate a comprehensive tracking system that observes all requests or samples a representative portion. Understanding how the application is being utilized provides crucial metrics, and these systems can further evolve through data analysis to proactively plan improvements. With the introduction of AI in these systems, self-correcting mechanisms can automatically take actions such as scaling up or down, blocking, or revoking actions in the metaverse to ensure safety and security standards are met. This observability and tracing support should extend from device telemetry and beyond.

- **Backward compatibility:** Managing backward compatibility is a complex endeavor, especially when it must be maintained across various devices, technologies, and a decentralized system. The decentralized nature adds intricacy, involving the upkeep of multiple contract versions across participants and efficiently routing requests to the appropriate components. To ensure seamless operations, it is imperative that all participants are aligned with the correct contract versions. Alternatively, a well-defined end of file for components, complete with clear endpoints and user consents for auto-upgrades, can simplify this process. In the dynamic and ever evolving metaverse, careful consideration of backward compatibility is important.

- **Feature introduction:** Traditionally, a feature-toggle[25] approach is employed to introduce features gradually and toggle them on and off until they mature. While this approach may be effective in delivering features quickly, but it becomes complex in the metaverse, given the involvement of multiple development layers, from hardware to software. Managing these toggles can turn into a nightmare. Hence, it is advised to explore more sophisticated methods for handling feature dynamism within the design. It's important to limit the number of feature toggles. Regularly cleaning up toggles is recommended to maintain a streamlined and efficient system.

While the practices outlined here offer a strong foundational framework for metaverse development, it is essential to recognize that they represent just a portion of the overall landscape. Developing specific application types, employing particular tools and technologies, may introduce additional nuances and considerations. The metaverse is a dynamic and ever-evolving space, requiring adaptability and responsiveness to emerging tech trends for sustained success.

Testing practices

In the metaverse, testing and quality assurance are integral to the development process, closely intertwined with the development phases. The closer we bring testing and development and broaden the base of the testing pyramid[26], the more we embrace a shift-left approach[27], the better we produce. The cohesiveness allows for faster, more efficient development, mirroring best practices in software engineering while adapting them to the unique challenges and capabilities of the metaverse. Here, we will understand some aspects of testing that deserve focused attention within the context of metaverse solutions, setting them apart from traditional software testing practices:

- **Identifying spatial context:** Metaverse applications are inherently spatial context-aware, often requiring users to physically move around to utilize functionality. This introduces a challenge for application developers and test, who need to test the application while designing these features. Development kits for metaverse applications offer emulators capable of simulating movement and spatial interactions, in a nascent stage. It is essential to identify functional specifications that can be tested with these emulators and those that cannot, strategizing automated and manual testing differently for each. Few applications might ask to test only the actual environment, it is better to design fake environment or build some remote collaborative testing practices.

- **Unit testing:** Unit testing remains at the core of comprehensive testing practices, with developers writing code to meet test cases closely tied to specific units of code. Unity engine and other development tools support unit testing, allowing developers to employ mock testing frameworks for rigorous testing. These frameworks help simulate dependencies and interactions, ensuring the functional units are robust.

- **Automation testing:** Automated testing can script the functionality that can be tested through emulators or unit testing frameworks. These tests can run programmatically, either at scheduled intervals or in response to specific triggers, such as code changes. While established automation frameworks like Selenium[28] and Appium[29] exist, customization is often necessary to meet the evolving needs of metaverse applications. Arium[30], for instance, is an automation testing framework specifically designed for writing automated tests for Unity applications and performing various user interactions programmatically in 3D space.
- **Integration testing:** Integration testing encompasses both automated and manual tests, focusing on the interconnected components of a solution. These tests come into play once all unit tests have passed, signifying the handover point for developers to initiate testing. The metaverse solutions involved interconnected components for various types from software to hardware, and integration tests rigorously examine all interaction points within the system, ensuring inputs and outputs align seamlessly with other systems.
- **Functional testing:** Functional testing typically follows integration testing, confirming the correct functionality of external dependencies. Like integration tests, functional tests come in both automated and manual forms. However, metaverse solutions present unique challenges in ensuring that functionality remains robust in varied real-world settings. Testers must assess functionality across diverse environments, varying lighting conditions, noise levels, indoor and outdoor settings, and even while moving within the environment. Acceptance criteria for immersive stories would differ significantly from standard software stories, introducing a host of new factors to consider:
    - Maintaining user immersion during interactions.
    - Achieving acceptable performance across diverse environmental conditions.
    - Recognizing that feature performance can vary in different contexts, impacting user immersion and expectations
    - Adapting acceptance criteria to match the evolving product.

These are just a few of the practices in testing, and the list is endless. The more we test metaverse solutions, the more challenges we will discover, leading to the development of new testing practices. Next, we will delve into the critical aspect of testing metaverse solutions: *user experience.*

Planning for user experience testing is crucial for gaining valuable insights and validating hypotheses with users. This approach provides a deeper understanding of the impact, benefits, limitations, and flexibility of spatial solutions. User experience testing also focuses on collaboration and assesses the effectiveness of the developed concept in terms of its usefulness and usability. This can be broken down into several components:

- **User research:** Conduct a thorough analysis of the user's current behaviors, interactions, and tools relevant to the problem statement. We also need to understand user expectations within the evolving environment.
- **Usability testing:** Assess how well the solution engages users and concentrate on its usability and usefulness.

Some best practices to enhance the overall user experience testing process involves both quantitative and qualitative analyses:

- Recruit a diverse group of users.
- Develop detailed questionnaires, plan user interviews before and after testing.
- Involve independent testers and use surveys for quantitative analysis.
- Create a test execution plan with scenarios.
- Observe user behavior during testing.
- Collect observations after multiple trials.
- Meticulously map and summarize testing reports.

In summary, robust user experience testing is essential for refining metaverse solutions and ensuring they meet the needs and expectations of users. Overall, testing practices are vital for ensuring the quality and user experience in metaverse development. Continuous testing, user feedback, and adapting to evolving tech trends are crucial. Tight integration of testing with development streamlines processes.

Continuous operations practices

Continuous Integration and Continuous Delivery/Deployment (CI/CD) practices, which in modern days are often referred to as DevOps[31] or even less commonly as DevSecOps[32], play a pivotal role in bridging the gap between development and operations teams by automating the building, testing, and deployment of applications.

In the context of metaverse development, setting up a robust CI/CD system at the outset offers substantial benefits throughout the development lifecycle. This practice serves as the linchpin for streamlining development operations, facilitating the automated execution of test suites, and the effortless deployment of code. One of the key strengths of CI/CD is its adaptability, making it well-suited for a wide range of development tools and environments. While traditional CI tools remain a mainstay for web applications, metaverse development, particularly in AI-driven and specialized hardware projects, may necessitate more specialized tooling. Additionally, the flexible nature of CI infrastructure allows for seamless management of resources for distributed, centralized, or decentralized need. As the metaverse development landscape advances, the integration of AI-assisted CI infrastructure[33] is poised to become a common and indispensable practice, ensuring your project remains agile, efficient, and ready to meet the demands of the evolving technological frontier.

In decentralized metaverse development, additional DevOps considerations become crucial. Defining a node deployment strategy (private/public cloud) upfront is essential, as changing it later can be challenging without risking data loss. Securely storing secrets, clearly outlining access management processes, and conducting frequent audits are vital. Secret rotation can be a costly affair in decentralized applications, and automating it is a wise approach to avoid expensive manual errors. Ensuring version compatibility across deployments is also a challenge, and backup/restore and recovery processes are complex. Maintaining high availability during a new deployment may also be challenging especially in decentralized systems like blockchain, where node indexes are key to the overall system's functionality. Addressing these considerations necessitates dedicated teams to tackle these unique challenges. Additionally, meticulous planning is required for legal compliance, GDPR, device compliance, SLAs for each participant, and thorough security testing and audits. Effective coordination with participants' infrastructure teams is also crucial.

Metaverse practices are a continuously evolving domain. We have discussed practices for requirements definition, development, testing, and operationalization, but they will continue to evolve as we explore, utilize, and push the boundaries of the metaverse. The dynamic nature of metaverse underscores the vulnerability of these practices, yet it is through practice and adaptation that best practices are forged. Next, we will discuss the evolving standards and protocols within the metaverse.

Emerging standards and protocols

Emerging standards and protocols are the foundation of a well-structured technological landscape. They serve as a set of guiding rules, specifications, and compliance requirements that the emerging technology solutions must adhere to. These standards and protocols have emerged over the years to address various industry considerations and continue to evolve. Whether it is the W3C[34] defining the very essence of the web or the specific specifications governing hardware connectivity such as USB[35] and Bluetooth[36], these standards enable seamless interoperability across devices and technologies. In the context of metaverse development, the need for greater streamlining and cohesion is paramount. In this section, we will discuss the pivotal standards and protocols that warrant special attention in the metaverse domain. While we provide some examples, it is important to acknowledge that this is a continually evolving landscape, and we discuss specific categories of standards and protocols that are particularly pertinent.

Electromagnetic safety standards

Safety is paramount in the metaverse, where a multitude of electronic devices using various radio waves are omnipresent. The interconnected nature of these devices can lead to **electromagnetic interference** (**EMI**) that not only disrupts operations but also poses safety risks to users. To mitigate this, governments and independent body like **International Standardization Organization** (**ISO**) have implemented strict regulations governing the amount of EMI that commercially available products can emit.

In the United States, the **Federal Communications Commission** (**FCC**)[37] defines EMI standards, while the European Union enforces the **Conformité Européene** (**CE**)[38] certification. India, through organizations like the **Bureau of Indian Standards** (**BIS**)[39] plays a similar role. These entities establish empirical tests and product evaluations to ensure EMI compliance, thereby maintaining safe levels of interference in the electromagnetic environment. As the metaverse advances and introduces innovative, modular, and wearable, and implantable technologies, it is crucial to balance these innovations with safety. Stricter regulations and adherence to safety standards will be indispensable to guarantee a seamless and secure metaverse experience, ensuring that the next generation of interconnected devices operates smoothly while preserving user safety.

Environment specific safety standards

Ensuring device safety in various environments, such as medical and healthcare settings or rugged conditions, requires adherence to specific standards. Medical device safety standards are defined by organizations like ISO[40] and BIS[41], among others. These standards are critical to guarantee the safety and reliability of devices used in healthcare.

Similarly, for rugged environments, distinct standards have been established to assess devices' capacity to withstand challenging conditions. Semi-rugged devices are built to endure low to moderate environmental hazards, while fully rugged devices are specifically engineered to handle severe environmental challenges, including resistance to water, vibrations, shock, and dust. Ultra-rugged devices, designed for deployment in military and heavy industrial contexts like mines, oil refineries, and manufacturing facilities, can withstand the most extreme conditions. Methods and standards like MIL-STD-810[42] and Ingress Protection Codes[43] are used to define ruggedness ratings. As metaverse devices continue to evolve, it is crucial to raise awareness and implement appropriate safety measures across all metaverse appliances to ensure user well-being in various operational settings.

Data safety standards

As the metaverse advances, data becomes an integral part of virtually every product, serving as the lifeblood that it maintains, consumes, produces, and transfers. Data protection is paramount to establishing trust in the metaverse and its solutions. In *Chapter 12, Identity Preservation and Privacy Protection*, we explored the significant related, along with other security considerations tied to data. Several data protection laws and standards have emerged to address these concerns.

General Data Protection Regulation (GDPR)[44], **California Consumer Privacy Act (CCPA)**[45], **Digital Personal Data Protection Act (DPDP)**[46] , and Online Safety bill[47] are some of the overarching standardisation effort in this direction. For healthcare data, the **Health Insurance Portability and Accountability Act (HIPAA)**[48], HL7[49] etc. applies, while financial data transactions adhere to the **Payment Card Industry (PCI)**[50] standards. These and similar others domain specific standards lay the foundation for safeguarding sensitive data in the metaverse, however they are not enough.

As the metaverse evolves and data manipulation techniques become increasingly sophisticated, more robust standards and certified metaverse solutions are required. Most standards needs a re-evaluation of privacy, security, and consumer protection laws that apply to the metaverse. The metaverse's propensity to blur the lines between reality and simulation calls for heightened protection measures against AI manipulation, exemplified by innovations like PhotoGuard[51] from MIT. It subtly alters photos to be imperceptible to the human eye while restricting AI systems from modifying them. Furthermore, the metaverse necessitates anti-AI technology systems[52] to guard against the negative aspects of generative AI and deepfakes[53]. Legislation and regulations, such as the evolving AI acts in the **European Union (EU)**[54], the US[55] and others, will continue to shape the landscape of data protection and privacy worldwide.

Security standards

In the world of web security, entities like IEEE[56] and OWASP[57] have defined a set of standards to promote awareness and facilitate the development of tools that proactively scan web applications for vulnerabilities, pre-empting potential breaches. In the context of the metaverse, a parallel framework of security standards is imperative. Zero Trust security practices should be integrated across the entire metaverse technology landscape to ensure a robust security posture.

ISO/IEC 23005 (MPEG-V)[58] represents a crucial step in standardizing interfaces between the real and virtual worlds, fostering seamless information exchange, simultaneous reactions, and interoperability. As a complement to ISO/IEC 23005, IEEE 2888[59] outlines information formats and **application program interfaces (APIs)** for controlling actuators and acquiring sensory data, forming the foundation for secure interactions between the virtual and physical realms in metaverse systems.

Most systems rely on passive defence mechanisms, such as security patching strategies, leaving systems susceptible to continuous exploitation. With the prevalence of cyber-physical attack surfaces in the metaverse, current security defences can prove fragile and expensive in practical use. To mitigate these challenges, a paradigm shift toward self-protection, self-evolution, and autoimmunity capabilities is crucial. By considering security and privacy factors during the system design phase, the future metaverse can better withstand the ever-evolving array of known and unknown security vulnerabilities and privacy concerns. One example of such security measures is **quantum key distribution (QKD)**[60], which employs channel-based secret keys, leveraging quantum entanglement properties to address information disclosure in wireless transmissions. **National Institute of Standards and Technology** (**NIST**)[61] is actively involved in the standardization of such approaches, while IEEE continues to establish blockchain standards[62] in a similar vein.

Usability standards

Usability standards are indispensable tools for metaverse designers aiming to create solutions that align with accessibility, usability, and inclusivity requirements. The W3C's **Web Accessibility Initiative** (**WAI**)[63] has delineated usability standards for the web, with the overarching goal of ensuring that the web is accessible and functional for all users. Building on this foundation, ISO 9241-11:2018[64] provides a more comprehensive definition of usability, emphasizing effectiveness, efficiency, and user satisfaction within the context of ergonomics and human factors.

A prominent international standard for enhancing web content accessibility is the **Web Content Accessibility Guidelines** (**WCAG**)[65]. These guidelines encompass a wide range of aspects, such as color schemes, element placement, spacing, and reach, all with the aim of creating a more accessible digital environment. The amalgamation of these web-focused standards serves as a fundamental building block for shaping usability standards in the metaverse. Additionally, the **American National Standards Institute** (**ANSI**) has compiled a collection of Augmented reality standards[66], offering valuable insights and practices for immersive development in the metaverse.

JTC 1[67] is an emerging standard that addresses various facets of the metaverse, encompassing ISO/IEC standards for virtual world representation, visualization, humanoid animation, semantic comprehension of the world, and secure information processing. As the metaverse ecosystem matures, organizations like the Extended Reality Institute[68] are taking shape, providing certification for ergonomic aspects of immersive solutions. These evolving usability standards are crucial in crafting metaverse experiences that cater to a broad and diverse user base.

Ethical standards

As explored in *Chapter 13, Metaverse and Sustainability*, metaverse solutions must adhere to the real-world rules and regulations when replicating aspects of our physical world. The digital realm also necessitates age-appropriate content regulations, recognizing that not all content is suitable for all age groups. Safety standards for metaverse solutions should be tailored to different age groups due to the potential impacts they may have. UNICEF has provided guidelines[69] for the industry regarding child online protection and published reports highlighting how immersive metaverse solutions might affect children[70]. They emphasize the importance of assessing and adjusting regulations and regulatory frameworks to safeguard children's rights in the metaverse. Implementing parental controls for various solutions is now a standard practice, although challenges remain in managing addiction and fostering safe usage practices.

Another ethical consideration is the drive to establish an open metaverse. The OpenXR[71] standard and the efforts of the Metaverse Standards Forum[72] are leading the way in ensuring the interoperability of content within the metaverse. The open metaverse ecosystem should define standards that ensure safe and inclusive usage, much like the internet functions today. The emergence of a *green metaverse* is also gaining attention. IEEE Global Initiatives produced a report on the ethics of XR[73], advocating for the development of a sustainable metaverse. This report recommends ethical assessments for XR technology solutions, focusing on establishing a governance system to identify and report on human rights measures, environmental suitability, and the impact of various software, hardware, and tools on the ecosystem. Collaboration with government legislation and adherence to legal compliance are central to these considerations.

In summary, the landscape of emerging standards and protocols for the metaverse is vast and continually evolving. This section has touched upon just a few facets, which are poised to develop further through collaborative efforts and initiatives involving various stakeholders. The next section will delve into specific initiatives and collaborations shaping the metaverse.

Collective initiatives shaping the metaverse

Community and social collaboration lie at the heart of the metaverse, as we collectively usher in the next era of the internet. In the recent years, the rise of social media has offered a platform for like-minded individuals and groups with shared interests to come together and collaborate. We will now discuss various initiatives supported by organizations, industry experts, and individuals who are committed to enhancing the metaverse. These endeavors take the form of open initiatives, consortiums, workshops, sessions, conferences, and the acknowledgment of efforts directed at advancing the metaverse.

Metaverse associations and consortiums

Over time, metaverse associations and consortiums come into light, and become valuable social capital, providing opportunities for networking, business growth, product launches, and product marketing. Here are some noteworthy metaverse associations and consortiums:

- **VR/AR Association (VRARA)**[74]: A global industry association dedicated to VR and AR, it features various industry-specific chapters and communities, and produces reports, podcasts, newsletters, and organizes events like the Immerse Global Summit, making it a prominent hub for metaverse and XR enthusiasts.
- **X Reality Safety Intelligence (XRSI)**[75]: XRSI is a safety initiative committed to ensuring safety, privacy, security, and inclusion in emerging technologies. It collaborates with other associations and organizations in the metaverse domain.

- **Responsible Metaverse Alliance (RMA)**[76]: RMA is a social enterprise and international movement with a focus on responsible metaverse development. It engages with politicians, government officials, regulators, and policymakers to address metaverse concerns and promote responsible practices.

- **Metaverse standards forum**[77]**:** This forum's primary goal is to bring together leading standard organizations and industry players to promote open and interoperable metaverse development.

- **Geatherverse**[78]: It places humanity-first standards at the core and focuses on accessibility, education, equality, community development, safety and privacy, wellness, and ethics within the metaverse and emerging technologies.

- **Metavethics institute**[79]: This community-driven, not-for-profit think tank is dedicated to research and the democratization of knowledge. Its mission is to equip individuals with the right tools to design, build, deliver, and run sustainable, ethical, and inclusive digital, virtual, and immersive environments and metaverses.

- **World Metaverse Council (WMC)**[80]: The WMC serves as a platform for leading discussions on equitable and inclusive life in the decentralized metaverse.

- **Consortium for VR/AR/MR Engineering (CAVE)**[81]: It promote XR technology development and adoption with best practices and dialogue with all stakeholders, government policy makers, and research institutions.

This list represents just a fraction of the numerous metaverse associations and consortiums actively shaping the metaverse landscape, with more emerging as the metaverse continues to evolve.

Government and academic initiatives

Active participation of government and academia is pivotal in shaping the future technology landscape of the metaverse. Their roles are multifaceted and extend beyond borders with the potential to foster innovation and skill development. Here are some key initiatives, which serve as examples but are by no means limited to any specific country:

- **Training and skill development ecosystem:** Establishing a robust training and onboarding platform is essential. Governments can dedicate a department or ministry to skill development and collaborate with other training partners, like **National Skill Development Corporation** (**NSDC**)'s partner program[82]. The World Bank has also recognized the need for such initiatives[83]. Meanwhile, academia is at the forefront of technological advancements, continually adapting and offering courses to prepare individuals for the metaverse's future.

- **Hackathons and skill assessment:** Skill assessment through practice and experimentation is a crucial step. Events like the Smart India Hackathon[84] serve as the world's largest open platform for innovators and entrepreneurs to tackle real-world challenges, fostering innovation at scale. Many groundbreaking ideas have emerged from the use of metaverse technologies, making it a prime example of government, academia, and industry working together to drive innovation.

- **Supporting startup ecosystem:** Once innovative ideas are generated, support is needed to transform them into valuable products. Governments and academia can collaborate to bolster the startup ecosystem, working in tandem with the industry. Collaborative efforts, such as the Meta and Meity Startup Hub XR Startup Program[85], in partnership with academic institutions like FITT[86], XTIC[87] at IIT, exemplify this approach. This program's aim is to accelerate India's contribution to the metaverse and nurture **Extended Reality** (**XR**) technologies.
- **Metaverse centers of excellence:** The establishment of **Centers of Excellence** (**CoE**) dedicated to metaverse technologies can significantly raise awareness. Organizations like NASSCOM CoE[88] provides a model for this concept, bringing states and educational institutes together under a common **Memorandum of Understanding** (**MoU**) to work toward a shared goal. These CoEs facilitate mentorship, connect mentees with mentors, and provide access to experts.

While the examples provided here are drawn from India, countries worldwide are taking various initiatives and crafting strategies for the metaverse[89], for example South Korea, Spain, China, and USA spending heavily on metaverse and XR initiatives. In the following section, we delve into the active industry investments in various metaverse programs.

Development programs and active investors

The adoption of metaverse technology is not solely reliant on exceptional devices; it hinges on the growth of a robust content and solution development ecosystem. This ecosystem has seen a surge in active investments aimed at shaping the metaverse. Some notable initiatives include:

- **The Snapdragon™ metaverse fund[90]:** Qualcomm is at the forefront of enabling the spatial internet through fundamental technologies[91]. The Snapdragon™ Metaverse Fund serves as a launchpad for XR developers and companies dedicated to building the foundational technologies and content ecosystem that will underpin the metaverse's development.
- **Developer platforms:** Leading technology providers offer open access to developer communities, often for non-commercial use. Examples include Unity, Lightship ARDK[92], and others development kits that provide accessible tools and resources. Initiatives like JioGlass developer program[93] and Ajnalens creator program[94] aim to drive adoption while making their devices available for sale. Apple's development kit for VisionOS is also on the horizon, further contributing to the metaverse landscape.

- **Support for student clubs:** Tech giants like Google[95] and Mozilla actively support student clubs. These clubs have gained popularity in various academic settings, with IEEE boasting a significant student community[96]. Their contributions are vital to the growth of the metaverse.

These programs are just few example, making up the developer platforms are a common practice along with the devices. Investments are instrumental in fostering metaverse adoption. Alongside these investments, an active community of investors is essential. Major players such as Apple, Microsoft, Meta, Google, Samsung, Lenovo, HTC, Magic Leap and Varjo have made substantial investments in the metaverse technology solutions. Moreover, new players continually join the ranks. Qualcomm, for instance, is diligently building an ecosystem that unites numerous partners who share a common vision. Companies like TCL, Raybon, Ajnalens, Reliance JioGlass, and even BMW have joined this ever-expanding list, solidifying the metaverse's future.

Conferences, summits, and tech-fairs

Conferences serve as vital platforms for showcasing innovations, networking, building brand recognition, and fostering collaboration. In metaverse, existing conference platforms are not only used to shape the metaverse but also to revolutionize the concept of conferences and collaboration. These events typically encompass speaking and listening opportunities, dedicated showcase spaces, workshops, and networking sessions to facilitate business growth, as well as recognizing outstanding products through public ratings. Here are some noteworthy conferences shaping the future:

- **Consumer Electronics Show (CES)[97]:** Widely regarded as the most influential event in the tech world, CES serves as a proving ground for breakthrough technologies and global innovators. Hosted annually by the Consumer Technology Association, CES unveils product launches, devices, and technological advancements, making it a hotbed for metaverse-related experiences.

- **Mobile World Congress (MWC):** This annual tradeshow, organized in various locations worldwide by the GSM Association, stands as the world's largest and most influential connectivity event. While primarily focused on mobile communication devices and telecom equipment, MWC plays a pivotal role in supporting internet and metaverse technologies. It features prominent exhibitors, keynotes from industry leaders, and influential voices in the field.

- **Augmented World Expo (AWE)[98]:** It has been known as the *family reunion* of the extended reality community. AWE offers an annual showcase of the latest hardware and software enabling AR and VR experiences. Attendees can explore cutting-edge demos and more.

- **SXSW conference[99]:** Although initially known as an annual music and interactive media festival, SXSW has evolved into a can't-miss conference for innovators across the digital landscape. With diverse tracks covering startups, tech domains, and the transformative metaverse, SXSW is a hub for change and innovation.

Attending these prominent conferences is a fascinating experience as depicted in *Figure 15.3*, and the list continues to grow.

Figure 15.3: *Attending conferences to experience the metaverse advancements*

Brands also host proprietary events that support metaverse development in various forms. Keep an eye out for annual announcements from events like Google I/O[100], Apple's **Worldwide Developers Conference** (**WWDC**)[101], Lenovo Tech World[102], and others. These gatherings provide opportunities to explore emerging solutions and the challenges that come with them. In the next section, we will discuss the emerging communities and the role of social influencers in shaping the metaverse.

Communities and social influencers

In recent years, social communities have redefined the dynamics of influence creation and propagation, with social influencers now wielding significant impact, at times surpassing that of traditional celebrities. Social media platforms have emerged as ideal environments for nurturing and expanding this influence. As awareness and adoption of metaverse technologies continue to rise, influencers and communities play a pivotal role in shaping metaverse solutions.

Influencers serve as content creators, offering their materials as a means of connection within various communities. Platforms like LinkedIn, X, Facebook, and Instagram host numerous metaverse-related communities where individuals join to stay updated, engage in discussions, and remain informed about the latest developments. Meetup groups also provide a platform for like-minded individuals to participate in events, fostering connections and shared interests.

Within these communities, influencers play a crucial role by sharing diverse content formats, such as media, live or recorded events, in-depth blogs, articles, and even books. They utilize these mediums to effectively communicate their knowledge, personal experiences, and entrepreneurial journeys. As they build their brands and engage with mentors and fellow community members, their influence grows through the collective support of a multitude of individuals and the engagement of influential figures, serving as a motivating factor for their continued efforts.

The scope of influencer activities within the metaverse is notably multifaceted, encompassing participation in various tech events, content distribution across platforms, valuable insights provided through newsletters, reviews, and key takeaways, engagement in specific topic discussions, sharing of research findings and analytical results, and the initiation of thought-provoking conversations. Influencers also craft and disseminate emotionally resonant content, conduct interviews, including engaging podcasts, and host live or recorded sessions for their audience. These activities underscore the influential and multifaceted role influencers play in shaping the evolving metaverse landscape.

The metaverse landscape is poised for further growth, with the anticipation of the rise of AI influencers presenting both opportunities and challenges that must be thoughtfully considered in the ongoing development of the metaverse. Overall, this section highlights a range of collective initiatives actively contributing to the development and shaping of the metaverse. These initiatives encompass metaverse associations, consortiums, government and academia programs, investments in development programs, and the impact of conferences, summits, and tech fairs. Furthermore, it explores the substantial role of communities and social influencers in influencing metaverse technology adoption and awareness, underlining the collaborative efforts and collective responsibility of diverse stakeholders in building the metaverse of the future.

Conclusion

In this chapter, we embarked on a journey into the metaverse's diverse facets, extending beyond the boundaries of software development. We unveiled a metaverse that encompasses both the digital and physical realms, forging new horizons.

We defined best practices for development, emphasizing user immersion and adapting criteria for evolving landscapes. Safety protocols and ethical considerations are to be integral to secure metaverse development. Collective initiatives and collaborations shaped the metaverse, fostering knowledge sharing and dynamic ecosystems through communities and influencers. Events like conferences and tech fairs became pivotal platforms for showcasing solutions and networking.

The metaverse, transcending traditional paradigms, thrives as a multidimensional entity, blending technology, ethics, and collaboration to shape a vibrant future where reality and imagination converge with endless possibilities for exploration and innovation.

Points to remember

Here are some points to remember from this chapter:

- The metaverse extends beyond the traditional software horizon, encompassing both digital and physical aspects of reality.
- Best practices in metaverse development include focusing on user immersion, performance optimization, and adaptable acceptance criteria.
- Emerging standards and protocols are crucial for ensuring the metaverse's safety and ethical development.
- Standards address various concerns, such as electromagnetic interference regulations and data protection, safeguarding users and ensuring a harmonious metaverse experience.
- Collective initiatives and collaborations play a significant role in shaping the metaverse's future, fostering communities and encouraging influencer participation.
- Conferences, summits, and tech fairs offer platforms for showcasing metaverse solutions, networking, and exploring emerging technologies.
- The metaverse represents a multidimensional entity where technology, ethics, and human collaboration converge to shape a dynamic and vibrant future.
- The metaverse continues to push the boundaries between reality and the digital realm, offering endless possibilities for exploration and innovation.

In this *Part 5 - Shaping the Metaverse: Standards and Practices,* we explored key aspects related to the development and shaping of the metaverse.

- **Getting started with metaverse development:** We explored the essential components and development kits, the role of the operating system, modular devices, and enterprise integration. It emphasized the dynamic nature of the metaverse and its transformative potential.
- **Metaverse practices, standards, and initiatives:** we delved into best practices, emerging standards, collective initiatives, and the roles of communities and influencers in metaverse development. It highlighted the importance of security, ethics, and collaboration.

As we conclude *Part 5,* next we will discuss how we can find the way forward in the metaverse, and get most out of it, while being conscious of the challenges it brings on the way.

References

1. https://www.forbes.com/advisor/business/what-is-waterfall-methodology/
2. https://agilemanifesto.org/
3. https://cmmiinstitute.com/
4. https://www.softkraft.co/software-development-standards/
5. https://www.asyncagile.org/the-book
6. https://www.eebo.org/# key-metrics
7. https://www.thoughtworks.com/en-in/insights/books/agile-it-organization-design
8. https://martinfowler.com/articles/lean-inception/
9. https://lawsofux.com/jakobs-law/
10. https://www.csse.canterbury.ac.nz/andrew.cockburn/2d3d.html
11. https://medium.com/xrpractices/understanding-human-anatomy-bed07677b587
12. https://medium.com/xrpractices/understanding-human-anatomy-bed07677b587
13. https://medium.com/xrpractices/understanding-human-anatomy-bed07677b587
14. https://developer.apple.com/design/human-interface-guidelines/designing-for-visionos/
15. https://docs.spaces.qualcomm.com/unity/handtracking/design/BestPractices.html
16. https://thinkreality.uds-dev.lenovo.com/design/
17. https://martinfowler.com/bliki/TestDrivenDevelopment.html
18. https://learn.microsoft.com/en-us/archive/msdn-magazine/2009/february/best-practice-an-introduction-to-domain-driven-design
19. https://www.agilealliance.org/glossary/xp/
20. https://martinfowler.com/books/refactoring.html
21. https://github.com/joelparkerhenderson/architecture-decision-record
22. https://www.thoughtworks.com/en-in/insights/books/building-evolutionary-architectures
23. https://ethereum.org/en/developers/tutorials/logging-events-smart-contracts/
24. https://dl.acm.org/doi/abs/10.1145/3416262
25. https://martinfowler.com/articles/feature-toggles.html

26. https://martinfowler.com/articles/practical-test-pyramid.html
27. https://www.thoughtworks.com/en-in/insights/blog/transitioning-conventional-shift-left-testing
28. https://www.selenium.dev/
29. https://appium.io/docs/en/2.1/
30. https://github.com/thoughtworks/Arium
31. https://aws.amazon.com/devops/what-is-devops/
32. https://www.devsecops.org/
33. https://thinkuldeep.com/post/ai-generated-xr-content/# ai-assisted-3d-modeling
34. https://www.w3.org/
35. https://www.usb.org/about
36. https://www.bluetooth.com/specifications/specs/
37. https://www.fcc.gov/
38. https://single-market-economy.ec.europa.eu/single-market/ce-marking_en
39. https://www.bis.gov.in/
40. https://www.greenlight.guru/blog/iso-standards
41. https://pharmaceuticals.gov.in/sites/default/files/Public%20Notice_BIS%20Standards.pdf
42. https://www.crystalrugged.com/mil-std-810/
43. https://www.iec.ch/ip-ratings
44. https://gdpr-info.eu/
45. https://oag.ca.gov/privacy/ccpa
46. https://www.meity.gov.in/writereaddata/files/Digital%20Personal%20Data%20Protection%20Act%202023.pdf
47. https://www.legislation.gov.uk/ukpga/2023/50/enacted
48. https://www.cdc.gov/phlp/publications/topic/hipaa.html
49. https://www.hl7.org/implement/standards/index.cfm
50. https://www.itgovernance.co.uk/pci_dss
51. https://www.technologyreview.com/2023/07/26/1076764/this-new-tool-could-protect-your-pictures-from-ai-manipulation/?truid=3faf134729d4639341022b1ba12a1a34
52. https://atlas-bench.com/the-market-for-anti-ai-technology/

53. https://www.infoworld.com/article/3574949/what-are-deepfakes-ai-that-deceives.html

54. https://www.computerworld.com/article/3699311/eu-parliament-approves-ai-act-moving-it-closer-to-becoming-law.html

55. https://www.whitehouse.gov/briefing-room/presidential-actions/2023/10/30/executive-order-on-the-safe-secure-and-trustworthy-development-and-use-of-artificial-intelligence/

56. https://standards.ieee.org/

57. https://owasp.org/www-project-top-ten/

58. https://www.iso.org/standard/73581.html

59. https://sagroups.ieee.org/2888/

60. https://www.techtarget.com/searchsecurity/definition/quantum-key-distribution-QKD

61. https://www.nist.gov/news-events/news/2022/07/nist-announces-first-four-quantum-resistant-cryptographic-algorithms

62. https://innovate.ieee.org/ieee-blockchain-standards-collection/

63. https://www.w3.org/WAI/fundamentals/accessibility-usability-inclusion/

64. https://www.iso.org/standard/63500.html

65. https://www.w3.org/WAI/standards-guidelines/wcag/

66. https://blog.ansi.org/metaverse-technology-augmented-reality-standards/#gref

67. https://jtc1info.org/jtc-1-standards-and-standardization-for-the-metaverse/

68. https://www.xr-institute.cz/en/researches/ergonomics-laboratory

69. https://www.unicef.org/media/66616/file/Industry-Guidelines-for-Online-ChildProtection.pdf

70. https://www.unicef.org/globalinsight/reports/metaverse-extended-reality-and-children

71. https://www.khronos.org/openxr/

72. https://metaverse-standards.org/

73. https://standards.ieee.org/wp-content/uploads/2022/06/XR_Metaverse_Governance.pdf

74. https://www.thevrara.com/

75. https://xrsi.org/

76. https://responsiblemetaverse.org/

77. https://metaverse-standards.org/
78. https://gatherverse.org/
79. https://www.metavethics.com/
80. https://wmetac.com/
81. https://touchlab.iitm.ac.in/index.php/consortium-for-xr-vr-ar-mr-engineering-mission-in-india-cxremi/
82. https://nsdcindia.org/partners
83. https://www.worldbank.org/en/topic/skillsdevelopment
84. https://www.sih.gov.in/
85. https://msh.meity.gov.in/program/mshcorporate/xr-startup-program
86. https://fitt-iitd.in/web/home
87. https://xtic.org/
88. https://www.coe-iot.com/
89. https://www.xrtoday.com/mixed-reality/which-countries-have-the-top-metaverse-strategies/
90. https://www.qualcomm.com/news/releases/2022/03/qualcomm-launches-100m-snapdragon-metaverse-fund
91. https://www.qualcomm.com/products/technology/metaverse
92. https://lightship.dev/
93. https://tesseract.in/developers
94. https://ajnacreator.com/
95. https://developers.google.com/community/gdsc
96. https://students.ieee.org/
97. https://www.ces.tech/
98. https://www.awexr.com/
99. https://www.sxsw.com/
100. https://io.google/
101. https://developer.apple.com/wwdc23/
102. https://www.lenovo.com/us/en/events/techworld/

Chapter 16
Metaverse: A Way Forward

Introduction

As we reach the culmination of this insightful journey through the metaverse, this final part of the book serves as the concluding chapter, providing a recap of our exploration. With a profound understanding of the metaverse, encompassing both its benefits and concerns, we are now equipped to make informed decisions on its utilization. However, it is crucial to recognize that staying distant from the metaverse is not a viable option for the future. This offers an action plan that encourages everyone to responsibly embrace and contribute to the evolving landscape of the metaverse.

Structure

In this chapter, we will discuss the following topics:

- Navigating the metaverse: A recap
- The future
- A collective action plan

Navigating the metaverse: A recap

Throughout this book, we embarked on a comprehensive exploration of the metaverse in five key parts. We began by defining the metaverse, tracing its historical roots, and dispelling common misconceptions. Our journey highlighted that the metaverse is not a fixed set of tools or technologies but an evolving concept, a continuous journey that leads us toward a future where the boundary between reality and virtual realms becomes indistinguishable.

The second part of our exploration focused on the pivotal role of technological advancements in propelling the metaverse forward. We discussed how immersive reality, spatial computing, AI, IoT, cloud technologies, and decentralization are shaping the metaverse ecosystem. It became evident that with widespread high speed internet and integrated spatial computing of future, we will transcend the confines of 2D screens. Our devices will take on real-world forms, enhancing our sensory perception and cognitive capabilities, enabling us to interact with and understand the world in unprecedented ways.

The third part of the book discussed various use cases where we explored how metaverse solutions are set to transform our beliefs and harness the extended capabilities we gain. We examined domains spanning gaming, entertainment, fitness, healthcare, and education, emphasizing their potential to address the ever-evolving skill requirements in a dynamic world. We recognized the profound impact on metaverse commerce and the economy. Businesses are already leveraging the metaverse as a powerful tool, with enterprises leading the way to harness its potential.

However, this newfound power brings along a significant responsibility.

The next part was all about the social impact and identity concerns associated with the metaverse, emphasizing the imperative of building a sustainable and responsible metaverse. Achieving this necessitates the establishment of standards, best practices, and the rigorous implementation of rules and regulations. We highlighted the need for collective responsibility, where individuals, governments, institutions, and industries collaborate to shape a responsible and sustainable metaverse.

As we come to the conclusion of the book, we may now acknowledge that the metaverse is not merely a technological concept but a profound transformation that challenges the boundaries of reality. However, our journey does not conclude here; we stand at the threshold of the metaverse understanding, and the question that lingers is, *What is next*?

The future

At this juncture, it is natural to be in a state of uncertainty. Do we truly need metaverse technologies when they come with the known concerns? How do we address these concerns? What should be our next course of action?

In reality, nothing comes without its costs, and every tool or technology we utilize may carry its own set of consequences. The key lies in finding a balance. The same holds true for the metaverse and its solutions. The answer is not to avoid using these solutions altogether, but rather to use them with a conscious awareness of their benefits and potential side effects. Just as excessive use of everyday technologies like mobile phones, laptops, even earbuds, or Wi-Fi connections can be challenging, the metaverse presents similar dynamics.

Responsible use and adoption of technology lies in our hands. The metaverse, often described as the next internet, offers incredible potential for positive impact, economic sustainability, and growth. Yet, like the internet, it can also be a tool for harm if misused. The path we choose to take with the metaverse is in our hands.

A collective action plan

The metaverse is a collective responsibility, involving technologists, consumers, and governance alike. To ensure its safe adoption and transformation, we can all play our part by taking actions from following plan:

1. **Continuous experience through experimentation:** First and foremost, gaining first-hand experience with metaverse solutions is essential. To understand the future, invest your time in exploring these technologies. For developers, dive into metaverse tools and create solutions. Content creators can contribute by crafting content for metaverse platforms and observing how it is consumed. Business professionals should contemplate using viable business models for metaverse applications. User experience designers can embark on building spatial user interfaces to transform the digital realm into the metaverse. Metaverse challenges existing beliefs, and the only way to truly grasp its impact and concerns is through continuous experimentation. It is an ongoing journey to understand the metaverse and form well-informed opinions.

2. **Continuous feedback by sharing:** Once you have experienced metaverse technologies and solutions, it is crucial to share your experiences. Create awareness by sharing what you liked and what you found lacking. Share ideas for new use cases or address concerns that need further exploration. Engage with creators and provide them with valuable feedback on their innovations. Be a part of communities and actively participate in social groups to share your metaverse experiences. Socializing your experiences is a vital step in creating awareness and ensuring the safe adoption of metaverse technologies. The feedback loop between

communities and users is a win-win situation, benefiting both parties and driving progress. *Figure 16.1* depicts the collective action plan for the metaverse.

Figure 16.1: *A collective action plan for the metaverse*

3. **Continuous improvement through acceptance:** Measuring and tracking how the metaverse is being utilized is critical. User feedback is invaluable for creators to further refine and enhance metaverse solutions. Accepting and acting on feedback leads to continuous improvement. Products and solutions in the metaverse need to have robust feedback and review systems, as well as community engagement. Those that lack these elements will find it challenging to thrive in the metaverse. Accepting feedback and continuously improving products and services will contribute to the collective betterment of the metaverse.

All the challenges, from privacy and security to sustainability, will go through these cycles. Soon, not using the metaverse will not be an option, so it is essential to prepare for this transformative digital frontier.

Conclusion

In conclusion, it is important to note that there can be no final conclusion on the metaverse. It is a continually evolving landscape. This book serves as an effort to create awareness, and the commitment is to maintain that awareness, to continue trying, experimenting, and sharing insights with creators, all while striving for continuous improvement. The metaverse is not an isolated moment but a journey that every one of us will embark on, knowingly or unknowingly, in the near future. Our journey does not conclude here; it is a call for all of us to play our part and actively engage in shaping this transformative journey.

Index